COOKING WITH
Bon Appétit

COOKING WITH

Bon Appétit

Recipe Yearbook 1991

Editors' Choice of Recipes from 1990

THE KNAPP PRESS
Publishers
Los Angeles

Bon Appétit Books offers cookbook stands. For details on ordering please write:
  Bon Appétit Books
  Premium Department
  Sherman Turnpike
  Danbury, CT 06816

On the Cover: *Chocolate-Peanut Butter "Pound Cake."*
Photographed by Kathryn Kleinman.

Printed and bound in the United States of America
10   9   8   7   6   5   4   3   2   1

❦ Contents

❦ Foreword

In this, our fifth annual collection of recipes from *Bon Appétit* magazine, you'll find more than 200 terrific ways to prepare everything from appetizers to desserts. Each recipe was carefully selected by the editors to represent the year's most interesting trends and the best of all that was featured over the 12 months of 1990. Join us for a trip down memory lane: You're bound to come across something—or more likely, several things—to add to your own collection of all-time favorite recipes.

It may surprise you to notice that our selections vary from the very easy to the more elaborate and from the down-home simple to the restaurant-style sophisticated. There's a little something here for everyone, since we've culled these recipes from virtually every area of the magazine, including popular departments like "Too Busy to Cook?" and "Cooking Healthy," as well as entertaining, travel and restaurant features. So in the same chapter (Appetizers), look for both the quick and easy Parmesan Cheese Twists and the strikingly elegant Roulade of Prosciutto, Figs, Stilton and Goat Cheeses with Port Glaze.

You'll find most every type of dish here, too, including soups, salads, entrées, side dishes, breads and more, along with an international array of cuisines, among them French, Italian, regional American, Mexican and Thai, to name a few. Turn to the section on main-dish salads by way of example: You'll see exotic Thai Beef Salad there along with California Grilled Game Hen, Orange and Arugula Salad and refreshing Japanese Noodle, Shrimp and Cucumber Salad.

The relatively recent trend toward lighter, healthier cooking is evident throughout the book, and in particular in recipes like Baked Red Snapper with Fennel-scented Tomato Sauce and Cannelloni with Spinach and Mushrooms with Low-Calorie Tomato Sauce. Likewise, the fact that people seem to have less and less time to spend in the kitchen these days is acknowledged here by fast, simple-to-cook dishes such as Jumbo Shrimp with Chive Butter, Fettuccine with Chicken and Wild Mushroom Sauce and Fried Peppers, Onions and Sausages. Also, many of the recipes include do-ahead tips for the busy cook.

All of which brings us to what is probably the book's most valuable attribute—its versatility. Whether you're looking for something new to do with chicken tonight for a family dinner or planning an innovative menu for an upcoming dinner party, chances are you'll come across the ideal dish (or dishes) for the occasion right here.

And since this is our version of the traditional yearbook, we've included a section at the back of the book called "News '90—The Year of Food and Entertaining in Review." You'll find all sorts of interesting bits of information about new food products and services, restaurants and people, travel tips, diet news and more—everything that struck us as the year's most interesting. (All the prices, addresses and other details have been updated as of this book's publication date.)

So here's to a delicious culinary trip back to the very recent past, one that stretches from the first month of 1990 to the last.

1 ❦ Appetizers

An appetizer, like a special dessert, isn't the kind of thing you make every day; chances are you save your favorites for entertaining, be it a cocktail party, a brunch, a dinner party, whatever. So it's likely you want recipes that stray a little from the ordinary, that offer sensational taste and great looks—but not at a high price in terms of time spent in the kitchen. Well, look no further: That's what this chapter is all about.

If you're in the process of planning a dinner party, there are plenty of sophisticated starters here to get things going in style. Consider the Roulade of Prosciutto, Figs, Stilton and Goat Cheeses with Port Glaze, which can be made ahead, or Celery Root Pancakes with Smoked Salmon and Sour Cream. Brie and Chive Fondue is another elegant choice. If it's just a casual affair, maybe a group of friends around to watch a game or a movie, try the Spiced Pecans or Salsa Deviled Eggs.

Then there's the possibility that these recipes may inspire you to throw a cocktail party, which is always a great way to entertain. Be sure to include any or all of the following: delicious Eggplant and Gorgonzola Crostini, savory Cheese-filled Pastries, and Cold Poached Shrimp with Fennel Aioli, all of which can be prepared at least in part ahead.

Cheese-filled Pastries

These cheese-filled pastries, known as börek, are usually filled with feta. In this version, smoked Gouda and Emmenthal are substituted.

Makes about 50

1 extra-large egg
¼ bunch fresh parsley, minced
2 large garlic cloves, minced
¾ teaspoon dried crushed red pepper
6 ounces smoked Gouda cheese, finely grated

6 ounces Emmenthal cheese, finely grated
12 (about) frozen phyllo pastry sheets, thawed
1½ cups (3 sticks) unsalted butter, melted

Whisk egg in medium bowl to blend. Mix in parsley, garlic and crushed red pepper. Mix in both cheeses. Place 1 phyllo sheet (keep remainder covered with plastic wrap and damp cloth) on work surface. Brush with butter. Cut lengthwise into 2½-inch-wide strips using heavy large knife. Place 1 rounded teaspoon of filling at end of each phyllo strip. Fold corner of phyllo over filling, forming triangle. Continue folding down entire length of strip as for flag, creating triangular-shaped pastry. Transfer to heavy large cookie sheet. Brush pastry with melted butter. Set phyllo pastry aside.

Repeat buttering, filling and folding process with remaining phyllo, melted butter and filling. (*Can be prepared ahead. Refrigerate 1 day or freeze up to 1 week in airtight container between double sheets of waxed paper. Arrange frozen phyllo triangles in single layer on heavy large cookie sheets. It is not necessary to thaw phyllo triangles before baking.*)

Preheat oven to 350°F. Bake phyllo pastries until golden brown, about 30 minutes. Transfer to platter. Serve warm.

Roulade of Prosciutto, Figs, Stilton and Goat Cheeses with Port Glaze

This is a beautiful and very rich appetizer.

6 servings

4 fresh figs or 3 ounces dried black figlets, halved
2½ cups Port
⅓ cup crumbled Stilton cheese (about 2 ounces)
⅓ cup soft fresh goat cheese, such as Montrachet, crumbled (about 2 ounces)

3 ounces cream cheese, room temperature
6 ounces thinly sliced prosciutto Pepper
4 additional fresh figs, quartered (optional)

Place figs in bowl. Add Port. Soak figs overnight.

Blend all cheeses in processor until smooth. Place large sheet of plastic wrap on work surface. Arrange prosciutto slices on plastic, forming 8 × 10-inch rectangle and overlapping slices slightly. Carefully spread cheese mixture over prosciutto leaving ½-inch border on sides. Season with pepper. Drain figs; reserve Port. Finely chop figs. Sprinkle figs over cheese. Roll prosciutto up tightly beginning at one long side, using plastic as aid. Wrap in plastic and refrigerate until firm, about 4 hours. (*Can be prepared 1 day ahead.*)

Bring reserved Port to boil in heavy small saucepan. Reduce heat and simmer until thick, syrupy and reduced to ⅓ cup, about 15 minutes. Cool to room temperature. Remove plastic from roulade. Slice roulade crosswise into 18 rounds. Place 3 rounds on each plate. Drizzle rounds lightly with glaze. Garnish each plate with fresh fig quarters if desired.

Eggplant and Gorgonzola Crostini

For a terrific appetizer, slices of Italian bread are spread with purchased pesto and seasoned eggplant, then topped with Gorgonzola and provolone and broiled.

Makes 14 to 16

1 eggplant, peeled, diced
1 teaspoon salt

3 tablespoons olive oil
1 tablespoon minced garlic
1 tablespoon dried basil, crumbled
  Pepper

½ cup purchased pesto sauce
1 8-ounce loaf Italian bread, sliced
4 ounces provolone cheese, grated
2 ounces Gorgonzola cheese, crumbled
  Fresh basil leaves

Spread eggplant on paper towel. Sprinkle with salt. Let stand 30 minutes to drain. Pat eggplant dry with paper towels.

Heat oil in heavy large skillet over medium-high heat. Add eggplant, garlic and dried basil and sauté until eggplant is tender and beginning to brown, 8 to 10 minutes. Season with pepper. (*Can be prepared 1 day ahead. Cover and refrigerate. Reheat eggplant mixture before using.*)

Preheat broiler. Spread 1½ teaspoons pesto sauce over one side of each bread slice. Top each with 1 tablespoon eggplant mixture, then with 1 tablespoon provolone and ½ tablespoon Gorgonzola. Place on cookie sheet. Broil until cheese melts, 3 to 4 minutes. Garnish with fresh basil.

Celery Root Pancakes with Smoked Salmon and Sour Cream

8 servings

1 red bell pepper
⅔ cup fresh or frozen corn kernels (from about 1 large ear)
1 12¼-ounce jar shredded celery root in vinegar,* drained and patted dry

1 egg
  Pinch of salt and pepper
5 tablespoons all purpose flour
3 tablespoons (about) unsalted butter
  Sour cream
  Smoked salmon slices

Char pepper over gas flame or in broiler until blackened on all sides. Wrap in plastic bag and let stand 10 minutes to steam. Peel and seed pepper. Cut into matchstick-size strips. Set aside.

Cook corn in small saucepan of boiling water for 3 minutes. Drain. Rinse under cold water. Drain and pat dry.

Mix bell pepper, corn, celery root, egg and salt and pepper in large bowl. Stir in flour. (*Can be prepared 2 hours ahead. Cover and refrigerate.*) Melt 1 tablespoon butter in heavy large skillet over medium heat until just beginning to brown. Spoon ⅓ cup celery root mixture into one half of skillet. Repeat to form second pancake, spacing evenly. Flatten with back of spatula. Cook until golden brown, about 3 minutes per side. Transfer to plates. Repeat with remaining celery root mixture, adding more butter to skillet as necessary. Top each pancake with sour cream. Cover with smoked salmon and serve.

*Available at specialty foods stores.

Salsa Deviled Eggs

Folks who normally keep a close watch on their egg intake seem to throw caution to the wind when confronted by a big platter of deviled eggs, especially this zesty variation with irresistible salsa flavors.

Makes 20

10 hard-boiled extra-large eggs, peeled, halved
⅓ cup mayonnaise
1 teaspoon Dijon mustard
¼ cup finely chopped drained oil-packed sun-dried tomatoes

1 tablespoon finely chopped pickled jalapeño peppers
2 green onions, thinly sliced
6 Kalamata olives,* pitted, chopped

Remove yolks from eggs and place yolks in medium bowl. Blend in mayonnaise and mustard. Stir in all remaining ingredients. Spoon mixture into pastry bag fitted with large plain or star tip. Pipe mixture into egg white halves. (*Can be prepared 4 hours ahead. Cover tightly and refrigerate.*)

*Black brine-cured olives, available at Greek and Italian markets and some supermarkets.

Parsley-Basil Cheese Spread

From the Piedmont region of Italy comes this agliata, an unusual "pesto" of parsley, celery leaves, basil, garlic and onion accented with lemon. Traditionally it is blended with fresh Robbiola cheese or unaged mountain pecorino, but soft, fresh goat cheese is a delicious and more readily available substitute.

12 servings

3 large garlic cloves
1¼ cups loosely packed fresh Italian parsley
1 cup loosely packed fresh basil leaves
¾ cup celery leaves
¼ cup olive oil (preferably extra-virgin)
2 tablespoons fresh lemon juice
1 pound soft fresh goat cheese (such as Montrachet)

¼ cup minced red onion
Salt and pepper

Fresh Italian parsley sprigs
Fresh basil sprigs
Additional fresh celery leaves
Olive oil (preferably extra-virgin)

Italian bread slices
1 garlic clove, halved

Chop 3 garlic cloves in processor. Add 1¼ cups parsley, 1 cup basil, ¾ cup celery leaves and ¼ cup olive oil and process until finely chopped but not pureed. Transfer mixture to medium bowl. Add lemon juice. Mix in cheese and onion. Season with salt and pepper. Cover and chill overnight.

Mound cheese mixture on platter. Surround with parsley sprigs, basil sprigs and celery leaves. Using thumb, make small indentation in top of cheese. Fill indentation with olive oil.

Prepare barbecue (high heat) or preheat broiler. Brush 1 side of each bread slice with olive oil and rub with halved garlic. Grill or broil bread until lightly toasted on both sides. Serve grilled garlic bread with cheese spread.

Sweet Potato Ribbon Chips

A sophisticated do-ahead hors d'oeuvre.

8 servings

4 medium orange-fleshed sweet potatoes (sometimes known as yams), peeled

Vegetable oil (for deep frying)
Salt

Place potato flat on work surface, holding one end. Using vegetable peeler and starting at center of potato, shave into long, wide ribbons in quick strokes. Turn potato and continue shaving opposite end. Turn potato over and repeat process for each side. Repeat with remaining potatoes.

Heat oil to 375°F in heavy, wide, 4-inch-deep pot. Shake one handful of potatoes in oil; do not crowd. Fry until crisp and slightly golden, stirring occasionally, 30 to 60 seconds. Remove with slotted spoon; drain on paper towels. Season with salt. Repeat with remaining potatoes in batches. (*Can be prepared 6 hours ahead. Cover lightly and store at room temperature.*)

White Bean Dip with Chips and Sticks

A new twist on the ubiquitous bean dip.

12 servings

3 garlic cloves
3 15-ounce cans cannellini beans (white kidney beans), rinsed, drained
¼ cup fresh lemon juice
½ cup olive oil
2¼ teaspoons ground cumin
1½ teaspoons chili powder
Salt and pepper

3 tablespoons minced fresh cilantro
Additional minced fresh cilantro
Fresh vegetables (such as carrot sticks, celery sticks and cauliflower)
Tortilla chips

Finely chop garlic in processor. Add beans and lemon juice and puree. Mix in oil, cumin and chili powder. Season with salt and pepper. Add 3 tablespoons cilantro and mix in using on/off turns. Transfer to large bowl. (*Can be prepared 1 day ahead. Cover and refrigerate.*) Sprinkle dip with additional minced cilantro. Serve with vegetables and chips.

Baked Radicchio and Herbed Goat Cheese

Serve this appetizer with crusty Italian bread.

4 servings

2 medium heads radicchio, cut into ¼-inch-thick strips
¼ pound goat cheese, cut into ½-inch pieces
¼ cup olive oil
1 garlic clove, flattened

1 teaspoon dried basil, crumbled
1 teaspoon dried marjoram, crumbled
½ teaspoon dried rosemary, crumbled
Pepper
Sliced Italian bread

Preheat oven to 400°F. Place radicchio in large shallow baking dish. Arrange goat cheese over. Heat oil in heavy small saucepan over medium heat. Add garlic and sauté until golden, about 1 minute. Discard garlic. Add basil, marjoram and rosemary to oil. Season with pepper. Drizzle over goat cheese and radicchio. Bake until cheese begins to melt, about 15 minutes. Serve with bread slices.

Roasted Red Bell Pepper Dip

This simple, flavorful dip is ready in minutes.

Makes about 2½ cups

1 green onion, cut into 1-inch pieces
2 7-ounce jars roasted red peppers, drained
1½ tablespoons fresh lemon juice
1 cup whipped cream cheese

Toasted French bread slices
Steamed broccoli florets

Finely chop onion in processor. Add peppers and lemon juice and blend until finely chopped. Add cream cheese and blend to coarse puree. Transfer to bowl. Cover and refrigerate at least 1 hour. (*Can be prepared 2 days ahead.*)

Place bowl with dip in center of platter. Surround with bread and broccoli.

Cold Poached Shrimp with Fennel Aioli

Shrimp and bell pepper strips are perfect partners for the dipping sauce. If you're running short on time, use cooked shrimp.

20 servings

Aioli

- 2 medium fennel bulbs (about 1½ pounds), roots trimmed
- 1½ cups plus 3 tablespoons olive oil
- 1½ teaspoons fennel seeds, chopped
- 1½ tablespoons white wine vinegar
- 3 garlic cloves, sliced
- 3 large egg yolks
  Salt and white pepper

Shrimp

- 2 carrots, chopped
- 2 teaspoons fennel seeds, crushed
- 2 teaspoons coriander seeds, crushed
- 2 cups dry white wine
- 2½ pounds uncooked shrimp, peeled, deveined (tails left intact), shells reserved
- 8 cups water

  Yellow or red bell pepper strips
  Fennel fronds or fresh dill sprigs

For aioli: Cut stalks off fennel bulbs. Chop stalks and reserve. Cut fennel bulbs into thin slices. Heat 3 tablespoons oil in heavy large skillet over medium heat. Add fennel, fennel seeds and vinegar. Sauté 10 minutes, stirring frequently; do not let color. Add 1½ garlic cloves and remaining 1½ cups oil. Reduce heat to low and cover. Cook until fennel is tender, stirring occasionally, about 35 minutes. Uncover and cool slightly.

Place remaining 1½ garlic cloves and yolks in blender. Add cooked fennel using slotted spoon. Process until smooth. Gradually add oil from fennel in slow steady stream. Process until emulsified. Season aioli with salt and pepper. Cover and refrigerate. (*Can be prepared 3 days ahead.*)

For shrimp: Place first 4 ingredients plus reserved shrimp shells and reserved fennel stalks in heavy large pot. Add 8 cups of water. Boil 25 minutes. Strain. Immediately return liquid to pot and add shrimp. Let stand until pink and opaque, about 5 minutes. Drain. Cover shrimp and refrigerate until well chilled. (*Can be prepared 1 day ahead.*)

Transfer aioli to medium bowl. Place bowl on platter. Hang shrimp on bowl rim. Arrange bell pepper strips around bowl. Garnish aioli with fennel or dill.

Eggplant Timbale with Two Sauces

Sauces of broccoli and Gorgonzola cheese complement this lovely starter.

4 servings

Timbale

- 6 tablespoons olive oil
- 1 garlic clove, minced
- 1 medium eggplant, peeled, cut into 2-inch cubes
- ⅔ cup whipping cream
- ½ cup plus 2 tablespoons freshly grated Parmesan cheese
- 1 egg
  Salt and pepper

Broccoli Sauce

- 3 tablespoons olive oil
- 1 teaspoon minced shallot
- 3 cups broccoli florets (about 1 pound)
- ¾ cup low-salt chicken broth
- ¼ cup whipping cream
  Salt and pepper

Gorgonzola Sauce

- ½ cup whipping cream
- 2 tablespoons Gorgonzola cheese
- 1 tablespoon unsalted butter
  Salt and pepper

  Arugula
  Chopped tomato

For timbale: Preheat oven to 375°F. Spray four 4-ounce timbale molds very generously with nonstick spray or spread with butter. Heat olive oil in heavy large skillet over medium-high heat. Stir in garlic. Add eggplant and cook until tender and slightly caramelized, stirring often, about 25 minutes.

Add cream to eggplant and cook until absorbed, about 5 minutes. Transfer mixture to processor and puree until smooth. Transfer to bowl. Stir in cheese, then egg. Season with salt and pepper. Spoon puree into prepared molds. (*Can be prepared 6 hours ahead. Cover and refrigerate. Bring to room temperature before continuing with recipe.*)

Set molds in roasting pan. Pour enough water into pan to come halfway up sides of molds. Bake until timbales are firm to touch and tester inserted in centers comes out clean, about 40 minutes, covering if browning too quickly.

Meanwhile, prepare broccoli sauce: Heat olive oil in heavy large skillet over medium heat. Stir in shallot. Add broccoli and chicken broth and cook until broccoli is crisp-tender, about 5 minutes; do not overcook or broccoli will lose color. Transfer to processor. Add cream and puree until smooth. Season with salt and pepper. Set sauce aside.

For Gorgonzola sauce: Stir cream, cheese and butter in heavy small skillet over medium heat until cheese and butter melt and sauce thickens, about 3 minutes. Season with salt and pepper. Set aside.

To serve: Spoon broccoli sauce onto each plate. Unmold timbale atop sauce. Spread Gorgonzola sauce atop each timbale. Garnish with arugula and tomato.

Parmesan Cheese Twists

These delicate cheese-flavored crisps, which use prepared puff pastry, are a snap to make.

Makes about 34

½ 17¼-ounce package frozen puff pastry (1 sheet), thawed

¼ cup freshly grated Parmesan cheese (about 1 ounce)

Preheat oven to 400°F. Place dough sheet on lightly floured work surface. Sprinkle cheese over half of dough. Lightly brush dough edges with water. Fold dough lengthwise, covering cheese completely. Press edges gently to seal. Roll dough out to ⅛-inch-thick rectangle. Fold pastry in quarters lengthwise. Cut pastry into ⅓-inch-wide strips. Unfold each strip and twist several times with hands. Place twisted strips on heavy cookie sheet, pressing ends onto pan to secure twists. (*Can be prepared ahead. Cover with plastic wrap and refrigerate up to 3 hours or freeze up to one week.*)

Bake twists until golden brown, about 12 minutes for refrigerated and 15 minutes for frozen. Transfer to rack and cool. (*Can be prepared 1 day ahead. Store in airtight container.*) Serve warm or at room temperature.

Liptauer Cheese

A favorite spread in Austria. Serve it slathered on chewy brown bread, or as a dip for raw vegetables.

Makes about 2 cups

1 8-ounce container small-curd cottage cheese
1 cup (2 sticks) unsalted butter, room temperature
2 tablespoons minced fresh parsley
1 tablespoon prepared mustard, preferably German
1 tablespoon Hungarian sweet paprika

1 tablespoon caraway seeds
1 small garlic clove, minced
¾ teaspoon salt
¼ teaspoon white pepper
Pinch of cayenne pepper
Milk or whipping cream (optional)

Mix cottage cheese and butter in blender or food processor until well blended. Add parsley, mustard, paprika, caraway, garlic, salt, pepper and cayenne and blend until smooth and uniform in color. Thin with milk if desired. Cover and refrigerate at least 3 hours to combine flavors. (*Can be prepared 1 day ahead.*) Bring to room temperature before using.

Spiced Pecans

Makes about 2½ cups

1 10-ounce package pecan halves
2 tablespoons (¼ stick) unsalted butter
1½ teaspoons ground cumin

¼ teaspoon cayenne pepper
2 tablespoons sugar
1 teaspoon salt

Preheat oven to 300°F. Place pecans in medium bowl. Melt butter in heavy small saucepan. Add cumin and cayenne and stir until aromatic, about 15 seconds. Pour over pecans. Add sugar and salt and stir to coat. Transfer to baking pan. Bake until nuts are toasted, stirring occasionally, about 20 minutes. Serve warm or at room temperature. (*Pecans can be prepared 5 days ahead. Store airtight.*)

Brie and Chive Fondue

This version of the classic dish uses brie instead of Swiss cheese and fresh grapefruit juice to replace the wine. The sweet tartness of the juice complements the rich cheese nicely. Serve with pumpernickel, sourdough or rye bread cubes. Cooked shrimp, blanched asparagus spears, Belgian endive leaves and boiled baby rose potatoes are all good "dippers" as well.

Makes about 4 cups

2 pounds chilled slightly firm brie cheese
2 tablespoons all purpose flour

1 tablespoon unsalted butter
3 tablespoons minced shallots or green onions
1½ cups (or more) fresh pink grapefruit juice

White pepper
¼ cup chopped chives
1 teaspoon minced grapefruit peel

Pumpernickel, sourdough or rye bread cut into 1-inch cubes

Remove rind from cheese. Tear cheese into pieces and place in large bowl. Add flour to bowl and toss to coat cheese.

Melt butter in heavy medium saucepan over medium heat. Add shallots and sauté until golden, about 4 minutes. Add grapefruit juice. Simmer until liquid is reduced to 1 cup, about 15 minutes. Turn heat to medium-low. Add 1 handful of cheese to saucepan and stir constantly until cheese melts, about 5 minutes. Repeat with remaining cheese, 1 handful at a time. Season with pepper. (*Can be prepared 1 day ahead. Cover and refrigerate. Reheat over medium-low heat, stirring frequently. Thin with 2 tablespoons grapefruit juice.*) Stir in chopped chives and minced grapefruit peel.

Pour cheese mixture into fondue pot. Set over candle or canned heat. Serve with skewers of bread cubes for dipping.

2 ❦ Soups and Salads

A funny thing has happened to soups and salads over the last few years. Soups have gotten less complicated and time-consuming now that they don't require hours of stove-top simmering, and salads, no longer just tosses of greens and dressing, have gotten more interesting. In the process, they both became wonderfully versatile menu items, switching from side dishes to main courses to starters with ease. You'll find light, refreshing first-course soups here along with hearty, satisfying main-dish versions and, likewise, salads that make terrific appetizers or side dishes and others that serve as quick and simple main courses.

For an intriguing beginning to an elegant dinner, try Chilled Brie Soup with Toasted Brioche and Caviar or colorful Yam Soup with Cardamom Cream. To warm you up on a chilly night there's Hearty Rutabaga, Carrot, Parsnip and Sausage Soup or Two-Bean Soup with Pappardelle. To round out your instant soup supper, just add a loaf of good, crusty bread and a fresh salad.

Speaking of salads, you're sure to find the perfect accompaniment here—maybe Tangerine and Green Salad, a lively mix of romaine, curly endive, red leaf lettuce, tangerines, red onion, avocado and jicama, or Belgian Endive and Snow Pea Salad. There are new takes on classic potato salad, including one with blue cheese, to accompany hamburgers or hot dogs, as well as sophisticated starters, among them Lima Bean, Prosciutto and Mint Salad and the vibrantly colored Artichoke, Green Bean and Sweet Potato Salad with Beet Vinaigrette.

There are also some terrific main-dish salads here. Try New Potato, Kielbasa and Gruyère Salad or Warm Wild Rice and Chicken Salad for a quick meal after a long day at work.

 *Soups*

Creamy Onion and Garlic Soup

4 servings

Soup

5 tablespoons unsalted butter
2 large onions, halved, thinly sliced
2 large garlic cloves, minced
2 tablespoons flour
½ cup dry white wine
3 cups beef stock or canned broth
1 cup whipping cream
Salt and white pepper

Croutons

3 tablespoons unsalted butter, room temperature
2 ounces blue cheese, crumbled (about ½ cup)
1 small onion, halved, thinly sliced
2 tablespoons dry white wine

8 ½-inch-thick French bread baguette slices, toasted

For soup: Melt butter in heavy large saucepan over medium heat. Add onions and garlic. Sauté until tender (do not brown), stirring occasionally, about 8 minutes. Sprinkle flour over onions. Turn heat to low and cook 4 minutes, stirring constantly. Add wine and boil 2 minutes. Add stock and cream. Cook over medium heat until slightly thickened, stirring occasionally, about 20 minutes. Season with salt and pepper. (*Can be prepared 1 day ahead. Cover and refrigerate.*)

For croutons: Using fork, blend 2 tablespoons butter with cheese in small bowl until smooth. Set aside. Melt remaining 1 tablespoon butter in heavy small skillet over medium heat. Add onion and sauté until golden brown, stirring occasionally, about 12 minutes. Add wine and cook until liquid evaporates, stirring occasionally. Transfer onion to another bowl. (*Can be made 1 day ahead. Cover and chill cheese mixture and onion separately.*)

Reheat soup over low heat if necessary. Preheat broiler. Spread toasts with cheese mixture and top with onions. Broil until cheese melts and onion heats through. Ladle soup into bowls and garnish with toasts.

Roasted Garlic Soup

4 servings

4 garlic heads (about ½ pound total), unpeeled
¼ cup olive oil

6 tablespoons (¾ stick) unsalted butter
4 leeks (white part only), chopped
1 onion, diced
6 tablespoons all purpose flour

4 cups chicken stock or canned broth, heated
⅓ cup dry Sherry

1 cup whipping cream
Fresh lemon juice
Salt and white pepper
2 tablespoons chopped fresh chives

Preheat oven to 350°F. Cut off top ¼ inch of each garlic head. Place garlic heads in small shallow baking dish. Drizzle oil over. Bake until golden, about 1 hour. Cool garlic slightly. Press individual garlic cloves between thumb and finger to release garlic. Chop garlic. Set aside.

Melt butter in heavy large saucepan over medium heat. Add garlic, leeks and onion and sauté until onion is translucent, about 8 minutes. Reduce heat to low. Add flour and cook 10 minutes, stirring occasionally. Stir in hot stock and

Sherry. Simmer 20 minutes, stirring occasionally. Cool slightly. Puree soup in batches in blender or processor. (*Can be prepared 1 day ahead. Refrigerate.*)

Return soup to saucepan. Add cream and simmer until thickened, about 10 minutes. Add lemon juice to taste. Season with salt and pepper. Ladle into bowls. Garnish garlic soup with chives.

Two-Bean Soup with Pappardelle

This is a refined version of the hearty Tuscan classic "pasta e fagioli," or pasta and bean soup. Start soaking all beans one day ahead.

4 servings

½ cup (generous) dried pinto beans
½ cup (generous) dried black-eyed peas

4 to 6 cups chicken stock, canned low-salt chicken broth or water
2 medium plum tomatoes, chopped
1 small carrot, chopped
1 celery stalk, chopped
½ small onion, chopped
6 large garlic cloves, minced
Salt and pepper

2 tablespoons olive oil
2 large garlic cloves, minced
12 large fresh basil leaves, minced
2 tablespoons minced fresh parsley

4 to 6 ounces egg pappardelle or fettuccine
Additional olive oil

Place pinto beans in one bowl and black-eyed peas in another. Add enough water to each to cover beans and peas completely. Let soak overnight. Drain pinto beans and black-eyed peas.

Place pinto beans in heavy medium saucepan. Add 4 cups stock, tomatoes, carrot, celery, onion and 6 garlic cloves. Simmer until beans are tender, adding up to 2 cups additional stock as necessary to keep beans covered, about 1½ hours (time will vary depending on age of beans). Transfer bean mixture to processor and puree. Press through medium sieve into saucepan. Season with salt and pepper. (*Can be prepared 1 day ahead. Cool, cover and refrigerate.*)

Meanwhile, place black-eyed peas in another medium saucepan. Cover with water and salt lightly. Simmer gently until tender but not mushy, about 1½ hours (time will vary depending on age of peas). Drain well.

Heat 2 tablespoons olive oil in heavy medium skillet over medium heat. Add 2 minced garlic cloves and stir 1 minute. Add black-eyed peas, basil and parsley and cook until mixture is heated through.

Cook pasta in boiling salted water until just tender but still firm to bite. Drain, then toss with enough olive oil to coat. Add to skillet and toss with black-eyed pea mixture. Season with salt and pepper.

Reheat pinto bean soup. Ladle soup into bowls. Spoon pasta and pea mixture in center of each. Drizzle with olive oil. Serve immediately.

Roquefort and Spinach Soup

2 servings

5 tablespoons unsalted butter
1 medium onion, halved and thinly sliced
2 tablespoons brandy
2 cups chicken stock or canned low-salt broth
3 ounces Roquefort cheese
2 cups fresh spinach leaves, cut into matchstick-size strips

2 plum tomatoes, seeded and diced
1 teaspoon minced fresh thyme or ¼ teaspoon dried, crumbled
6 tablespoons whipping cream
Pepper
Additional Roquefort cheese, crumbled

Melt 2 tablespoons butter in heavy large saucepan over medium heat. Add onion and cook until golden brown, stirring frequently, about 15 minutes. Remove pan from heat. Add brandy; ignite with match. When flames subside, return pan to heat. Add stock and 3 ounces cheese and bring to boil, stirring frequently. Reduce heat to low and stir until cheese melts. Cool soup slightly. Puree in batches in blender. Return soup to saucepan.

Melt 1 tablespoon butter in heavy medium skillet over medium heat. Add spinach, tomatoes and thyme and sauté until spinach wilts, about 2 minutes. Add cream and spinach mixture to soup and bring to simmer over medium heat. Season with pepper. Add remaining 2 tablespoons butter and swirl until melted. Ladle soup into bowls. Garnish with additional cheese and serve.

Cream of Fennel Soup

6 servings

1½ pounds fennel bulbs with leafy tops (about 2 medium)
¼ cup (½ stick) unsalted butter
½ cup minced onion
2 tablespoons Pernod
2 tablespoons dry white wine
5 cups chicken stock or canned low-salt broth
2¼ cups milk

6 tablespoons (¾ stick) unsalted butter, room temperature
⅔ cup all purpose flour
1 cup whipping cream
2 egg yolks
Salt and pepper

Finely chop leafy fennel tops. Discard tough outer layer of bulb. String and core fennel. Cut each fennel bulb into quarters. Melt ¼ cup butter in heavy large saucepan over medium heat. Add onion and sauté 5 minutes. Add fennel bulbs and leafy tops and cook until fennel begins to soften, stirring frequently, about 8 minutes. Add Pernod and wine and cook 1 minute. Add stock and milk and simmer 15 minutes. Remove fennel quarters and coarsely chop; reserve. Strain soup into heavy medium saucepan.

Mix 6 tablespoons butter with flour in bowl. Bring soup to simmer. Add butter-flour mixture by tablespoonfuls, stirring until completely incorporated. Cook soup until thickened, stirring frequently, about 5 minutes. Whisk cream with yolks and add to soup. Mix in chopped fennel bulb. Stir to heat through. Season with salt and pepper. (*Can be prepared 1 day ahead. Refrigerate.*)

Chilled Brie Soup with Toasted Brioche and Caviar

An intriguing starter.

4 to 6 servings

3 tablespoons butter
2 leeks, white part only, chopped
2 inner celery stalks, chopped
1 medium onion, chopped
4 large mushrooms, stemmed and chopped
3 garlic cloves, sliced
1 small bunch fresh thyme or basil
  White pepper

2 cups sweet fruity white wine, such as Sauternes or Beaumes-de-Venise
2 cups chicken stock or canned low-salt broth
4 cups (or more) whipping cream
¼ pound Brie cheese, rind removed

4 to 6 slices brioche or egg bread, toasted
  Black caviar

Melt butter in heavy medium saucepan over medium-low heat. Add leeks, celery, onion, mushrooms, garlic and thyme. Season with pepper. Cook until vegetables soften slightly, stirring occasionally, about 5 minutes. Add wine and boil until reduced by half. Add stock and boil until reduced by ¾. Add 4 cups cream and simmer until slightly thickened. Strain mixture through fine sieve. Transfer to processor or blender. Add Brie and puree. Transfer to bowl. Cover and refrigerate until well chilled. (*Can be prepared 1 day ahead.*)

Thin soup with more cream if too thick; if no longer silken, sieve again. Ladle soup into bowls. Serve immediately with toast spread with caviar.

Classic Black Bean Soup

8 servings

1 pound dried black beans, rinsed, picked over

¼ cup (½ stick) unsalted butter
2 large onions, chopped
1 celery stalk, finely chopped
2 garlic cloves, minced
8 cups chicken stock or canned broth

1¾ pounds smoked ham hocks
2 bay leaves
2 whole cloves
8 whole black peppercorns
  Salt and pepper

6 tablespoons Madeira
2 hard-boiled eggs, finely chopped
8 thin lemon slices

Place beans in large pot. Add enough cold water to cover by 3 inches and let soak overnight. Drain beans. Set aside.

Melt butter in heavy large pot over medium-high heat. Add onions, celery and garlic and sauté 10 minutes. Mix in stock. Add drained beans, ham hocks, bay leaves, cloves and peppercorns and bring to boil. Reduce heat, cover partially and simmer until beans are tender, stirring occasionally, about 2 hours 15 minutes. Remove ham hocks and bay leaves from soup (reserve ham hocks for another use). Puree soup in batches in processor. Return puree to pot. Season with salt and pepper. (*Soup can be prepared up to 2 days ahead. Cover soup tightly and then refrigerate.*)

Add Madeira to soup and bring to simmer. Ladle into bowls. Sprinkle with chopped egg. Garnish soup with lemon and serve.

Hearty Rutabaga, Carrot, Parsnip and Sausage Soup

This wintry soup can be enhanced with any sausage you like. It works especially well with the lowfat turkey sausages now available.

2 servings

2 tablespoons olive oil
6 ounces smoked turkey sausage, cut into ½-inch dice
1 large onion, chopped
3 small parsnips, peeled, diced
1 medium rutabaga, peeled, diced
1 large carrot, peeled and diced

1 14½-ounce can beef broth
1 14½-ounce can chicken broth

¼ cup half and half
½ teaspoon dried thyme, crumbled
Salt and pepper

Heat oil in heavy large saucepan over medium-high heat. Add sausage and sauté until brown on all sides, about 7 minutes. Transfer to plate using slotted spoon. Add onion to saucepan. Reduce heat to medium and cook until tender, stirring occasionally, about 8 minutes. Add parsnips, rutabaga and carrot and cook 5 minutes, stirring occasionally. Add broths. Bring to boil. Reduce heat and simmer until vegetables are tender, about 40 minutes.

Puree soup in batches in processor. Return to saucepan. Mix in half and half and thyme. Season with salt and pepper. Add sausage. (*Can be prepared 1 day ahead. Cover and chill.*) Heat through. Ladle into bowls and serve.

Yam Soup with Cardamom Cream

A cardamom-flavored sour cream adds a delicious touch to this starter.

6 servings

7 cups (about) chicken stock or canned broth
3½ pounds yams, peeled, diced
1 large onion, chopped
¼ cup (½ stick) unsalted butter

¼ teaspoon (or more) ground nutmeg
Salt and pepper

1 cup sour cream
¼ teaspoon ground cardamom

Bring 6 cups stock to boil in heavy large saucepan. Add yams, onion and butter. Reduce heat. Cover and simmer until yams are very soft, about 35 minutes. Cool slightly. In processor, puree yams with stock in batches. Return soup to saucepan. Thin with additional stock if desired. Add ¼ teaspoon nutmeg. Taste, adding more nutmeg if desired. Season with salt and pepper. (*Can be prepared 1 day ahead. Cover with plastic wrap and refrigerate.*)

Mix sour cream and cardamom in small bowl. Bring soup to simmer. Ladle into individual tureens or bowls. Top each with dollop of sour cream and serve.

Fresh Corn and Lobster Soup

Order lobster shells from your local fish market.

4 servings

6 large ears yellow corn or 3 cups frozen yellow corn kernels
Lobster Cream Base*
Salt and pepper
¼ cup milk (optional)

1 small zucchini
⅓ cup ⅛-inch cubes peeled carrot
⅓ cup ⅛-inch cubes peeled turnip
⅓ cup ⅛-inch cubes celery

Bring large pot of salted water to boil. Add corn ears or frozen corn kernels and cook until just tender, about 3 minutes. Drain, refresh under cold water, then drain again. Cut kernels from cobs. Transfer kernels to processor and puree. Pour into 2-quart saucepan. Add lobster base and bring to boil, stirring occasionally. Strain into clean saucepan, pressing on solids to extract as much pulp as possible. Season with salt and pepper. Thin with milk if desired. (*Can be prepared up to 1 day ahead. Cover and refrigerate.*)

Cut peel from zucchini in ⅛-inch-thick strips; cut strips into ⅛-inch squares. Bring small pot of salted water to boil. Add carrot, turnip and celery and cook 2 minutes. Add zucchini peel and cook 1 minute. Drain, refresh under cold water, then drain again. (*Can be prepared 8 hours ahead; refrigerate.*)

Divide vegetable mixture among 4 bowls. Gently reheat soup and ladle over vegetables. Serve soup immediately.

*Lobster Cream Base

Makes about 2½ cups

3 **pounds lobster shells, coarsely chopped**	3 **tablespoons minced shallot**
¾ **cup finely chopped unpeeled carrot**	½ **small bunch fresh parsley, stemmed**
¾ **cup finely chopped celery**	1 **tablespoon coarse salt**
¾ **cup finely chopped leek (white and pale green parts only)**	1 **teaspoon whole black peppercorns**
¾ **cup finely chopped unpeeled turnip**	1 **cup dry white wine, preferably Chardonnay**
½ **cup finely chopped onion**	5 **cups whipping cream**

Heat heavy large pot over high heat 1 minute. Add lobster shells, carrot, celery, leek, turnip, onion, shallot, parsley, salt and peppercorns. Cook 5 minutes, stirring frequently. Add wine and bring to boil. Reduce heat and simmer 10 minutes, stirring occasionally. Add enough water to cover ingredients completely. Boil until liquid is reduced to 1 cup, about 45 minutes.

Add cream to lobster shell liquid and bring to boil. Reduce heat and simmer until liquid is reduced to 2½ cups, about 30 minutes. Strain through fine sieve, pressing on solids to extract as much liquid as possible. (*Can be prepared 2 days ahead. Cool slightly, cover and refrigerate; do not freeze.*)

Nip-Nip Soup

The parsnips and turnips give this soup not only its name, but its creamy texture as well.

Makes about 10 cups

6 **tablespoons (¾ stick) unsalted butter**	**Vegetable oil (for deep frying)**
1 **large onion, chopped**	1 **leek (white and pale green parts only), cut into ¼-inch slices**
1 **pound parsnips, peeled, chopped**	**All purpose flour**
1 **pound turnips, peeled, chopped**	**Salt and pepper**
½ **cup dry Sherry**	⅓ **cup chopped fresh chives**
4 **cups chicken stock or canned broth**	**Toasted sliced almonds**

Melt butter in heavy large saucepan over medium heat. Add onion. Cook until tender and golden, stirring occasionally, about 8 minutes. Add parsnips and turnips. Stir to combine. Add Sherry and reduce heat to low. Place foil directly on vegetables. Cover with tight-fitting lid. Steam vegetables until tender, adding up to 1 cup stock by tablespoons if too dry, about 45 minutes.

Puree vegetables with remaining stock in batches in processor until smooth. Strain into large bowl. (*Can be prepared 1 day ahead. Cover and chill.*)

Heat 1 inch of oil in heavy medium saucepan to 375°F. Separate sliced leeks into rings. Place flour in small bowl. Season with salt and pepper. Add leeks to flour and toss to coat; shake off excess. Add leeks to oil and deep-fry until golden, about 45 seconds. Transfer to paper towels using slotted spoon.

Bring soup to simmer over medium heat. Season with salt and pepper. Ladle into bowls. Garnish each serving with chives, almonds and fried leeks.

🍎 Side-Dish Salads

Italian Chopped Salad

4 to 6 servings

1 large head romaine lettuce, finely chopped
4 large plum tomatoes, seeded, finely chopped
1 green bell pepper, finely chopped
4 ounces Italian dry salami, finely chopped
1 cup drained canned garbanzo beans (chick-peas)
4½ ounces mozzarella, diced
½ cup pitted black olives, finely chopped

½ cup pimiento-stuffed green olives, finely chopped
¾ cup olive oil
2 tablespoons red wine vinegar
1½ tablespoons minced fresh basil or 1 teaspoon dried, crumbled
1 tablespoon Dijon mustard
2 teaspoons fresh lemon juice
Pinch of sugar
Salt and pepper

Combine first 8 ingredients in large bowl. Blend oil with next 5 ingredients in small bowl. Season with salt and pepper. Pour over salad and toss thoroughly.

Curried Corn, Zucchini and Bell Pepper Salad

8 servings

¼ cup vegetable oil
2 tablespoons curry powder
2 garlic cloves, flattened
⅓ cup mayonnaise
⅓ cup sour cream or plain yogurt
2 tablespoons honey
1 tablespoon fresh lemon juice
1½ teaspoons salt
¾ teaspoon pepper

2 large red bell peppers
5 large zucchini, quartered lengthwise
2 tablespoons olive oil
8 ears of corn or 2 10-ounce packages frozen whole kernel corn, thawed
½ cup chopped red onion

Combine vegetable oil, curry powder and garlic in heavy small skillet. Stir over medium-low heat until fragrant, about 5 minutes. Cool completely; discard garlic. Whisk mayonnaise, sour cream, honey, lemon, salt and pepper to blend in small bowl. Stir in curry mixture. (*Can be prepared 1 day ahead. Refrigerate.*)

Prepare barbecue (medium-high heat) or preheat broiler. Grill or broil peppers until charred and blackened on all sides. Wrap in paper bag and let stand 10 minutes to steam. Peel and seed. Rinse if necessary; pat dry. Cut peppers into ¼-inch-wide strips. Set aside.

Brush zucchini with 2 tablespoons olive oil. Grill or broil until brown and tender, about 4 minutes per side. Cool slightly. Cut into ½-inch pieces.

Using sharp knife, cut corn kernels from cobs. Place kernels in large bowl. Add peppers, zucchini and onion. Pour curry mixture over vegetables and toss to coat. (*Can be prepared 6 hours ahead. Cover and refrigerate. Bring salad to room temperature before serving.*)

New Potato Salad with Bacon and Mustard Seeds

Hearty, crunchy and slightly smoky, this potato salad is a useful addition to many menus. Spanish Sherry wine vinegar is robust and flavorful, but you can substitute red wine vinegar or balsamic vinegar if you have those on hand.

8 servings

2 tablespoons mustard seeds
⅓ cup (or more) Sherry wine vinegar
12 ounces thick-sliced bacon, chopped

3½ pounds small red new potatoes
1 tablespoon plus ½ teaspoon salt
⅔ cup olive oil
½ cup chopped fresh parsley
2 teaspoons pepper

Soak mustard seeds in ⅓ cup vinegar in small bowl 1 hour.

Cook bacon in heavy large skillet over medium heat until crisp and brown, stirring occasionally, about 8 minutes. Using slotted spoon, transfer bacon to paper towels; drain thoroughly.

Cover potatoes with water in heavy large saucepan. Add 1 tablespoon salt. Boil until potatoes are just tender, about 20 minutes. Drain and cool slightly. Cut potatoes into quarters and place in large bowl. Stir remaining ½ teaspoon salt into vinegar mixture. Pour over warm potatoes; toss to coat completely. Cool potatoes to room temperature.

Mix bacon, olive oil, parsley and pepper into potatoes. Taste, adding more vinegar if desired. (*Can be prepared 6 hours ahead. Cover and refrigerate.*) Serve potato salad at room temperature.

Lima Bean, Prosciutto and Mint Salad

2 servings

1 cup dried lima beans
3½ cups water
1½ tablespoons olive oil
Salt and pepper
2 tablespoons Sherry wine vinegar
1 teaspoon Dijon mustard
¼ cup olive oil

2 Belgian endive heads, cut into matchstick-size strips
½ small head romaine lettuce, cut into matchstick-size strips
½ bunch watercress, stems trimmed
3 ounces thinly sliced prosciutto, cut into matchstick-size strips
10 large mint leaves, cut into matchstick-size strips

Place beans in heavy large saucepan with enough cold water to cover by 3 inches; let beans stand overnight.

Drain beans. Return to saucepan. Add 3½ cups water and bring to boil. Reduce heat and simmer until beans are very tender, about 45 minutes. Drain. Toss with 1½ tablespoons oil. Season generously with salt and pepper. Cover and refrigerate until well chilled. (*Can be prepared 1 day ahead.*)

Whisk vinegar and mustard in small bowl. Gradually whisk in ¼ cup oil. Season dressing with salt and pepper.

Combine beans, endive and next 4 ingredients in large bowl. Add dressing and toss to coat. Serve immediately.

Blue Cheese Potato Salad

This tangy take on potato salad can be prepared ahead.

12 servings

5 pounds red new potatoes
½ cup dry white wine
  Salt and pepper
1¼ cups mayonnaise
1¼ cups sour cream

2½ tablespoons Dijon mustard
2½ tablespoons cider vinegar
½ pound blue cheese, crumbled
5 green onions, minced
1½ cups chopped celery

Place potatoes in large pot. Cover with cold water. Boil until tender. Drain. Cool slightly. Peel potatoes. Cut into 1-inch pieces. Transfer to large bowl. Add wine, season with salt and pepper and toss to coat. Cool.

Combine all remaining ingredients. Mix with potatoes. Adjust seasoning. (*Can be prepared 1 day ahead. Cover and refrigerate. Let stand 30 minutes at room temperature before serving.*)

Belgian Endive and Snow Pea Salad

A light and refreshing first-course salad.

8 servings

3 tablespoons red wine vinegar
2 tablespoons Dijon mustard
½ teaspoon salt
½ cup plus 1 tablespoon olive oil
3 tablespoons chopped shallots
  Pepper

1 pound snow peas, ends trimmed diagonally, strings removed

6 heads Belgian endive

Whisk vinegar, mustard and salt in small bowl. Gradually whisk in oil. Mix in shallots. Season with pepper. (*Can be prepared 8 hours ahead. Let stand at room temperature. Whisk before using.*)

Blanch snow peas in large pot of boiling salted water 30 seconds. Drain. Refresh under cold water. Drain and pat dry. Transfer to large bowl.

Peel off outer leaves from Belgian endive and arrange in spoke fashion on large platter. Cut remaining endive into matchstick-size strips. Add to snow peas. Add enough dressing to season to taste and toss well. Mound salad in center of endive-lined platter and serve.

Artichoke, Green Bean and Sweet Potato Salad with Beet Vinaigrette

4 servings

1 tablespoon fresh lemon juice
1 large artichoke

2 ounces green beans

¼ cup plus 3 tablespoons olive oil
1 cup matchstick-size strips of peeled sweet potato (about ½ sweet potato)

4 ounces fresh goat cheese (such as Montrachet), cut into 4 slices

⅓ cup dry breadcrumbs

1 tablespoon red wine vinegar
8 cups bite-size assorted greens, such as romaine, red leaf and curly endive
½ cup sliced button mushrooms
4 fresh shiitake mushrooms, stemmed and sliced
  Beet Vinaigrette (see recipe)
¼ cup sliced red onion

Bring medium pot of water to boil over high heat. Add lemon juice. Reduce heat to medium. Add artichoke. Cover and cook until leaves pull away easily, about 40 minutes. Drain and cool. Peel off leaves and reserve for another use. Scoop out choke and discard. Thinly slice artichoke heart.

Cook beans in small saucepan of boiling water until just tender, about 3 minutes. Drain. Refresh under cold water and drain again. Coarsely chop beans. (*Can be prepared 1 day ahead. Cover and refrigerate sliced artichoke heart and beans separately.*) Set beans aside.

Preheat oven to 350°F. Heat ¼ cup oil in heavy large skillet over high heat. Add sweet potato and sauté until golden brown, about 5 minutes. Using slotted spoon, transfer potato to paper towels and let drain completely.

Meanwhile, roll goat cheese in breadcrumbs, coating completely. Transfer to baking sheet. Bake until heated through, about 5 minutes.

Mix remaining 3 tablespoons oil and 1 tablespoon vinegar in large bowl. Add greens and mushrooms and toss to coat. Spoon Beet Vinaigrette onto 4 plates. Top with greens and mushrooms. Garnish with artichoke, green beans, sweet potato and onion. Top each with goat cheese and serve.

Beet Vinaigrette

Makes about 1 cup

¾ **pound beets, stems trimmed**

¼ **cup (or more) water**
1 **tablespoon red wine vinegar**

1 **egg yolk**
1 **teaspoon Dijon mustard**
½ **teaspoon minced shallot**
¼ **cup olive oil**

Cook beets in large pot of boiling salted water until just tender. Drain and cool. Peel beets; cut into 1-inch pieces. (*Can be prepared 1 day ahead. Refrigerate.*)

Puree beets in processor. Measure puree and return ½ cup to processor. (Reserve any remainder for another use.) Mix in ¼ cup water and next 4 ingredients. Gradually mix in oil. Thin vinaigrette with additional water if desired. (*Can be prepared 2 hours ahead. Cover and let stand at room temperature. Rewhisk vinaigrette before using.*)

Tangerine and Green Salad

6 servings

Dressing
7 **tablespoons corn oil**
¼ **cup red wine vinegar**
3 **tablespoons (scant) honey**
1¼ **teaspoons ground cumin**
1¼ **teaspoons chili powder**
½ **teaspoon (generous) aniseed, chopped**
Pinch of cayenne
Salt and pepper

Salad
1 **small romaine lettuce head**
1 **curly endive head, outer leaves discarded**
1 **small red leaf lettuce head**
4 **tangerines or 4 small oranges, peeled, divided into segments**
1 **small red onion, thinly siced**
1 **avocado, cut into ½-inch cubes**
1 **cup coarsely grated jicama (about 6 ounces)**
2 **green onions, minced**

For dressing: Whisk oil, vinegar, honey and spices in medium bowl. Season with salt and pepper. (*Can be prepared up to 2 days ahead. Cover dressing tightly and let stand at room temperature.*) Set dressing aside.

For salad: Tear lettuces into bite-size pieces and place in large bowl. Add tangerine segments, red onion, avocado and jicama. Toss gently to combine. Whisk green onions into dressing. Pour over salad and toss to coat.

Pear and Curly Endive Salad

2 servings

2 teaspoons Sherry wine vinegar
1 teaspoon Dijon mustard
3 tablespoons olive oil
¼ teaspoon dried thyme, crumbled
Salt and pepper

5 cups bite-size pieces curly endive (about ¼ medium head)
1 large ripe pear, cut into quarters, cored, sliced crosswise

Combine vinegar and mustard in small bowl. Gradually whisk in oil. Mix in thyme. Season with salt and pepper.

   Combine endive and pear in large bowl. Add dressing and toss to coat.

❦ *Main-Dish Salads*

Creamy Farfalle Salad with Smoked Salmon and Caviar

Bow tie-shaped farfalle pasta is mixed with cream, lemon juice, dill, chives, cucumber, smoked salmon and caviar to make an elegant meal. In smaller servings, this is a terrific first course.

4 servings

Dressing
10 fresh chives, cut into 1-inch lengths
¼ cup packed fresh dill
2 shallots or green onions, cut into 1-inch pieces
1 cup whipping cream
3 tablespoons fresh lemon juice
2 tablespoons milk
Salt and pepper

Salad
4 pickling cucumbers, ends cut flat
8 ounces farfalle pasta, cooked, rinsed, drained, tossed with 1 teaspoon vegetable oil and chilled
6 ounces smoked salmon, coarsely chopped
Boston lettuce leaves
1 2-ounce jar American golden caviar
4 lemon wedges

For dressing: Place chives and dill in work bowl of processor. With machine running, drop shallots through feed tube and process until minced. Scrape down sides of bowl. Add cream, lemon juice and milk. Season with salt and pepper. Process just until blended well, using about 5 on/off turns. (*Can be prepared 2 hours ahead. Refrigerate. Reblend before using if necessary.*)

For salad: Stand cucumber in feed tube of processor and shred using medium pressure. Transfer cucumbers to kitchen towel. Wrap tightly and squeeze to remove as much moisture as possible. Combine cucumbers and farfalle in large bowl. (*Can be prepared 2 hours ahead. Refrigerate.*)

   Add dressing and salmon to pasta and cucumbers. Toss to combine. Adjust seasoning. Line 4 chilled serving plates with lettuce. Divide salad among plates. Spoon 1 tablespoon caviar atop each. Garnish with lemon.

Thai Beef Salad

A simple salad made special with a few exotic ingredients and two colorful, easy-to-make garnishes.

2 servings

2 fresh Anaheim chilies*

2 small tomatoes

1 fresh lemongrass stalk**

3 tablespoons fish sauce (nam pla)**

3 tablespoons fresh lime or lemon juice

2 tablespoons finely chopped fresh mint

1 tablespoon honey

3½ teaspoons minced garlic

1 teaspoon minced serrano chili with seeds

8 tablespoons olive oil

2 6-ounce ½-inch-thick beef tenderloin steaks

1 teaspoon pepper

1 small romaine lettuce head, torn into bite-size pieces

1 small radicchio head, torn into bite-size pieces

1 small Belgian endive head, cut into bite-size pieces

2 green onions, finely chopped
Green Onion Brushes (see recipe)
Serrano Chili Fans (see recipe)

Char Anaheim chilies over gas flame or in broiler until blackened on all sides. Wrap in paper bag and let stand 10 minutes to steam. Peel, core and seed chilies. Cut into ½-inch pieces. Set chilies aside.

Blanch tomatoes in medium saucepan of boiling water for 10 seconds. Transfer to bowl of cold water using slotted spoon. Drain. Pull off tomato skins using small sharp knife. Cut tomatoes crosswise in half. Squeeze tomatoes gently to remove seeds. Finely dice tomatoes and set aside.

Peel tough outer leaves from lemongrass stalk. Finely chop enough lemongrass to measure 1 tablespoon.

Whisk lemongrass, fish sauce, lime juice, mint, honey, 1½ teaspoons garlic and serrano chili in medium bowl. Gradually whisk in 6 tablespoons oil. (*Can be prepared 6 hours ahead. Cover and refrigerate Anaheim chilies, diced tomatoes and salad dressing separately.*)

Brush both sides of steaks with remaining 2 tablespoons oil. Rub pepper and remaining 2 teaspoons garlic onto steaks. Heat heavy large skillet over medium-high heat. Add steaks and cook to desired degree of doneness, about 2 minutes per side for rare. Transfer steaks to cutting board. Let stand until cool, approximately 15 minutes.

Cut steaks diagonally into thin slices. Transfer to large bowl. Pour 3 tablespoons dressing over steak; toss gently to coat. Combine Anaheim chiles, tomatoes, romaine, radicchio, endive and chopped green onions in another bowl. Toss with remaining dressing. Divide salad between plates. Arrange beef atop salads. Garnish with Green Onion Brushes and Serrano Chili Fans.

*Also called California chilies. Anaheim chilies are available at Latin American markets, specialty foods stores and some supermarkets.

**Available at oriental markets and some specialty foods stores.

Green Onion Brushes

Makes about 8

4 green onions (white and pale
green parts only)

Cut green onions into 2½-inch-long pieces. Make several 1-inch-long lengthwise cuts on one end of each onion piece. Gently peel back cut pieces to resemble flower. Soak in ice water until ends curl, about 15 minutes. (*Can be prepared 1 day ahead. Cover and refrigerate in water.*) Drain and pat dry before using.

Serrano Chili Fans

Makes 4

2 red serrano, jalapeño or other
small chilies

2 green serrano, jalapeño or other
small chilies

Using small sharp knife and starting just below stem end, make several lengthwise cuts down length of chili, spacing cuts ⅛ inch apart. Carefully scrape out seeds. Place chili in bowl of cold water. Repeat cutting with remaining chilies. Let chilies stand in water until ends curl, about 15 minutes. (*Can be prepared 1 day ahead. Cover and refrigerate in water.*) Drain and pat dry before using.

New Potato, Kielbasa and Gruyère Salad

Offer with crusty French bread and you have a satisfying supper. The creamy dressing is a lower-fat version, using half yogurt and half mayonnaise.

2 servings

1¾ pounds medium white-skinned
boiling potatoes (about 6)
2 tablespoons cider vinegar
4 green onions, chopped

4 tablespoons plain yogurt
4 tablespoons mayonnaise
4 teaspoons prepared white
horseradish

1 teaspoon caraway seeds
½ pound kielbasa sausage, sliced
into rounds
5 ounces Gruyère cheese, diced
Salt and pepper
Curly endive

Cook potatoes in large saucepan of boiling water until tender, about 20 minutes. Drain and cool slightly. Peel and slice potatoes. Transfer to large bowl. Gently mix in vinegar and green onions, using rubber spatula. Cool.

Combine yogurt, mayonnaise, horseradish and caraway. Mix into potatoes. Add kielbasa and cheese. Season with salt and pepper. Line plates with endive. Spoon salad atop. Serve immediately.

California Grilled Game Hen, Orange and Arugula Salad

12 servings

Hens

8 Cornish game hens, quartered
1½ cups fresh orange juice
  (about 3 oranges)
1 cup peanut oil
3 tablespoons soy sauce
3 garlic cloves, minced
3 teaspoons minced fresh ginger

Dressing

¼ cup Sherry vinegar
2 tablespoons oriental sesame oil
1½ teaspoons oriental chili oil
  Salt and pepper

Salad

4 ounces fresh shiitake mushrooms

1 head radicchio, torn into pieces
1 bunch arugula leaves
3 oranges, peeled, cut into
  segments
4 green onions, chopped
  Toasted almonds or cashews,
  chopped
  Grated peel from 1 orange

For hens: Arrange game hens in a single layer in glass baking dish. Mix ½ cup orange juice, ¼ cup peanut oil, 2 teaspoons soy sauce, 1 minced garlic clove and 1 teaspoon minced ginger in medium bowl. Pour marinade over hens. Cover tightly and refrigerate for at least six hours or overnight.

For dressing: Whisk remaining 1 cup orange juice, ¾ cup peanut oil, 2 tablespoons plus 1 teaspoon soy sauce, 2 minced garlic cloves and 2 teaspoons ginger in medium bowl. Stir in vinegar, sesame and chili oils. Whisk to blend. Season dressing with salt and pepper. (*Can be prepared 1 day ahead. Cover dressing and store at room temperature.*)

For salad: Bring hens to room temperature before grilling. Prepare barbecue (medium-high heat). Remove hens from marinade; reserve marinade. Arrange hens on grill. Cook until crisp and cooked through, turning occasionally, breast pieces about 10 minutes and leg pieces about 15 minutes. Transfer to platter. Brush mushrooms with reserved marinade; place on grill. Cook until tender and light brown, about 1 minute per side.

Arrange radicchio and arugula on another platter. Place hens atop greens. Surround with mushrooms and orange segments. Sprinkle with green onions, almonds and orange peel. Drizzle enough dressing over salad to moisten. Serve, passing remaining dressing separately.

Japanese Noodle, Shrimp and Cucumber Salad

12 servings

Dressing

⅔ cup rice wine vinegar
¼ cup soy sauce
¼ cup vegetable oil
3 tablespoons sugar
1 teaspoon dry mustard
  Pinch of cayenne pepper

Salad

1 pound fresh bean sprouts
14 ounces dried chuka soba
  noodles*
¼ cup oriental sesame oil

2 pounds cooked bay shrimp
3 large cucumbers, peeled, halved,
  thinly sliced
6 green onions, sliced
  Red cabbage leaves

For dressing: Whisk together vinegar, soy sauce, oil, sugar and mustard in small bowl. Season with cayenne pepper. (*Can be prepared up to 1 day ahead. Cover dressing and store at room temperature.*)

For salad: Blanch bean sprouts in boiling water 30 seconds. Drain and refresh in cold water. Drain. Bring large pot of salted water to boil. Add noodles and boil until tender, stirring occasionally, about 3 minutes. Drain noodles. Refresh in cold water. Drain and place in large bowl. Add sesame oil and toss to coat. (*Can be prepared up to 6 hours ahead. Cover and refrigerate bean sprouts and oriental noodles separately.*)

Add bean sprouts, shrimp, cucumbers and onions to noodles. Drizzle with dressing. Toss gently to combine. Line platter with cabbage leaves and mound salad in center. Serve immediately.

*Available at oriental markets and in oriental section of many supermarkets.

Warm Wild Rice and Chicken Salad

A light chicken salad with interesting textures makes a pleasing lunch or supper.

4 servings

Wild Rice
⅔ cup wild rice
2 cups water
¼ teaspoon salt

Chicken
3 large boneless chicken breast halves, skinned
   Salt and pepper
½ cup chicken stock or canned broth

Salad
1 large tart apple (unpeeled), cored, cut into 1-inch chunks
⅓ small red onion, halved
½ large red bell pepper, diced
½ cup dried currants
½ cup toasted pecan pieces
2 tablespoons balsamic vinegar or 1½ tablespoons red wine vinegar
2 tablespoons olive oil
½ teaspoon salt
   Pepper
   Red leaf lettuce leaves

For rice: Rinse rice. Place in small saucepan with water and salt. Bring to boil. Reduce heat, cover and simmer until rice is just tender, about 35 minutes. Transfer rice to large bowl. (*Can be prepared 1 day ahead. Cool, cover and chill.*)

For chicken: Season both sides of chicken with salt and pepper. Place in medium skillet. Add stock. Cook over medium-high heat until springy to touch, about 4 minutes per side. (**Or to microwave:** Place seasoned chicken breasts in 9-inch microwave-safe dish. Add stock. Cook covered on High 3 minutes. Turn and cook covered until almost completely opaque, about 1½ minutes. Let stand 5 minutes. Uncover and pierce with knife to be sure juices run clear.) (*Can be prepared 1 day ahead. Cover chicken and then refrigerate.*) Cut chicken into 1-inch chunks and add to rice.

For salad: Coarsely chop apple and onion in processor using on/off turns. Add to chicken. Mix in bell pepper, currants, pecans, vinegar, oil and salt. Season with pepper. Adjust seasonings. (*Can be prepared 4 hours ahead. Cover and refrigerate. Reheat covered in microwave on High for 3 minutes.*) Arrange lettuce on 4 dinner plates or 1 platter. Top with warm salad and serve.

3 ❦ Pasta, Pizza and Sandwiches

Over the past couple of years, there's been a real return in this country to so-called comfort food, the kind of simple, soul-satisfying fare that just plain tastes great. And from our experience, high on everybody's list of favorite comforts are pasta, pizza and sandwiches.

You're sure to find a pasta recipe here that proves irresistible and sends you in the direction of the kitchen to start the water boiling. Perhaps it will be Linguine with Spicy Tomato and Clam Sauce or Cheesy Pasta Shells with Chicken and Vegetables. The added benefit is that both make a quick and delicious supper when you add bread and a crisp green salad. Some elegant first-course pastas round out the selection.

When a pizza craving strikes, many of us reach for the phone, but there are some recipes here that might have you baking up a homemade version tonight, complete with olives, mushrooms and bell peppers.

If you thought sandwiches were only for lunch boxes, look again. Here you'll find hearty, main-course interpretations, including Grilled Flank Steak, Onion and Bell Pepper Sandwiches on Grilled French Bread Rolls and Broiled Tomato and Basil Sandwiches.

 Pasta

Spaghetti all'Amatriciana

4 servings

⅓ cup olive oil
½ pound pancetta* or bacon, cut into ¼-inch-wide strips
1 small onion, minced
2 garlic cloves, minced
1½ teaspoons minced jalapeño chilies with seeds

1 pinch (generous) of rubbed or ground dried sage
¾ cup dry white wine
3 cups prepared spaghetti sauce

1 pound spaghetti
1 tablespoon chopped fresh parsley
Freshly grated Parmesan cheese

Heat oil in heavy large deep skillet over medium heat. Add pancetta and cook until brown and slightly crisp, stirring frequently, about 10 minutes. Add onion, garlic, jalapeño and sage and sauté 3 minutes. Pour off oil from skillet. Add wine and bring to boil, scraping up any browned bits. Boil until liquid is reduced by half, about 2 minutes. Add spaghetti sauce and simmer 5 minutes. (*Can be prepared 1 day ahead. Cover and refrigerate. Rewarm sauce before continuing.*)

Cook pasta in large pot of boiling salted water until just tender but still firm to bite. Drain well. Transfer to large bowl. Mix parsley into sauce. Pour sauce over pasta and toss to coat. Serve, passing Parmesan separately.

*Italian unsmoked bacon cured in salt, available at Italian markets and some specialty foods stores.

Wild Mushroom and Orzo "Risotto"

Orzo—rice-shaped pasta— is easier to find than Arborio rice (the traditional ingredient in risotto) and makes a delicious risotto-style side dish.

6 servings

⅞ to 1 ounce dried porcini mushrooms*
1½ cups hot water

3 tablespoons olive oil
1 medium onion, chopped
2 cups orzo

3½ to 4 cups canned low-salt chicken broth

½ cup freshly grated Parmesan cheese (about 1¼ ounces)
Salt and pepper
Minced fresh parsley

Rinse mushrooms briefly with cold water. Place in small bowl. Add 1½ cups hot water and let soak until softened, about 30 minutes. Drain mushrooms, reserving soaking liquid. Squeeze mushrooms and chop.

Heat oil in heavy medium saucepan over medium heat. Add onion and sauté until tender, about 8 minutes. Add orzo and stir until coated with oil. Mix in chopped mushrooms. Set aside.

Meanwhile, combine 4 cups broth and mushroom soaking liquid in another medium saucepan. Bring to simmer. Reduce heat to low and keep hot.

Add 1 cup liquid to orzo, adjust heat so liquid simmers slowly and cook until orzo absorbs liquid, stirring occasionally. Continue adding liquid 1 cup at a time, simmering until each addition is absorbed before adding next and stirring occasionally until orzo is just tender and liquid is creamy, about 30 minutes. Stir in Parmesan. Season with salt and pepper. Garnish with parsley.

*Porcini mushrooms are available at Italian markets and specialty foods stores.

Mostaccioli with Spinach and Feta

4 to 6 servings

1 tablespoon butter
8 tablespoons olive oil
⅓ cup pine nuts
5 garlic cloves, minced
2 10-ounce packages frozen chopped spinach, thawed, well drained

4 large plum tomatoes, seeded, finely chopped
1 pound mostaccioli or penne pasta, freshly cooked
12 ounces feta cheese, crumbled
   Salt and pepper

Melt butter with 2 tablespoons oil in heavy large skillet over medium heat. Add pine nuts and garlic and sauté until pine nuts are light brown, about 5 minutes. Add spinach and tomatoes and sauté until heated through, about 3 minutes. Place mostaccioli in serving bowl. Add remaining 6 tablespoons oil to pasta and toss. Pour spinach-pine nut mixture over and toss to coat. Add feta. Season with salt and pepper and toss thoroughly. Serve immediately.

Pasta with Roasted Eggplant

Eggplant roasted on the grill and then marinated gets tossed with hot pasta just before serving—a lovely play of different tastes and temperatures.

12 servings

3 large eggplants or 7 Japanese eggplants, cut into ½-inch-thick rounds
   Salt

1 medium-size red onion, cut into ½-inch-thick rounds
¾ cup olive oil (preferably extra-virgin)
   Pepper

1 cup chopped red onion
2 large garlic cloves, minced
¼ cup fresh lemon juice

¼ teaspoon dried crushed red pepper

1½ pounds penne rigate or other tubular pasta
3 large tomatoes, seeded, cut into ¼-inch-wide strips
½ cup plus 2 tablespoons (about 4 ounces) toasted pine nuts
½ cup chopped fresh oregano
½ cup chopped fresh basil
1½ cups freshly grated Romano cheese (about 6 ounces)

Arrange eggplant rounds on triple layer of paper towels on large cookie sheet. Sprinkle both sides of eggplant with salt. Cover with more paper towels. Place cutting board over eggplant; weight with heavy objects (books or cans work well). Let stand at least 12 hours and up to 48 hours to drain.

Prepare barbecue (high heat). Brush eggplant and onion rounds with ½ cup olive oil. Grill until brown and eggplant is soft, about 2½ minutes per side. Transfer to large pan. Sprinkle with salt and pepper. Cool slightly.

Cut grilled vegetables into ½-inch-wide strips. Transfer to large bowl. Add chopped red onion, garlic, lemon juice, crushed red pepper and remaining ¼ cup olive oil. Let stand 1 hour. (*Can be prepared 1 day ahead. Cover and refrigerate. Let mixture stand at room temperature 2 hours before continuing.*)

Cook penne in boiling salted water until tender but still firm to bite, stirring occasionally. Drain well. Add pasta to eggplant mixture. Mix in tomatoes, pine nuts and herbs. Add cheese. Season with salt and pepper.

Cheesy Pasta Shells with Chicken and Vegetables

Rotelle *or* radiatore *("radiators") would work well here, too. This can easily be doubled.*

2 servings

8 ounces shell, rotelle or radiatore pasta

5 tablespoons olive oil

3 medium zucchini, cut into ½-inch cubes

½ teaspoon salt

4 boneless, skinless chicken breast halves, cut into 1 × 2-inch strips

1 teaspoon dried marjoram, crumbled

3 garlic cloves, minced

1 cup chicken stock or canned broth

⅔ cup drained rinsed canned garbanzo beans (chick-peas)

⅔ cup frozen whole kernel corn, thawed, drained

⅓ cup sliced green onions

8 ounces hot pepper cheese (such as hot pepper Jack or Havarti), grated

2 tablespoons freshly grated Parmesan cheese

Cook pasta in large pot of boiling salted water until just tender but still firm to bite, stirring occasionally to prevent sticking. Drain well.

Meanwhile, heat 3 tablespoons olive oil in heavy large skillet over medium-high heat. Add zucchini and cook until brown, stirring frequently, about 7 minutes. Add ¼ teaspoon salt and toss well. Using slotted spoon, transfer zucchini to small bowl and reserve.

Heat remaining 2 tablespoons oil in same skillet. Add chicken and marjoram and sauté 2 minutes. Add garlic, reduce heat to medium and sauté until chicken is cooked through, about 3 minutes. Add remaining ¼ teaspoon salt. Increase heat to high. Add stock and bring to boil, scraping up browned bits.

Add pasta, zucchini, garbanzo beans and corn to chicken mixture. Cook until pasta has absorbed most of liquid, stirring frequently, about 4 minutes. Add green onions, pepper cheese and Parmesan. Remove from heat. Cover and let stand 1 minute. Divide between plates and serve immediately.

Orecchiette Pasta with Vegetables and Cream

Orecchiette *means "little ears" in Italian. If you can't find this curved pasta in your market, any shell-shaped one will do.*

4 servings

¼ cup diced peeled carrot

¼ cup diced broccoli

4 asparagus, trimmed and diced

2 tablespoons (¼ stick) unsalted butter

2 garlic cloves, minced

¼ cup diced yellow bell pepper

¼ cup diced red bell pepper

¼ cup diced zucchini

1 cup whipping cream

4 teaspoons purchased pesto sauce
Salt and pepper

8 ounces orecchiette pasta

½ cup freshly grated Romano cheese (about 2 ounces)
Additional freshly grated Romano cheese

Cook carrot in small saucepan of boiling salted water until just tender, about 3 minutes. Add broccoli and asparagus and cook 30 seconds. Drain.

Melt butter in heavy large skillet over medium heat. Add garlic and sauté 1 minute. Add all vegetables and sauté 3 minutes. Mix in cream and pesto. Season with salt and pepper. Boil until slightly thickened, about 5 minutes.

Meanwhile, cook pasta in large pot of boiling salted water until just tender but still firm to bite. Drain pasta well. Transfer pasta to large bowl.

Pour sauce over pasta. Add ½ cup Romano and toss to coat. Serve, passing additional Romano cheese separately.

Fettuccine with Chicken and Wild Mushroom Sauce

4 servings

3 tablespoons unsalted butter
2 garlic cloves, minced
3 boneless chicken breast halves, skinned, cut into 1-inch pieces
5 ounces fresh shiitake mushrooms, stemmed and sliced, or 5 ounces fresh oyster mushrooms, sliced

3 tablespoons chopped green onions
3 tablespoons dry Madeira
1¼ cups whipping cream
3½ ounces goat cheese, crumbled
Salt and pepper

12 ounces fettuccine

Melt butter in heavy large skillet over medium-high heat. Add garlic and sauté 30 seconds. Add chicken, mushrooms and green onions and sauté 5 minutes. Add Madeira and stir 1 minute. Mix in cream and goat cheese and cook until sauce thickens slightly and chicken is cooked through, about 4 minutes. Season sauce with salt and pepper.

Meanwhile, cook fettuccine in large pot of boiling water until just tender but still firm to bite, stirring occasionally. Drain well. Transfer to large bowl. Add sauce and toss well. Serve immediately.

Linguine with Spicy Tomato and Clam Sauce

This is as delicious with mussels as it is with clams.

2 servings

1 28-ounce can Italian plum tomatoes, drained
4 tablespoons olive oil
½ red onion, chopped
3 large garlic cloves, minced
¼ teaspoon dried crushed red pepper
Salt and pepper

2 tablespoons chopped fresh marjoram or 1½ teaspoons dried, crumbled
2 tablespoons chopped fresh Italian parsley
1 pound fresh clams

8 ounces linguine

Gently squeeze tomatoes to remove juices, then chop. Heat 3 tablespoons oil in heavy large saucepan over medium heat. Add onion and sauté until tender, about 5 minutes. Add garlic and sauté until soft, about 4 minutes. Add dried red pepper and stir 20 seconds. Mix in tomatoes and simmer until sauce thickens, stirring frequently, about 5 minutes. Season with salt and pepper. Stir in half of marjoram and half of parsley. Add clams to sauce. Cover and cook sauce until clams open, approximately 5 minutes.

Meanwhile, cook linguine in large pot of boiling salted water until just tender but still firm to bite. Drain well. Transfer to large bowl. Add remaining 1 tablespoon oil and toss to coat. Pour clams and sauce over, discarding any clams that do not open. Sprinkle with remaining chopped fresh herbs.

 *Pizza*

Pesto, Tomato and Cheese Pizza Bites

Makes about 30

Herb Oil
- ⅔ cup olive oil
- 4 garlic cloves, finely chopped
- 3 tablespoons minced fresh basil or 1 tablespoon dried, crumbled
- 3 tablespoons minced fresh oregano or 1 tablespoon dried, crumbled

Pizzas
- 2 8-ounce sourdough baguettes, sliced into ½-inch-thick rounds

- ¾ cup (about) Basil and Olive Pesto (see recipe)
- 1 pound smoked mozzarella cheese, thinly sliced
- 1 cup (about) Tomato-Anchovy Sauce (see recipe)
- ½ pound Gorgonzola cheese, crumbled
- 8 ounces lox trimmings
- 15 oil-packed sun-dried tomatoes, drained and cut into strips

For oil: Mix all ingredients in small bowl. Cover and let stand 4 hours at room temperature. (*Can be prepared 3 days ahead. Cover and refrigerate.*)

For pizzas: Preheat oven to 450°F. Arrange bread slices on heavy large cookie sheets. Brush tops with herb oil. Bake until tops are crusty, about 4 minutes. Maintain oven temperature.

Spread 1 teaspoon pesto over each toasted bread round. Top each with slice of mozzarella, trimming to fit. Top each with 1½ teaspoons tomato sauce. Sprinkle with Gorgonzola. Top half of pizzas with lox trimmings and half with sun-dried tomato strips. (*Can be prepared ahead. Cover and refrigerate 4 hours or freeze pizzas on cookie sheet until firm. Cover with foil and return to freezer. Thaw before continuing with recipe.*) Bake pizzas until cheese melts and topping is heated through, about 10 minutes. Transfer to platter and serve.

Basil and Olive Pesto

Makes about 1½ cups

- 1 cup packed fresh basil leaves
- 6 tablespoons pine nuts
- ¼ cup walnuts (about 1 ounce)
- 12 black olives (preferably Gaeta*), pitted
- 2 garlic cloves

- ½ cup freshly grated Parmesan cheese (about 2 ounces)
- ¼ cup freshly grated Romano cheese (about 1 ounce)
- ½ cup olive oil
- Pepper

Puree first 5 ingredients in processor. Blend in cheeses. Gradually add oil, blending until smooth. Season with pepper. (*Can be prepared 3 days ahead. Transfer to jar. Add enough oil to cover pesto; chill. Mix before using.*)

*Gaeta olives are available at Italian markets and some specialty foods stores.

Tomato-Anchovy Sauce

Makes about 5 cups

2 pounds ripe tomatoes

1½ tablespoons olive oil
1 2-ounce can anchovies, drained, oil reserved, anchovies chopped
2 small onions, finely chopped
2 celery stalks, finely chopped
4 large garlic cloves, finely chopped
½ cup water
3½ tablespoons tomato paste

1½ tablespoons chopped fresh oregano or 1 teaspoon dried, crumbled
1 bay leaf
1 teaspoon fennel seeds
Pepper
5 tablespoons freshly grated Parmesan cheese (about 1 ounce)
⅓ cup chopped fresh Italian parsley
8 fresh basil leaves, finely chopped

Blanch tomatoes in large saucepan of boiling water for 10 seconds. Transfer to bowl of cold water using slotted spoon. Drain. Pull off tomato skins using small knife. Quarter tomatoes. Set aside.

Heat olive oil and reserved anchovy oil in heavy large skillet over medium-low heat. Add onions, celery and garlic and sauté until soft, about 15 minutes. Mix in chopped anchovies, tomatoes, water, tomato paste, oregano, bay leaf and fennel seeds. Season with pepper. Cover and bring to boil. Uncover, reduce heat and simmer 40 minutes to blend flavors and thicken sauce, adding Parmesan during last 5 minutes and stirring occasionally. Mix in parsley and basil. Cool sauce completely. (*Can be prepared 1 day ahead. Cover and refrigerate.*)

Mesquite-grilled Pizza

Makes one 14-inch pizza

1 envelope dry yeast
¾ cup plus 2 tablespoons warm water (105°F to 115°F)
2 tablespoons olive oil
2½ cups (or more) bread flour
1 teaspoon salt

Olive oil

1 cup purchased pizza sauce
¾ cup pitted black olives, halved
¼ cup pitted green olives, halved
12 ounces mozzarella cheese, shredded (about 3½ cups)

½ cup freshly grated Parmesan cheese
⅓ pound mushrooms, sliced
½ green bell pepper, cut into matchstick-size strips
½ red bell pepper, cut into matchstick-size strips
1 tablespoon olive oil
Minced fresh herbs such as oregano, basil and rosemary (optional)

½ cup mesquite chips soaked in water 30 minutes and drained

Sprinkle yeast over warm water in small bowl; stir to dissolve. Let stand 5 minutes. Stir in 2 tablespoons oil. Mix 2½ cups flour and salt in processor using on/off turns. With machine running, pour yeast mixture through feed tube and process until combined, about 10 seconds. Knead dough on lightly floured surface until smooth and elastic, adding more flour if sticky, about 5 minutes.

Brush large bowl with olive oil. Add dough, turning to coat entire surface. Cover and let rise in warm draft-free area until doubled in volume, about 1½ hours. (*Can be prepared 1 day ahead. Punch dough down; cover and refrigerate. Bring to room temperature before continuing with recipe.*)

Prepare covered barbecue grill (medium-high heat). Brush 14-inch pizza pan with 1-inch-high sides with olive oil. Punch dough down and knead 2 minutes. Roll dough out on lightly floured surface to 16-inch round. Transfer to prepared pan. Spread sauce over dough; sprinkle with black and green olives. Top with both cheeses, then mushrooms and bell peppers. Drizzle with 1 tablespoon oil. Sprinkle with minced herbs if desired.

Add mesquite chips to fire. Open bottom barbecue vent. Place pizza on rack on lowest rung. Cover, leaving top vent half open. Bake until crust is golden brown, checking occasionally, about 15 minutes. Serve immediately.

Double-Cheese, Mushroom and Tapenade Pizza

6 to 8 servings

Tapenade
  1 cup black olives (preferably Gaeta*), pitted
  ¼ cup capers, rinsed, drained
  4 anchovy fillets
  2 tablespoons olive oil
  1 tablespoon fresh lemon juice
    Pepper

Pizza
  2 tablespoons (¼ stick) unsalted butter

  6 ounces mushrooms, sliced
  1 Whole Wheat Pizza Crust (see recipe)
  1 cup (generous) grated mozzarella (about 4 ounces)
  2 tablespoons chopped fresh basil or 2 teaspoons dried, crumbled
  2 teaspoons grated lemon peel
  1 cup (generous) grated Monterey Jack cheese (about 4 ounces)

For tapenade: Place olives, capers and anchovies in blender. Process until finely chopped. With machine running, gradually add oil. Puree until mixture binds together. Add lemon juice. Season with pepper. (*Can be prepared 1 day ahead. Cover tightly and refrigerate.*) Set tapenade aside.

For pizza: Melt butter in heavy medium skillet. Add mushrooms and cook until golden brown, stirring occasionally, about 6 minutes. Cool slightly.

Position rack in lowest third of oven and preheat to 500°F. Spread tapenade over Whole Wheat Pizza Crust. Sprinkle with mozzarella. Top with mushrooms. Distribute basil and lemon peel over mushrooms. Sprinkle with Monterey Jack cheese. Bake until crust is golden brown, about 20 minutes.

*Gaeta olives are available at Italian markets and some specialty foods stores.

Whole Wheat Pizza Crust

Freeze the extra crusts for quick pizza dinners.

Makes five 10-inch pizza crusts

Sponge
  2 cups warm water (105°F to 115°F)
  2½ tablespoons dry yeast
  ¾ cup whole wheat flour

Dough
  1¼ cups whole wheat flour
  ¾ cup olive oil
  2 teaspoons salt
  3¼ cups (or more) unbleached all purpose flour

For sponge: Mix water, yeast and ¾ cup whole wheat flour in large bowl. Cover and let stand in warm draft-free area until foamy, about 15 minutes.

For dough: Stir 1¼ cups whole wheat flour into sponge. Add oil, salt and 3 cups all purpose flour. Stir to combine. Dust work surface with ¼ cup all purpose flour. Turn dough out onto floured surface and knead until smooth and elastic, adding more flour if dough is very sticky, about 5 minutes.

Transfer dough to large bowl. Cover lightly with towel. Let rise in warm draft-free area until doubled in volume, about 1 hour. Divide dough into 5 equal pieces. Roll each piece out on lightly floured surface to 10-inch round. Transfer to 10-inch pizza pan. Press to build rim. (*Can be prepared 2 weeks ahead. Wrap pizza crusts individually and freeze. Thaw at room temperature before using.*)

❦ Sandwiches

Pizzette

The Pesto Sauce keeps in the refrigerator up to four days. Toss the remainder with freshly cooked pasta for a simple supper.

4 servings

1 medium eggplant, cut crosswise into ¼-inch-thick rounds
1 small red onion, cut into ½-inch-thick slices
3 medium tomatoes, thinly sliced
7 tablespoons olive oil
1 teaspoon dried thyme, crumbled
Salt and pepper

1 9-ounce French bread baguette
½ cup olive oil

6 tablespoons Pesto Sauce (see recipe)
4 ounces mozzarella cheese, thinly sliced
¾ cup freshly grated Romano cheese (about 3 ounces)
¼ cup Kalamata olives,* pitted and sliced
¼ cup chopped green onions

Prepare barbecue (medium-high heat). Arrange eggplant, onion and tomatoes on cookie sheets. Brush both sides using 7 tablespoons oil; sprinkle with thyme. Season with salt and pepper. Place onion slices on grill and cook until tender, about 4 minutes per side. Place eggplant on grill and cook until tender, about 2 minutes per side. Grill tomato until lightly charred, about 45 seconds per side.

Preheat oven to 350°F. Halve bread lengthwise using serrated knife. Gently pull out soft bread, leaving ½-inch shell (reserve centers for another use). Brush each bread half with ¼ cup oil. Bake bread cut side up 4 minutes.

Increase oven temperature to 400°F. Spread 3 tablespoons Pesto Sauce on each bread half. Place alternating layers of grilled eggplant, mozzarella and grilled tomato on each bread half. Sprinkle with Romano cheese. Bake until crust is crisp and cheese melts, about 8 minutes. Top with olives and green onions. Halve bread crosswise. Transfer to plates. Serve with grilled onions.

*Black, brine-cured olives, available at Greek and Italian markets and some supermarkets.

Pesto Sauce

Makes about 1 cup

½ bunch fresh basil
½ bunch fresh parsley, stemmed
¼ cup pine nuts, toasted
2 tablespoons freshly grated Romano cheese

1 tablespoon finely chopped garlic
⅛ teaspoon salt
¼ teaspoon pepper
½ cup olive oil

Place first 7 ingredients in processor and chop finely. With machine running, gradually add oil through feed tube and blend until pesto is smooth. (*Can be prepared 4 days ahead. Transfer to bowl. Press plastic wrap onto surface of pesto to preserve color; refrigerate.*)

Grilled Flank Steak, Onion and Bell Pepper Sandwiches

12 servings

3 cups dry red wine
3 cups chopped onions
2¼ cups soy sauce
¾ cup olive oil
8 large garlic cloves, chopped
1 tablespoon plus 1½ teaspoons dry mustard
1 tablespoon plus 1½ teaspoons ground ginger

4½ pounds flank steaks
6 large bell peppers (red, yellow and/or green), cut into ¾-inch-wide strips
3 large red onions, cut into ½-inch-thick rings

Grilled French Bread Rolls (see recipe)

Combine first 7 ingredients in large bowl. Divide steaks, bell peppers and red onions among large shallow pans. Pour marinade over. Turn to coat. Cover with plastic wrap and refrigerate 3 to 6 hours.

Prepare barbecue (high heat). Drain steaks and vegetables. Grill steaks to desired degree of doneness, about 4 minutes per side for rare. Transfer to platter. Grill vegetables until beginning to brown, about 4 minutes per side. Slice steaks thinly across grain. Arrange steaks and vegetables on large platter. Serve with grilled rolls, allowing diners to assemble sandwiches.

Grilled French Bread Rolls

Makes 18

¾ cup olive oil
6 garlic cloves, flattened

18 large French bread rolls
Pepper

Heat olive oil in heavy medium skillet over medium-low heat. Add garlic and cook until light brown, about 4 minutes. Discard garlic.

Prepare barbecue (high heat). Split rolls in half horizontally. Brush cut surfaces with garlic oil. Sprinkle generously with pepper. Grill rolls, oiled side down, until golden brown. Serve hot or at room temperature.

Broiled Tomato and Basil Sandwiches

4 servings

4 large sourdough sandwich bread slices
4 teaspoons olive oil
3 tomatoes, thinly sliced
Salt and pepper

3 tablespoons minced fresh basil or 2 teaspoons dried, crumbled
3 ounces Monterey Jack cheese, cut into 8 slices
3 ounces mozzarella, cut into 8 thin slices

Preheat broiler. Brush 1 side of each bread slice with 1 teaspoon olive oil. Place bread oiled side up on cookie sheet. Broil until lightly toasted. Arrange tomato slices on bread. Season with salt and pepper. Sprinkle basil over. Top with cheese slices. Brown until cheese melts, about 2 minutes. Serve hot.

4 ❧ Main Courses

In this, the heart of the book, you'll find the kind of good, quick-to-cook recipes that will become mainstays in your repertoire of regular week-night meals along with showstopping dinner party fare, sure to please and impress. And whether you're looking for something new to do with chicken or a helping hand to guide you through a first effort with duck, you'll be sure to come across the ideal recipe here.

Steak goes elegant when it's sautéed and served with a creamy green peppercorn, horseradish and Cognac sauce. Or if you're of a mind to splurge on veal, try simple Herb-scented Grilled Veal Chops or luscious Veal with Leek and Roquefort Sauce. Lamb shoulder chops—readily available but often overlooked—are terrific braised in a garlicky blend of tomatoes and wine. And dinner couldn't be easier than Fried Peppers, Onions and Sausages, a one-dish meal that cooks in about 15 minutes.

If you're like a lot of us, chicken and seafood make regular appearances on your menus. For something simple but different, consider Basil-Buttermilk Fried Chicken; for something a little daring and innovative, how about Shrimp with Black Beans and Pineapple-Coconut Relish?

This chapter ends with a selection of delicious egg, cheese and vegetable entrées, ideal for those who are eating less red meat. Among them are the easy-to-make Chili Soufflé Roll with Chunky Tomato and Green Onion Sauce and a satisfying Mixed Mushroom and Potato Charlotte.

 # *Beef*

Deviled Herb-and-Mustard Beef Ribs

This recipe is great for a big family get-together. Kids adore these dinosaur-size meaty ribs, and grown-ups appreciate the great taste, as beef back ribs are cut from the prime. The seasoning mixture used to flavor these ribs is also good with steak and chicken. Serve with your favorite potato salad, sliced tomatoes with vinaigrette and crusty sourdough bread.

6 servings

Glaze

½ cup (1 stick) unsalted butter
¼ cup olive oil
6 green onions (white and green parts chopped separately)
1 cup finely minced yellow onion
3 large garlic cloves, pressed
¼ cup Worcestershire sauce
¼ cup dry Sherry
2 tablespoons firmly packed golden brown sugar
2 tablespoons fresh lemon juice
⅔ cup Dijon mustard
1 teaspoon cracked black peppercorns
¼ teaspoon cayenne pepper
2 tablespoons minced fresh parsley
2 tablespoons minced fresh tarragon or 2 teaspoons dried, crumbled
2 tablespoons minced fresh thyme or 2 teaspoons dried, crumbled
Salt

Seasoning

1½ tablespoons hickory-smoked salt*
1½ tablespoons grated orange peel
1 tablespoon sugar
1 tablespoon coarsely ground pepper
1 tablespoon grated lemon peel
1½ teaspoons ground allspice
1½ teaspoons dry mustard
1½ teaspoons ground ginger
1½ teaspoons ground coriander
1½ teaspoons paprika

3 beef back rib racks (about 9 pounds)
2 lemons, halved

Fresh parsley sprigs

For glaze: Melt butter with oil in heavy large saucepan over medium-high heat. Add chopped white part of green onions and minced yellow onion and sauté until translucent, about 5 minutes. Add garlic and sauté 2 minutes. Add Worcestershire, Sherry, sugar and lemon juice and cook until thick and bubbling, stirring constantly, about 5 minutes. Remove from heat. Whisk in mustard, peppercorns and cayenne. Add minced herbs and ¼ cup chopped green onion tops. Season with salt. (*Glaze can be prepared 1 day ahead; refrigerate. Before using, stir over low heat until heated through.*)

For seasoning: Mix first 10 ingredients in small bowl to blend.

Rub ribs with cut sides of lemons. Rub ribs with ½ cup seasoning. Cover and let stand at room temperature 45 minutes.

Prepare barbecue grill (medium-high heat). Lightly brush grill with oil. Place ribs on grill and sear 5 minutes per side. Continue grilling until meat is tender and ribs are lightly charred, turning occasionally and brushing with some of glaze during last 5 minutes, about 12 minutes. Transfer ribs to work surface. Cut into individual ribs. Arrange on platter. Garnish with parsley sprigs. Serve ribs with remaining glaze.

*Hickory-smoked salt is available in the spice section of most supermarkets.

Beer-braised Beef Short Ribs with Spicy Molasses Mop

A mop is a thin basting sauce, in this case a slightly sweet and spicy blend of molasses and hot pepper sauce. Succulent, meaty beef short ribs take a fair amount of cooking time to reach optimum tenderness, but that step can be done days ahead. A brief, ten-minute finish over a smoky fire then heats and crisps the ribs, while the mop glazes them a rich brown.

6 servings

5 pounds beef short ribs, surface fat trimmed
3½ cups canned beef broth
1 12-ounce bottle dark beer
1 medium onion, sliced
1 teaspoon salt
½ teaspoon dried thyme, crumbled

¼ cup unsulfured molasses
2 tablespoons balsamic vinegar or red wine vinegar
2½ teaspoons hot pepper sauce (such as Tabasco)
1 teaspoon salt

Preheat oven to 350°F. Combine first 6 ingredients in heavy large Dutch oven. Bring to boil over medium heat. Cover and bake until ribs are very tender, turning occasionally, about 2 hours 50 minutes. Cover and refrigerate until fat solidifies. (*Can be prepared to this point 2 days ahead.*)

Spoon off fat from surface of rib-braising liquid. Remove short ribs from liquid and pat dry. Strain braising liquid. Combine ¼ cup braising liquid, molasses, vinegar, hot pepper sauce and salt in small bowl.

Prepare barbecue (medium heat). Place ribs on grill. Cover with grill lid or heavy-duty foil. Cook until ribs are crisp and heated through, turning and basting frequently with molasses mixture, about 10 minutes. Serve hot.

Sautéed Beef Tenderloin with Cream of Shallot Sauce

Poached marrow makes a delicious garnish to this entrée. To keep it white, soak it in water overnight before cooking.

4 servings

8 marrow bones (optional)

Sauce
2 pounds veal bones (preferably shank end, cut up)
3 cups chicken stock or canned low-salt chicken broth
1 cup beef stock or canned unsalted beef broth

1 tablespoon butter
4 large shallots, minced
½ cup dry white wine
6 tablespoons (¾ stick) butter, cut into 6 pieces
Salt and pepper

Beef
4 8-ounce beef tenderloins
Coarse salt
3 tablespoons butter
1 tablespoon olive oil

Minced fresh parsley

Crack each marrow bone open. Remove marrow in as large a piece as possible. Transfer marrow to colander. Run under cold water. Transfer to bowl. Cover with cold water. Refrigerate marrow overnight.

For sauce: Preheat oven to 450°F. Place veal bones in roasting pan and roast until well browned, turning occasionally, about 45 minutes. Transfer bones to large pot. Set roasting pan over high heat. Add both stocks and bring to boil, scraping up browned bits. Pour into pot with bones. Simmer until reduced to 1 cup, about 2 hours. (*Can be prepared 1 day ahead. Chill.*)

Melt 1 tablespoon butter in heavy medium skillet over medium heat. Add shallots and sauté until golden brown, about 4 minutes. Add wine and boil until almost completely evaporated, about 4 minutes. Add reduced broth and boil until reduced to ⅔ cup, about 6 minutes. Whisk in 6 tablespoons butter 1 piece at a time. Season with salt and pepper. Remove from heat.

For beef: Pat beef dry. Sprinkle with coarse salt. Melt 3 tablespoons butter with oil in heavy large skillet over medium-high heat. Add beef and cook to desired degree of doneness, about 4 minutes per side for medium-rare.

Meanwhile, drain marrow and cut into ⅜-inch-thick pieces. Bring pot of salted water to boil. Reduce heat, add marrow and simmer until opaque, 5 minutes. Remove using slotted spoon.

Set beef tenderloin on each plate. Nap with sauce. Sprinkle with parsley. Garnish with marrow slices if desired.

Fillet of Beef with Sun-dried Tomato Aioli

6 servings

1 cup olive oil (preferably extra-virgin)
¾ cup dry red wine
1 tablespoon chopped fresh thyme or 1 teaspoon dried, crumbled
1 tablespoon minced garlic
1 tablespoon minced fresh parsley

½ teaspoon pepper
1 2-pound beef fillet (center cut)

1 tablespoon olive oil

Sun-dried Tomato Aioli (see recipe)

Mix first 6 ingredients in medium bowl. Place beef in shallow glass baking dish. Pour marinade over. Cover and marinate 2 hours, turning occasionally.

Preheat oven to 350°F. Remove beef from marinade. Heat 1 tablespoon oil in heavy large skillet over medium-high heat. Add beef and brown on all sides, about 5 minutes. Place beef on rack set in roasting pan. Roast beef until thermometer inserted in center registers 125°F for medium-rare, about 20 minutes. Transfer to heated platter. Let beef stand for 10 minutes.

Cut beef into thin slices. Divide among plates. Serve with aioli.

Sun-dried Tomato Aioli

Makes about 2 cups

¼ cup drained oil-packed sun-dried tomatoes
1 large egg
1 tablespoon minced garlic
1½ teaspoons Dijon mustard

1½ teaspoons fresh lemon juice
¾ cup olive oil (preferably extra-virgin)
Salt and white pepper

Finely chop sun-dried tomatoes in processor. Add egg, garlic, mustard and lemon juice and blend well. With machine running, gradually add oil through feed tube in slow steady stream. Blend until smooth and thick. Season with salt and pepper. (*Can be prepared 2 days ahead. Refrigerate.*)

Steaks with Green Peppercorn, Horseradish and Cognac Sauce

4 servings

1 cup chicken stock or canned low-salt broth
1 cup beef stock or canned unsalted broth

2 tablespoons olive oil
4 1½-inch-thick 8-ounce beef fillets
Salt and pepper

1 tablespoon butter

2 tablespoons chopped shallots
1 tablespoon dried green peppercorns, crushed
½ cup dry red wine vinegar
2 tablespoons Cognac
2 cups whipping cream
2½ tablespoons freshly grated horseradish or 2 tablespoons prepared horseradish

Boil both stocks in heavy medium saucepan until liquid is reduced to ½ cup, about 15 minutes. Set reduced stock aside.

Heat oil in heavy large skillet over medium-high heat. Season beef with salt and pepper. Add beef to skillet and brown well. Reduce heat to medium and cook about 5 minutes per side for medium-rare. Transfer beef to platter. Tent with foil to keep warm. Set aside.

Pour off oil from skillet. Add butter and stir over medium heat until melted. Add shallots and peppercorns and sauté until shallots are golden brown, about 5 minutes. Increase heat to high. Add vinegar and Cognac and boil until liquid is reduced to ¼ cup, about 4 minutes. Add reduced stock and cream and boil until reduced to thick sauce consistency, stirring occasionally, about 5 minutes. Mix grated horseradish into sauce. Season with salt. Spoon sauce over steaks.

Stifado

This Greek stew is typically served with french fries, but it would also be good with a simple rice pilaf.

4 servings

¼ cup olive oil
1½ pounds boneless beef chuck roast, cut into 1½-inch cubes
2 tablespoons all purpose flour
12 ounces small white boiling onions, peeled
1 pound tomatoes, peeled, seeded, chopped
3 garlic cloves, minced
2½ tablespoons chopped fresh thyme or 1 teaspoon dried, crumbled

2½ tablespoons chopped fresh oregano or 1 teaspoon dried, crumbled
2½ tablespoons chopped fresh rosemary or 1 teaspoon dried, crumbled
1 bay leaf, crumbled
1 teaspoon ground cumin
2 cups dry red wine

½ pound feta cheese, crumbled
Salt and pepper

Preheat oven to 350°F. Heat oil in heavy 4- to 5-quart Dutch oven over medium-high heat. Toss beef with flour in large bowl. Add beef to pan in batches and cook until brown, stirring occasionally, about 3 minutes per batch. Transfer browned beef to bowl. Add onions to pan and cook until light brown, stirring frequently, about 5 minutes. Add tomatoes, garlic, herbs and cumin to onions. Return beef and any juices in bowl to pan. Stir in wine and bring to boil. Cover and bake in oven until beef is tender, about 2 hours. (*Can be prepared 1 day ahead. Cover and refrigerate. Rewarm in 350°F oven before continuing.*)

Stir feta into stew. Return to oven and continue baking until cheese is heated through, about 10 minutes. Season with salt and pepper and serve.

Filet Mignon Hash

A warm cabbage salad is a good accompaniment.

2 servings

½ pound filet mignon
2 tablespoons (¼ stick) unsalted butter
2 tablespoons vegetable oil
¾ pound red new potatoes, peeled, sliced, boiled until just tender, drained
1 small onion, chopped

1 garlic clove, minced
1 teaspoon minced fresh thyme or ¼ teaspoon dried, crumbled
1 teaspoon minced fresh marjoram or ¼ teaspoon dried, crumbled
1 teaspoon minced fresh parsley
1 teaspoon caraway seeds
Salt and pepper

Wrap filet in plastic and freeze until firm but not solid. Slice across grain as thinly as possible. Cut slices lengthwise into fine slivers. Set aside.

Melt butter with oil in heavy large skillet over medium-high heat. Add filet mignon and sauté until brown, about 3 minutes. Transfer to platter using slotted spoon. Add potatoes and onion to skillet and sauté until brown, about 8 minutes. Mix in garlic and cook 2 minutes. Return filet mignon to pan. Mix in thyme, marjoram, parsley and caraway. Season hash with salt and pepper and serve.

Veal

Herb-scented Grilled Veal Chops

The secret of succulent veal chops is quick searing and then slow grilling until the chops are just blushed with pink inside. Marinate them overnight. Offer the chops with steamed broccoli.

12 servings

1 cup olive oil (preferably extra-virgin)
5 large garlic cloves
1 tablespoon plus 1 teaspoon grated orange peel
¼ teaspoon pepper

12 ½-inch-thick veal rib or loin chops
18 fresh sage leaves

Salt
1 small bunch sage leaves dipped in water

Combine olive oil, garlic, orange peel and pepper in processor. Process until garlic is finely chopped. Place chops in large shallow baking dish. Rub chops with 18 sage leaves. Pour oil mixture over. Refrigerate overnight.

Prepare barbecue (high heat). Drain chops. Sprinkle chops with salt. Grill 1 minute on each side. Raise grill or close vents to reduce barbecue temperature. Grill chops until almost cooked through, about 4 minutes per side. Place wet sage leaves directly on coals to create smoke. Continue grilling chops to desired degree of doneness, about 4 minutes per side for medium-rare. Season chops with salt and serve immediately.

Veal Saltimbocca

2 servings

6 veal scallops (about 9 ounces total)
1 teaspoon dried sage, crumbled
Pepper
6 paper-thin prosciutto slices

½ cup all purpose flour

3 tablespoons unsalted butter
¾ cup dry white wine
6 tablespoons (¾ stick) chilled unsalted butter, cut into pieces
Salt
Lemon wedges

Place 1 veal scallop between sheets of waxed paper. Flatten to thickness of ⅛ inch using mallet or rolling pin. Repeat with remaining veal. Season veal with sage and pepper. Place 1 slice of prosciutto atop each veal scallop. Fold each veal scallop in half crosswise. Secure open ends with toothpick.

Dredge veal in flour; shake off excess. Melt 3 tablespoons butter in heavy large skillet over medium heat. Add veal and cook until golden, 2 to 3 minutes per side. Transfer veal to platter; tent with foil. Pour off fat from skillet.

Add wine to skillet and bring to boil, scraping up any browned bits. Boil until liquid is reduced to ¼ cup, about 8 minutes. Reduce heat to low. Whisk in 6 tablespoons chilled butter 1 tablespoon at a time. Season sauce with salt and pepper. Remove toothpicks from veal. Pour sauce over. Garnish with lemon wedges and serve immediately.

Veal Chop Calabrese

2 servings

6 tablespoons olive oil
1 red bell pepper, cut into 2-inch-wide strips
4 garlic cloves, thinly sliced
2 tablespoons fresh lemon juice
2 tablespoons red wine vinegar

1 cup chicken stock or canned low-salt broth
2 8-ounce, 1-inch-thick veal chops
Salt and pepper

Heat 3 tablespoons oil in heavy medium skillet over medium heat. Add bell pepper and cook until brown on edges, turning occasionally, about 4 minutes. Add garlic and sauté until golden brown, about 2 minutes. Add lemon juice and vinegar and bring to boil. Add stock and bring to boil.

Heat remaining 3 tablespoons oil in heavy large skillet over medium-high heat. Season veal with salt and pepper. Add to skillet and cook to desired degree of doneness, about 5 minutes per side for medium. Transfer to plates; tent with foil to keep warm. Add bell pepper and stock mixture to veal skillet and bring to boil, scraping up any browned bits. Boil until liquid is reduced to thin sauce, stirring occasionally, about 10 minutes. Spoon peppers and sauce over veal.

Veal with Leek and Roquefort Sauce

In this elegant entrée, the leeks mellow to lend a bit of sweetness to the sauce.

8 servings

Sauce
3 tablespoons unsalted butter
2½ pounds leeks (white and pale green parts only), halved lengthwise, sliced into ½-inch pieces (about 6 cups)
1 tablespoon sugar
1 teaspoon dried thyme, crumbled
Salt and white pepper

2½ cups chicken stock or canned low-salt broth, boiled until reduced to ½ cup

Veal
8 1-inch-thick veal loin chops (about 8 ounces each), fat and sinew trimmed
Dried thyme, crumbled
Pepper
3 tablespoons unsalted butter
¼ cup brandy
¼ cup whipping cream
6 tablespoons unsalted butter, cut into 6 pieces, room temperature
1½ ounces Roquefort cheese, crumbled (about ½ cup)
Salt and white pepper

For sauce: Melt butter in heavy large skillet over medium heat. Add leeks, sugar and thyme. Season with salt and pepper. Cook until liquid evaporates and leeks begin to soften, stirring occasionally, about 10 minutes; do not brown. Transfer all but 1 cup leek mixture to bowl and reserve for garnish. Stir remaining leeks, reduce heat to low and cover. Cook until leeks are very soft and lightly caramelized, stirring occasionally, about 20 minutes.

Puree caramelized leeks and stock in blender until smooth. (*Can be prepared 1 day ahead. Cover reserved leeks and sauce separately and refrigerate.*)

For veal: Preheat broiler. Season veal with thyme and pepper. Melt 3 tablespoons butter in heavy large skillet over medium heat. Add veal and cook until just pink inside, about 4 minutes per side. Transfer to plate and cover to keep warm. Add brandy to skillet and cook until liquid is almost evaporated, scraping up any browned bits. Add cream and leek sauce and bring to simmer. Whisk in 6 tablespoons butter 1 piece at a time. Add cheese and any accumulated meat juices and whisk until smooth. Season with salt and pepper. Divide sauce among broilerproof plates. Top with veal and sprinkle reserved leeks over. Broil until leeks are heated through, about 1 minute.

 *Lamb*

Lamb Chops with Warm Garlic, Mint and Balsamic Vinaigrette

4 servings

1 cup chicken stock or canned low-salt broth
1 tablespoon olive oil (preferably extra-virgin)
½ tablespoon minced garlic
¼ cup balsamic vinegar*

1 tablespoon minced fresh mint leaves
1 tablespoon chopped fresh parsley
Salt and pepper

4 4-ounce lamb chops

Boil stock in heavy medium saucepan until reduced by half, about 8 minutes. Heat oil in heavy medium skillet over medium heat. Add garlic and sauté until golden brown, about 1 minute. Add reduced stock and vinegar and boil until liquid is reduced by half, about 5 minutes. Mix in mint and parsley. Season vinaigrette with salt and pepper. Set aside.

Prepare barbecue (medium-high heat) or preheat broiler. Season lamb chops with salt and pepper. Grill about 3 minutes per side for medium-rare. Transfer to plates. Spoon warm vinaigrette over lamb chops and serve.

*Available at specialty foods stores, Italian markets and some supermarkets.

Braised Lamb Shanks with Garlic

An aromatic tomato broth adds flavor to the lamb, and a sauté of garlic and cilantro with a sprinkling of lime juice finishes it off perfectly. This is one of those dishes that tends to taste even better the next day.

6 servings

3 tablespoons olive oil
6 1-pound lamb shanks, trimmed
½ teaspoon pepper
½ teaspoon ground allspice
½ teaspoon ground nutmeg
Seeds from 4 cardamom pods, cracked
2 cups beef stock or canned broth
2 cups chicken stock or canned low-salt broth

1 cup chopped peeled plum tomatoes
3 tablespoons tomato paste
1 pound carrots, cut into ½-inch cubes

6 garlic cloves, minced
1 cup chopped fresh cilantro
3 tablespoons lime juice

Heat 2 tablespoons oil in heavy large Dutch oven over medium-high heat. Add lamb and brown on all sides, about 6 minutes. Cover, reduce heat to medium-low and cook 20 minutes, stirring occasionally. Sprinkle lamb with pepper, allspice, nutmeg and cardamom. Add both stocks, tomatoes and tomato paste. Cover and cook 1 hour 20 minutes, turning lamb once. Add carrots; cover and cook 30 minutes. *(Can be prepared 1 day ahead. Cover and refrigerate. Rewarm in 350°F oven approximately 30 minutes.)*

Heat remaining 1 tablespoon oil in heavy medium skillet over medium heat. Add garlic and sauté until tender, about 1 minute. Add cilantro and sauté 1 minute. Sprinkle mixture over lamb. Cover and continue cooking until lamb is tender, about 10 minutes. Sprinkle lime juice over.

Rack of Lamb with Cumin-Caraway Sauce

4 servings

Sauce
- 2 racks of lamb, scraped between bones and trimmed of fat, scraps reserved
- 4½ pounds meaty lamb neck bones
- 1½ onions, chopped
- 1½ celery stalks, chopped
- 1½ carrots, chopped
- 1½ tablespoons chopped fresh thyme or 1 teaspoon dried, crumbled
- 2 garlic cloves, chopped
- 10 whole black peppercorns
- 1½ tablespoons tomato paste
- 4½ cups water
- 4½ cups canned low-salt chicken broth
  Salt and pepper

Lamb
- ¼ cup (½ stick) butter, room temperature
- ½ cup fresh white breadcrumbs
- ½ cup chopped pecans
  Salt and pepper
- 6 tablespoons whipping cream
- 1 teaspoon (generous) minced caraway seeds
- ½ teaspoon (scant) minced cumin seeds

For sauce: Cook lamb rack scraps and neck bones in heavy large Dutch oven over medium-high heat until brown, stirring occasionally, about 30 minutes. Pour off fat. Reduce heat to medium. Add onions, celery, carrots, thyme, garlic and peppercorns and cook until vegetables are tender, stirring occasionally, about 5 minutes. Add tomato paste and stir 1 minute. Add water and broth. Cover and simmer until liquid is reduced to about 2½ cups. Strain stock into clean saucepan. Simmer until stock is reduced to 1½ cups. Season the lamb stock reduction with salt and pepper. *(Can be prepared 1 day ahead. Cover and chill.)*

For lamb: Preheat oven to 425°F. Place butter in bowl. Finely grind breadcrumbs and pecans in processor. Stir into butter to form paste. Set lamb racks in roasting pan. Season with salt and pepper. Cover with paste. Roast 15 minutes. Reduce oven temperature to 375°F. Roast to desired doneness, 5 more minutes for medium-rare.

Meanwhile, add cream, caraway and cumin to lamb stock reduction. Boil until reduced to ¾ cup. Season with salt and pepper.

Cut each rack of lamb in half. Set half on each plate. Surround with some of sauce. Serve lamb immediately.

Lamb Shoulder Chops with Tomatoes and Marjoram

2 servings

- 2 1½-inch-thick round-bone shoulder lamb chops (about 14 ounces total)
  Salt and pepper
- 1 tablespoon olive oil
- 2 large garlic cloves, chopped
- ½ cup dry white wine
- 1 28-ounce can Italian plum tomatoes, drained, coarsely chopped
  Pinch of dried crushed red pepper
- 1½ tablespoons minced fresh marjoram or 1 teaspoon dried, crumbled

Season lamb chops with salt and pepper. Heat oil in heavy large skillet over high heat. Add lamb and cook until brown, about 2½ minutes per side. Transfer to plate. Reduce heat to medium-low. Add garlic and cook until beginning to color, about 30 seconds. Add wine and bring to boil, scraping up any browned bits. Add tomatoes and dried red pepper. Return lamb to skillet. Cover and simmer until tender, turning occasionally, about 30 minutes.

Transfer lamb to plates and keep warm. Boil sauce until thickened, stirring occasionally and adding any juices accumulated on lamb plates, about 8 minutes. Season with salt and pepper. Spoon sauce over lamb chops. Sprinkle with marjoram and serve immediately.

Pork

Glazed Pork Chops with Maple Syrup

Serve with steamed potatoes and red cabbage braised with apples.

4 servings

4 1-inch-thick loin pork chops
  Salt and pepper
2 tablespoons (¼ stick) butter
  All purpose flour

¼ cup cider vinegar
6 tablespoons maple syrup
10 tablespoons dark brown sugar

Preheat oven to 450°F. Pat pork chops dry. Season meat with salt and pepper. Melt butter in heavy large skillet over high heat. Dredge pork chops in flour, shaking off excess. Add to skillet and cook until brown, about 4 minutes per side. Transfer to roasting pan (do not wash skillet). Bake pork chops until thermometer inserted in thickest part registers 145°F, about 20 minutes.

Preheat broiler. Pour off drippings from skillet. Add vinegar to skillet and bring to boil, scraping up any browned bits. Add maple syrup. Reduce heat to low, cover and cook 10 minutes.

Meanwhile, transfer chops to broiler pan. Pack 2½ tablespoons brown sugar evenly atop each. Broil pork until sugar is dark brown and glazed, turning pan to brown evenly, about 1 minute. Serve, passing sauce separately.

Fried Peppers, Onions and Sausages

4 servings

¼ cup olive oil
6 large green or red bell peppers,
  cut into strips
2 medium onions, sliced

3 garlic cloves, minced
2 tablespoons red wine vinegar
  Salt and pepper

2 pounds hot Italian sausage

Heat oil in heavy large skillet over medium heat. Add peppers, onions, garlic and vinegar and sauté 10 minutes. Cover and cook until tender, about 5 minutes. Season to taste with salt and pepper.

Meanwhile, cook sausages in another heavy large skillet over medium-high heat until brown and cooked through, turning occasionally, about 15 minutes. Transfer to platter. Surround with peppers.

Kentucky-Whiskey-glazed Ribs

Real sour mash whiskey is the secret to this robust, savory glaze for pork spareribs. Serve with baked beans or a big pan of cheese-flavored grits, hot corn bread flecked with red and green bell peppers, grilled potato and tomato slices.

6 to 8 servings

Glaze
- ½ cup (1 stick) unsalted butter
- ⅓ cup vegetable oil
- 1 cup minced onion
- ⅔ cup catsup
- ⅔ cup whiskey or bourbon
- ½ cup cider vinegar
- ½ cup fresh orange juice
- ½ cup pure maple syrup
- ⅓ cup light unsulfured molasses
- 2 tablespoons Worcestershire sauce
- ½ teaspoon cracked black pepper
- ½ teaspoon liquid smoke flavoring
- ½ teaspoon salt
- 1 tablespoon finely grated orange peel

Ribs
- 3 pork sparerib racks (about 9 pounds), cut into 5-rib sections
- 4 teaspoons sugar
- 1½ teaspoons ground allspice
  Salt and pepper

  Green onions (optional)

For glaze: Melt butter in heavy large saucepan over medium heat. Add oil and heat 2 minutes. Add onion and sauté until pale golden, about 5 minutes. Add catsup, whiskey, vinegar, orange juice, maple syrup, molasses, Worcestershire, pepper, liquid smoke and salt. Bring to simmer, stirring frequently. Reduce heat to medium-low and cook until mixture is thick and glossy, stirring occasionally, about 1 hour. Add orange peel and cook 5 minutes, stirring occasionally. (*Glaze can be prepared 1 day ahead. Cover tightly and refrigerate. Before using, stir over low heat until glaze is heated through.*)

For ribs: Season both sides of ribs with sugar, allspice, salt and pepper. Cover and let stand at room temperature 45 minutes.

Prepare barbecue grill (medium-high heat). Lightly oil grill. Place ribs on grill and sear 5 minutes per side. Move ribs to outer edges of grill. Cover with grill lid or heavy-duty foil and continue grilling until meat is tender, turning ribs occasionally and brushing with some of glaze during last 5 minutes, about 30 minutes. Arrange ribs on platter. Garnish with onions. Serve with remaining glaze.

Salt- and Pepper-crusted Pork

Offer with mashed potatoes and some steamed broccoli.

2 servings

- 2 teaspoons pepper
- 1 teaspoon salt
- 1 teaspoon dried rosemary, crumbled
- 1 large garlic clove, minced
- 1 12-ounce (about) pork tenderloin
- 1 tablespoon olive oil

Combine pepper, salt, rosemary and garlic in small bowl. Rub over pork. Let pork stand at room temperature at least 15 minutes.

Preheat oven to 400°F. Heat oil in heavy medium ovenproof skillet over high heat. Add pork and brown on all sides, about 6 minutes. Transfer skillet with pork to oven and roast until pork is cooked through, turning occasionally, approximately 20 minutes. Slice and serve.

❧ Poultry and Game

Roast Duck with Bordelaise Sauce and Herb Sabayon

While this roast duck is delicious with both sauces, it would also be good with just the bordelaise if you wanted to simplify things.

4 servings

Bordelaise Sauce
- 2 tablespoons (¼ stick) butter
- 3 medium shallots, minced
- 1½ cups dry red wine
- 1 teaspoon minced fresh thyme leaves or ¼ teaspoon dried, crumbled
- 1 bay leaf
- 4 cups beef stock or canned unsalted broth

Ducks
- 2 4-pound ducks
  Salt and pepper

- 9 tablespoons butter
- 1 cup sliced fresh wild mushrooms, such as oyster, shiitake* or chanterelle (about 2 ounces)

Herb Sabayon (see recipe)

For bordelaise sauce: Melt 2 tablespoons butter in heavy medium saucepan over medium heat. Add shallots and sauté until soft, about 3 minutes. Increase heat to high. Add wine, thyme and bay leaf and boil until reduced to ⅓ cup, about 8 minutes. Reduce heat to medium-high. Add 3¾ cups stock and boil until reduced to ½ cup, about 35 minutes. (*Can be prepared 1 day ahead. Refrigerate.*)

For ducks: Preheat oven to 375°F. Rinse ducks; pat dry. Season inside and out with salt and pepper. Place ducks in shallow roasting pan and roast until meat thermometer inserted in breast registers 120°F, about 40 minutes. Cut breast meat from ducks and transfer to heated platter. Tent with foil. Continue roasting ducks until juices run clear when thighs are pierced, 10 minutes.

Transfer ducks to heated platter. Tent with foil to keep warm. Pour off all drippings from roasting pan. Melt 1 tablespoon butter in same pan over medium heat. Add mushrooms and cook until light brown, about 4 minutes. Add remaining ¼ cup stock and bring to boil, scraping up any browned bits. Boil until reduced to glaze. Add sauce to pan and bring to simmer. Reduce heat to low. Whisk in remaining 8 tablespoons butter 1 tablespoon at a time. Season bordelaise sauce with salt and pepper to taste.

Cut leg-thigh pieces from duck carcasses. Slice breast meat across grain. Arrange breast meat and leg-thigh pieces on plates. Serve duck, passing bordelaise sauce and sabayon separately.

*One-half ounce dried shiitake mushrooms can be substituted. Soak in hot water to cover 30 minutes. Drain mushrooms and squeeze dry before using.

Herb Sabayon

This sauce would be great with grilled fish, as well as with the roast duck here.

Makes about 1 cup

- ¼ cup dry white wine
- 2 egg yolks
- 1 tablespoon minced fresh tarragon or 1 teaspoon dried, crumbled

- 1 tablespoon minced fresh chives
- 1 tablespoon minced fresh parsley
  Salt and pepper

Whisk wine and yolks in top of double boiler over barely simmering water until thickened and doubled in volume, about 1 minute. Remove from over water and whisk 5 minutes to cool. Add tarragon, chives and parsley. Season sauce with salt and pepper. (*Can be prepared 2 hours ahead. Keep warm in double boiler over hot water or in vacuum bottle.*)

Basil-Buttermilk Fried Chicken

Dried basil infuses the chicken with its subtle flavor; garnish the platter with sprigs of fresh basil.

8 servings

2 cups buttermilk
5 tablespoons dried basil, crumbled
2 teaspoons hot pepper sauce (such as Tabasco)
2 3- to 3½-pound chickens, cut into serving pieces

2 cups all purpose flour
2 teaspoons salt
2 teaspoons pepper

Solid vegetable shortening (for deep frying)
Fresh basil sprigs

Combine buttermilk, 2 tablespoons dried basil and hot pepper sauce in large bowl. Add chicken; turn to coat with buttermilk mixture. Let stand at room temperature 2 hours, turning occasionally. (*Can be prepared 1 day ahead. Chill.*)

Place rack atop large cookie sheet. Combine flour, salt, pepper and remaining 3 tablespoons dried basil in large shallow dish. Drain chicken and dredge in flour mixture; shake off excess. Transfer chicken to rack. Chill 30 minutes.

Heat 2 inches of shortening in heavy large skillet or Dutch oven to 360°F. Fry chicken in batches (do not crowd) until cooked through and coating is golden brown, turning occasionally, about 20 minutes for white meat and 25 minutes for dark. Remove using tongs. Drain chicken on paper towels. Place on platter and garnish with basil. Serve warm or at room temperature.

Chicken Milanese

4 servings

4 boneless chicken breast halves, skinned
¾ cup plus 2 tablespoons freshly grated Parmesan cheese (about 2 ounces)
¾ cup fresh white breadcrumbs
1 tablespoon minced fresh parsley
⅛ teaspoon salt
⅛ teaspoon pepper

1 egg
½ cup milk

2 cups olive oil
2 tablespoons (¼ stick) unsalted butter
2 tablespoons fresh lemon juice
1 lemon, quartered
Fresh parsley sprigs

Flatten chicken breasts between sheets of waxed paper to thickness of ⅜ inch, using meat mallet or rolling pin. Mix cheese, breadcrumbs, minced parsley, salt and pepper in large bowl. Whisk egg with milk in medium bowl to blend. Dip chicken into egg, then into breadcrumb mixture, coating completely and pressing to adhere. Shake off excess breadcrumbs.

Heat oil in heavy large deep skillet to 375°F. Add chicken and cook until golden brown and cooked through, about 4 minutes per side. Using tongs, transfer to paper towels and drain. Transfer chicken to platter. Melt butter in small saucepan. Mix in lemon juice and pour over chicken. Garnish with lemon wedges and parsley sprigs. Serve immediately.

Chicken with Tomatoes and Shiitake Mushrooms

4 servings

½ cup dry-packed sun-dried tomatoes
½ cup dried shiitake mushrooms
 1 3- to 3⅓-pound chicken, cut into 8 pieces
All purpose flour
 3 tablespoons olive oil
 2 cups chicken stock or canned broth
 1 cup dry white wine
 3 carrots, peeled and thickly sliced

 1 teaspoon chopped fresh parsley
 1 teaspoon dried basil, crumbled
 1 teaspoon dried tarragon, crumbled
 1 bay leaf
 1 whole clove
Salt and pepper
 2 large tomatoes, coarsely chopped

 1 cup whipping cream
Freshly cooked rice or noodles

Soak sun-dried tomatoes and mushrooms in warm water 20 minutes.

Pat chicken dry. Dust lightly with flour. Heat oil in heavy Dutch oven over high heat. Add chicken (in batches if necessary) and cook until brown, turning frequently, about 5 minutes. Drain sun-dried tomatoes and mushrooms. Remove stems from mushrooms. Slice tomatoes and mushrooms and add to Dutch oven. Return all chicken pieces. Stir in stock and next 7 ingredients. Season with salt and pepper. Reduce heat to low. Cover and cook 20 minutes. Add fresh tomatoes; cover and cook until chicken is cooked through, about 10 minutes.

Remove bay leaf and clove. Transfer chicken and vegetables to platter using slotted spoon. Tent with foil to keep warm. Stir cream into liquid in Dutch oven. Boil until reduced to sauce consistency, about 20 minutes. Adjust seasoning. Pour sauce over chicken. Serve immediately with rice or noodles.

Chicken in Orange Sauce

2 servings

 1 cup fresh orange juice
 2 tablespoons minced shallot or green onion
1½ tablespoons white wine vinegar
 1 tablespoon dry white wine
 1 tablespoon firmly packed golden brown sugar

 2 tablespoons (¼ stick) unsalted butter
 2 boneless chicken breast halves

 5 tablespoons chilled unsalted butter, cut into 5 pieces
 1 2 × ¾-inch-wide strip orange peel (orange part only), cut into matchstick-size strips
Salt and pepper
Ground nutmeg

Bring first 5 ingredients to simmer in heavy small saucepan over medium heat, stirring until brown sugar dissolves. Increase heat and boil until sauce is reduced to ¼ cup, approximately 15 minutes.

Meanwhile, melt 2 tablespoons butter in heavy medium skillet over medium heat. Add chicken and cook until just springy to touch, about 4 minutes per side. Transfer chicken to plates.

Remove sauce from heat and whisk in 2 pieces chilled butter. Set pan over low heat and whisk in remaining 3 butter pieces 1 piece at a time, removing pan from heat briefly if drops of melted butter appear. (If sauce breaks down at any time, remove from heat and whisk in 2 tablespoons chilled butter.) Mix in orange peel. Season with salt, pepper and nutmeg. Spoon over chicken.

Shallot-stuffed Chicken on Savoy Cabbage

This gets garnished with Parsnip Chips and served with a rich, buttery sauce.

4 servings

Chicken
- 6 medium shallots, halved, peeled
- 1 tablespoon vegetable oil

- 4 boneless chicken breast halves
- 4 tablespoons chopped fresh basil
  Salt and pepper

Cabbage
- 6 cups thinly sliced savoy cabbage, about 1 pound

- 2 ounces (about 3 slices) bacon, finely chopped
- 1/4 cup (1/2 stick) unsalted butter

Assembly
- 2 tablespoons (1/4 stick) unsalted butter

  Buttery Thyme Sauce (see recipe)
  Parsnip Chips (optional, see recipe)

For chicken: Preheat oven to 450°F. Place shallots in center of large piece of foil. Drizzle shallots with oil. Enclose shallots in foil. Roast until shallots are tender when pierced with small sharp knife, about 35 minutes. Cool. (*Can be prepared 1 day ahead. Cover and refrigerate.*)

Pound chicken breasts between sheets of plastic wrap to thickness of 1/2 inch. Place breasts skin side down on work surface. Sprinkle each breast with 1 tablespoon chopped basil. Season with salt and pepper. Arrange 3 roasted shallot halves lengthwise down center of each breast. Fold long chicken breast sides in to enclose shallots completely. Tuck ends in, forming cylinder. Tie chicken at 1-inch intervals to secure. (*Chicken can be prepared up to 8 hours ahead. Cover tightly and refrigerate.*)

For cabbage: Bring large pot of salted water to boil. Add cabbage and return to boil. Simmer until cabbage is crisp-tender, about 2 minutes. Strain. Rinse cabbage under cold water. (*Cabbage can be prepared 4 hours ahead.*)

Cook bacon in heavy large skillet over medium-high heat until golden brown and crisp, stirring occasionally, about 5 minutes. Add 4 tablespoons butter and let melt. Add cabbage and cook until heated through, stirring occasionally, about 5 minutes. Set aside.

To assemble: Preheat oven to 500°F. Melt butter in heavy large ovenproof skillet over high heat. Add chicken and cook until brown, about 3 minutes per side. Season with salt and pepper. Place skillet with chicken in oven and roast until chicken is cooked through, about 15 minutes. Let chicken stand at room temperature in skillet for 5 minutes.

Meanwhile, reheat cabbage if necessary. Spoon about 2/3 cup cabbage mixture on each plate. Remove string from chicken. Slice chicken on diagonal in 3/4-inch-thick pieces. Arrange chicken slices atop cabbage on each plate. Spoon 1/4 cup sauce over each. Serve with Parsnip Chips if desired.

Buttery Thyme Sauce

Makes about 1 cup

- 1 pound chicken necks and backs
- 1 celery stalk, chopped
- 1/2 small carrot, chopped
- 2 medium shallots, chopped
- 1 garlic clove, chopped
- 1 fresh thyme sprig or 1 pinch dried, crumbled

- 1/4 cup dry white wine
- 4 cups chicken stock or canned low-salt broth

- 1/2 cup (1 stick) unsalted butter, room temperature

Preheat oven to 425°F. Place chicken necks and backs in heavy large ovenproof saucepan. Roast in oven until brown, about 20 minutes. Add celery, carrot, shallots, garlic and thyme and continue roasting until vegetables just begin to brown, approximately 5 minutes.

Remove pan from oven and place over medium-high heat. Add wine and boil until liquid is reduced to 2 tablespoons, stirring up any browned bits in pan. Pour in chicken stock. Simmer over medium-low heat until liquid is reduced to 1 cup, about 30 minutes. Strain, pressing on solids to extract as much liquid as possible. (*Can be prepared 2 days ahead; refrigerate.*)

Bring sauce mixture to boil in heavy medium saucepan. Add ½ cup butter. Boil until slightly thickened and reduced to 1 cup. Use immediately.

Parsnip Chips

4 servings

3 large parsnips, peeled

Vegetable oil (for deep frying)
Salt

Hold narrow tip of parsnip, resting thick end on work surface. Using vegetable peeler, shave parsnip into long thin ribbons. Turn parsnip and repeat process for each side. Repeat shaving with remaining parsnips.

Heat oil in heavy wide 4-inch-deep pot. Shake 1 handful of parsnips into oil; do not crowd. Fry until crisp and light golden, stirring occasionally, about 1 minute. Remove with slotted spoon; drain on paper towels. Season with salt. Repeat with remaining parsnips in batches. (*Parsnips can be prepared up to 6 hours ahead. Cover lightly and store at room temperature.*)

Turkey with Whole Wheat and Currant Stuffing

The stuffing that bakes inside the bird is nice and moist. The remainder gets baked in a separate dish, with extra stock added to impart the same texture. If using the Giblet Broth, instead of chicken stock or canned broth, in the gravy, you'll need to make it before starting turkey preparation.

6 servings

Turkey
1 **12-pound turkey (neck, heart and gizzard reserved for Giblet Broth* and liver reserved for gravy)**
1 **large orange, halved**
Salt and pepper
Whole Wheat and Currant Stuffing (see recipe)
2 **eggs**
⅔ **cup chicken stock or canned broth**
6 **tablespoons (¾ stick) unsalted butter, room temperature**

6 **tablespoons (¾ stick) unsalted butter, melted**

Gravy
6 **tablespoons all purpose flour**
3 **cups Giblet Broth, chicken stock or canned low-salt broth**

1 **tablespoon butter**
Heart and gizzard reserved from Giblet Broth
1 **hard-boiled egg, finely chopped (optional)**

For turkey: Preheat oven to 450°F. Butter 8-cup soufflé dish. Cut off turkey wing tips. Rinse turkey inside and out. Dry thoroughly. Place turkey on rack set in large roasting pan. Squeeze juice from orange over turkey and into cavity. Season turkey inside and out with salt and pepper. Spoon 4 cups stuffing into cavity of turkey. Mix 2 eggs and ⅔ cup stock into remaining stuffing in bowl. Transfer stuffing to prepared soufflé dish; cover and refrigerate. Rub 6 tablespoons room-temperature butter over turkey.

Roast turkey 45 minutes. Reduce oven temperature to 350°F. Roast turkey until meat thermometer inserted in thickest part of thigh registers 175°F, basting turkey occasionally with melted butter, about 1 hour 15 minutes (uncover stuffing in dish and place in oven for final 45 minutes).

Transfer turkey to platter; tent with foil. Remove stuffing from oven.

For gravy: Pour turkey pan juices into bowl; do not rinse pan. Degrease pan juices, reserving 6 tablespoons fat. Pour 6 tablespoons fat back into roasting pan. Place pan over medium heat. Add flour to pan and stir 3 minutes. Stir degreased pan juices and 3 cups Giblet Broth into pan and bring to boil, scraping up any browned bits and stirring constantly. Simmer until gravy thickens, stirring frequently, about 8 minutes. Pour into medium saucepan.

Melt 1 tablespoon butter in heavy small skillet over medium heat. Add liver and sauté until cooked through, about 6 minutes. Cool slightly. Chop liver. Mix liver and chopped heart, gizzard and egg into gravy. Bring to simmer. Serve turkey with Whole Wheat and Currant Stuffing and gravy.

*Giblet Broth

Makes 3 cups

8 cups water	1 1-inch-thick onion slice
1½ pounds turkey necks	1 celery stalk, chopped
Neck, heart and gizzard from 12-pound turkey	1 teaspoon dried thyme, crumbled

Combine water, turkey necks, heart and gizzard, onion, celery and thyme in heavy large saucepan. Bring to boil. Reduce heat and simmer 1½ hours. Strain, reserving heart and gizzard. Return broth to saucepan and boil until liquid is reduced to 3 cups, about 30 minutes. Chop heart and gizzard and reserve. (*Can be prepared 1 day ahead. Refrigerate broth, heart and gizzard separately.*)

Whole Wheat and Currant Stuffing

Makes about 12 cups

1¾ pounds whole wheat bread, crusts trimmed, bread broken into large pieces	1 cup dried currants
2 ounces dried shiitake mushrooms	1 cup lightly toasted unsalted shelled sunflower seeds
3 cups hot water	Ground nutmeg
1 cup (2 sticks) unsalted butter	Salt and pepper
¾ cup chopped shallots or green onions	
2 teaspoons dried thyme, crumbled	

Preheat oven to 350°F. Grind bread in batches in processor to coarse crumbs. Spread crumbs out on 2 heavy large cookie sheets. Bake until dry, stirring occasionally, about 20 minutes. Cool. Transfer to large bowl.

Place mushrooms in small bowl. Add 3 cups hot water. Let soak 30 minutes. Drain mushrooms; reserve 1 cup soaking liquid. Cut off mushroom stems and discard. Cut caps into ¼-inch-thick slices. Melt ½ cup butter in heavy large skillet over medium heat. Add shallots and sauté until soft, 5 minutes. Add remaining ½ cup butter and thyme and stir until butter melts.

Mix mushrooms, currants and sunflower seeds into breadcrumbs. Add butter mixture and stir until well mixed. Stir in 1 cup reserved mushroom soaking liquid. Season to taste with nutmeg, salt and pepper.

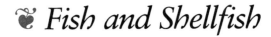

Fish and Shellfish

Fricassee of Scallops with Leek, Red Bell Pepper and Champagne Sauce

6 servings

6 tablespoons (¾ stick) unsalted butter
3 shallots, minced
1 large leek, trimmed, halved lengthwise, thinly sliced
⅓ cup diced red bell pepper
2 pounds large sea scallops
All purpose flour

½ cup Champagne or sparkling white wine

1½ cups whipping cream
1 tablespoon fresh lemon juice
⅛ teaspoon hot pepper sauce (such as Tabasco)
⅓ cup freshly grated Parmesan cheese (about 1¼ ounces)
Salt and pepper
2 tablespoons minced fresh Italian parsley

Melt 2 tablespoons butter in heavy large skillet over medium-high heat. Add shallots, leek and red bell pepper and sauté until tender, about 4 minutes. Remove vegetables from skillet using slotted spoon. Melt remaining 4 tablespoons butter in same skillet. Dredge scallops in flour, shaking off excess. Add scallops to skillet and cook until just firm to touch and golden brown, about 5 minutes. Remove scallops from skillet and set aside.

Pour Champagne into skillet. Boil until reduced by half, scraping up any browned bits. Add cream, lemon juice and hot pepper sauce. Reduce heat and simmer until liquid is reduced to 1 cup, about 10 minutes. Stir in Parmesan and reserved vegetables and simmer until cheese melts and mixture is reduced to 1½ cups, about 3 minutes. Return scallops to sauce and reheat gently. Season with salt and pepper. Divide scallops and sauce among plates. Sprinkle with parsley. Serve scallops immediately.

South Carolina Shrimp

4 servings

6 plum tomatoes

¼ cup olive oil
20 uncooked large shrimp, peeled, deveined, tails left intact
1 tablespoon minced shallot
1 tablespoon minced garlic
⅓ cup dry white wine

⅓ cup chopped fresh cilantro
2 tablespoons fresh lemon juice
½ cup whipping cream
6 tablespoons (¾ stick) unsalted butter, cut into pieces
Salt and pepper

12 ounces freshly cooked fettuccine

Drop tomatoes in large saucepan of boiling water for 10 seconds. Transfer to bowl of cold water using slotted spoon. Drain. Pull off skins using small knife. Peel, seed and chop tomatoes. Set tomatoes aside.

Heat oil in heavy large skillet over medium-high heat. Add shrimp and cook until just pink, turning occasionally, about 2 minutes. Transfer to platter. Tent with foil to keep warm. Add shallot and garlic to skillet and sauté 1 minute. Add tomatoes, wine, cilantro and lemon juice and cook until mixture is reduced by half, stirring frequently, about 2 minutes. Add cream and boil until mixture is reduced by half, stirring occasionally, about 3 minutes. Remove pan from heat. Add butter 1 piece at a time, whisking until melted. Season with salt and pepper.

Mound fettuccine on plates. Top with shrimp. Spoon sauce over.

Jumbo Shrimp with Chive Butter

6 servings

1 cup (2 sticks) butter
¼ cup Dijon mustard
¼ cup fresh lemon juice
6 tablespoons chopped fresh chives

Pepper

36 uncooked jumbo shrimp, peeled, deveined and butterflied
Whole chives

Preheat broiler. Melt butter in heavy small saucepan over low heat. Place mustard in bowl. Whisk in lemon juice. Gradually whisk in butter. Add chopped chives. Season butter mixture with pepper.

Arrange shrimp cut side up on broiler pan. Brush with some of butter mixture. Broil until just cooked through, about 4 minutes. Arrange on plates and garnish with whole chives. Serve, passing remaining butter separately.

Tuna with Spicy Coconut Sauce

4 servings

1 14-ounce can unsweetened coconut milk*
1 tablespoon vegetable oil
1 tablespoon chopped lemongrass* or 1½ teaspoons grated lemon peel
1 teaspoon chopped shallot
1 teaspoon shrimp sauce (nam pla)*

1 teaspoon fresh lime juice
1 teaspoon chopped peeled fresh ginger
¼ teaspoon (or more) sambal oelek* (ground fresh chili paste)
Salt and pepper

4 6-ounce ¾-inch-thick tuna steaks
Minced fresh cilantro

Boil coconut milk in heavy medium saucepan until reduced to 1 cup, stirring occasionally, about 8 minutes. Heat oil in heavy large skillet over medium-high heat. Add lemongrass and shallot and sauté 1 minute. Add coconut milk, shrimp sauce, lime juice, ginger and ¼ teaspoon sambal oelek. Bring to boil. Taste, adding more sambal oelek if spicier flavor is desired. Season sauce with salt and pepper to taste. Set sauce aside.

Prepare barbecue (high heat) or preheat broiler. Cook tuna to desired degree of doneness, about 2 minutes per side for medium. Transfer tuna to plates. Spoon sauce over. Sprinkle with cilantro and serve immediately.

*Available at Indian, Southeast Asian and specialty foods stores.

Baked Salmon with Champagne and Dill Mayonnaise

If you're running short on time, purchased mayonnaise can be substituted for the homemade. Just mix two cups mayonnaise with a little lemon juice and some minced fresh dill.

10 servings

Mayonnaise
4 egg yolks
2 tablespoons fresh lemon juice
4 teaspoons Dijon mustard
1½ cups vegetable oil
Salt and pepper
10 tablespoons chopped fresh dill

Salmon
Olive oil

1 6-pound whole salmon, scaled and cleaned, head and tail intact
Pepper
1 small bunch fresh dill, large stems trimmed
¼ cup (½ stick) butter, cut into pieces

½ cup Champagne or other sparkling wine

For mayonnaise: Blend yolks, lemon juice and mustard in processor. Gradually add oil in slow steady stream, blending until thick. Season with salt and pepper. Add dill and blend until just combined. Transfer to bowl. (*Can be prepared 2 days ahead. Cover and refrigerate. Let stand 30 minutes at room temperature.*)

For salmon: Preheat oven to 400°F. Grease large rimmed cookie sheet with olive oil. Brush salmon inside and out with oil. Season inside and out with pepper. Arrange dill in cavity. Top dill with butter pieces. Bake until salmon near backbone is no longer translucent (make small cut along backbone to check), about 30 minutes.

Increase oven temperature to 500°F. Pour Champagne over fish. Bake 5 minutes more. Remove from oven. Tent salmon with foil and let stand 15 minutes. Slide fish off cookie sheet and onto platter using metal spatula as aid. Peel skin off top of fish. Serve, passing mayonnaise separately.

Baked Red Snapper with Fennel-scented Tomato Sauce

2 servings

2 tablespoons olive oil
½ large onion, sliced
1 28-ounce can Italian plum tomatoes, drained
¼ cup dry white wine
2 2½ × 1-inch pieces orange peel (orange part only)

¼ teaspoon fennel seeds
⅛ teaspoon dried crushed red pepper
Salt and pepper

2 ¾-inch-thick red snapper or other firm-fleshed white fish fillets

Preheat oven to 400°F. Heat 1 tablespoon oil in heavy medium skillet over medium heat. Add onion and sauté until tender, about 8 minutes. Add tomatoes, wine, orange peel, fennel and crushed red pepper. Boil gently until reduced to chunky sauce, breaking up tomatoes with spoon, about 12 minutes. Season with salt and pepper. (*Can be prepared up to 1 day ahead. Cover and refrigerate. Rewarm sauce before continuing.*)

Pour remaining 1 tablespoon oil into small baking dish. Add fish and turn to coat with oil. Sprinkle with salt and pepper. Spoon warm sauce over fish. Bake until just cooked through, about 20 minutes.

Scallops with Sorrel and Tomato

If sorrel isn't available, try spinach or a combination of basil and arugula in this pretty and sophisticated dish.

2 servings

2 teaspoons butter
2 large tomatoes, peeled, seeded, chopped and pureed
Salt and pepper

16 medium sea scallops, connective tissue removed

1 cup matchstick-size strips of sorrel leaves
½ cup fish stock or bottled clam juice

12 tablespoons (1½ sticks) butter, cut into 6 pieces
1 teaspoon fresh lemon juice

Melt butter in heavy small skillet over medium heat. Add tomatoes and cook until thickened, stirring frequently. Season with salt and pepper. (*Can be prepared 1 day ahead. Cover and refrigerate.*)

Preheat oven to 450°F. Set large aluminum foil square on work surface. Pat scallops dry. Arrange in center of foil. Season with salt and pepper. Spoon tomatoes over. Sprinkle with sorrel and drizzle with stock. Bring all sides of foil to center and fold and crimp to seal tightly.

Set package in ovenproof skillet over high heat and cook until sizzling, about 2 minutes. Transfer skillet with package to oven and bake until scallops are cooked through, 5 to 10 minutes (time will vary depending on size of scallops). Remove scallops from package to 2 warm plates. Pour remaining contents into heavy medium saucepan and bring to boil. Whisk in butter 1 piece at a time. Add lemon juice. Pour over scallops and serve immediately.

Shrimp with Black Beans and Pineapple-Coconut Relish

Start marinating the shrimp for this colorful, tasty dish one day ahead.

4 servings

Shrimp
¼ cup fresh breadcrumbs
2 tablespoons minced fresh parsley
2 tablespoons minced fresh cilantro
2 tablespoons semidry Sherry
2 tablespoons olive oil
2 tablespoons fresh lemon juice
2 garlic cloves, minced
1 teaspoon pepper
½ teaspoon Hungarian hot paprika
½ teaspoon sea salt
⅛ teaspoon ground mace
Pinch of saffron threads
12 uncooked large shrimp, peeled and deveined, tail shells intact

Pineapple Relish
⅔ cup diced ripe pineapple
½ cup diced yellow bell pepper
½ cup diced red onion
½ cup diced poblano chili*
½ cup diced fresh ripe coconut or flaked unsweetened coconut
1 tablespoon Sherry vinegar

Cumin Butter
1 tablespoon cumin seeds
1 garlic clove

6 tablespoons dry white wine
3 tablespoons white wine vinegar
2 shallots, sliced
1 teaspoon cracked black pepper
1 bay leaf
½ cup whipping cream
½ cup (1 stick) unsalted butter, chilled and cut into 8 pieces
1 teaspoon (about) fresh lime juice
Salt

1 cup (or more) Black Beans with Cumin (see recipe)

Fresh cilantro sprigs

For shrimp: Mix all ingredients except shrimp in large nonaluminum bowl. Add shrimp and toss to coat. Cover and refrigerate overnight.

For relish: Combine all ingredients in bowl. Cover and let stand at room temperature until ready to serve. (*Can be prepared 8 hours ahead.*)

For butter: Toast cumin seeds in heavy small skillet over medium heat until fragrant, about 4 minutes. Transfer to mortar. Add garlic clove. Using pestle, pound cumin and garlic together to form paste.

Combine cumin-garlic paste, wine, vinegar, shallots, pepper and bay leaf in heavy small skillet over medium heat. Boil until reduced to 2 tablespoons. Add cream and boil until reduced to ½ cup. Reduce heat to low. Whisk in butter 1 piece at a time. Strain sauce. Add fresh lime juice to taste. Season with salt. Keep sauce warm in double boiler.

Preheat barbecue (high heat) or broiler. Warm beans in heavy saucepan over medium heat. Grill or broil shrimp until pink, about 1 minute per side.

Mound about ¼ cup beans (or more if desired) in center of each plate. Spoon cumin butter around beans. Arrange 3 shrimp halfway over beans on each plate. Top with relish. Garnish with cilantro sprigs and serve.

*A green chili, sometimes called a *pasilla*, available at Latin American markets and some supermarkets.

Black Beans with Cumin

The recipe yields more beans than you'll need to go with the shrimp, but they freeze beautifully and make a quick dinner when reheated and rolled in a tortilla with garnishes.

Makes 8 cups

2 cups dried black beans, sorted

⅓ cup cumin seeds

2 tablespoons olive oil
3 ounces smoked slab bacon, rind removed, finely diced
3 celery stalks, finely diced
1 green bell pepper, finely diced
1 yellow bell pepper, finely diced
2 jalapeño chilies, finely diced
1 poblano chili,* finely diced
1 red onion, finely diced

4 garlic cloves, minced
1 smoked ham hock
2 bay leaves
1 cup Madeira
1 tablespoon fresh thyme leaves or 1 teaspoon dried, crumbled
4 to 6 cups chicken stock or canned low-salt broth

1 tablespoon cracked black pepper
Salt

Place dried black beans in large bowl. Add enough cold water to cover. Let stand overnight. Drain beans. Set aside.

Toast cumin seeds in heavy small skillet over medium heat until fragrant, about 4 minutes. Transfer to spice grinder and grind finely.

Heat oil in heavy large pot over medium heat. Add bacon and fry until cooked but not crisp. Add celery, both bell peppers, chilies, onion and garlic and stir 1 minute. Mix in 3 tablespoons of ground toasted cumin, ham hock and bay leaves. Add beans and cook 3 minutes. Add Madeira and thyme and cook 1 minute. Pour in enough stock to cover beans by 1 to 2 inches. Simmer until tender, about 2 hours (time will vary depending on dryness of beans).

Remove ham hock from beans. Cut off skin; remove meat from bone. Dice or shred and return to pot. Add cracked pepper. Season with salt and serve. (*Can be prepared 3 days ahead. Refrigerate. Reheat just before serving.*)

*A green chili, sometimes called a *pasilla*, available at Latin American markets and some supermarkets.

Roast Monkfish with Cabbage

4 servings

1¼ pounds savoy cabbage, cored, quartered, trimmed and cut into thin strips

3 ounces smoked slab bacon, rind removed, cut crosswise into ½-inch pieces
1 large shallot, minced
1 cup fish stock or bottled clam juice
½ cup chicken stock or canned low-salt broth

2 pounds monkfish fillets (about ½ inch thick), trimmed
Salt and pepper
All purpose flour
2 tablespoons vegetable oil

1 cup (2 sticks) butter, cut into large pieces
2 tablespoons minced fresh chervil or tarragon

Preheat oven to 450°F. Bring large pot of salted water to boil. Add cabbage and blanch until wilted, about 1 minute. Drain. Transfer to 10 × 3-inch ovenproof and flameproof casserole. Set cabbage aside.

Fry bacon in heavy small saucepan over medium-high heat until light brown. Add minced shallot and stir 1 minute. Add half of fish stock and all of chicken stock and boil until reduced by ¾. Pour over cabbage.

Pat monkfish dry. Season with salt and pepper. Dredge in flour, shaking off excess. Heat oil in heavy large skillet over high heat. Add fish and brown well on all sides. Place atop cabbage in casserole.

Brian Leatart

Thai Beef Salad

Parsley-Basil Cheese Spread
and Pasta with Roasted
Eggplant

Brian Leatart

Espresso Cream and Chocolate Tartlets

Brian Leatart

Vanilla Crème Caramel

Clockwise from upper right: New Potato Salad with Bacon and Mustard Seeds; Basil-Buttermilk Fried Chicken; Curried Corn, Zucchini and Bell Pepper Salad; Salsa Deviled Eggs; Raspberry Brownies

Herb-scented Grilled Veal Chops

Brian Leatart

Add remaining ½ cup fish stock to casserole. Cover tightly and roast until fish is slightly firm to touch, 10 to 15 minutes (time will vary depending on thickness of fish). Transfer fish to plate and cover with aluminum foil.

Set casserole over medium heat and boil until cabbage is tender and liquid is syrupy, about 15 minutes. Whisk in butter several pieces at a time. Add chervil. Season with salt and pepper to taste.

Slice fish diagonally ¾ inch thick. Using slotted spoon, remove cabbage from sauce and mound on plates. Top with fish slices. Spoon sauce over.

Fried Oysters with Chili Corn Sauce

Crisp golden oysters served with a deliciously thick and rich sauce—enough to make anyone a fan of Creole-style cooking. The sauce would be a great accompaniment to many varieties of seafood.

2 servings

Sauce
- 3 cups whipping cream
- 2 tablespoons (¼ stick) butter
- ½ poblano chili* (about 1 ounce), cut into matchstick-size strips
- ½ red bell pepper, cut into matchstick-size strips
- ⅓ onion, cut into matchstick-size strips
  Kernels from 1 large corn ear
- 2 garlic cloves, minced
- 2 tablespoons tequila
- 2½ tablespoons chili powder
- 2 teaspoons ground cumin
  Salt and pepper
  Cayenne pepper

Oysters
- Vegetable oil (for deep frying)
- 1 cup instant masa mix*
- 1 cup all purpose flour
- 2½ tablespoons Cajun Seasoning Mix (see recipe)
- 24 shucked oysters

For sauce: Cook cream in heavy large saucepan over medium heat until reduced to 1½ cups, stirring occasionally, about 20 minutes. Set aside.

Melt butter in heavy medium skillet over low heat. Add chili, bell pepper, onion, corn and garlic and sauté until slightly softened, about 4 minutes. Transfer vegetables to bowl. Add tequila to skillet and bring to boil, scraping up any browned bits. Mix in reduced cream, vegetables, chili powder and cumin. Season with salt, pepper and cayenne and simmer until thickened to sauce consistency, about 2 minutes. Keep warm in double boiler over warm water.

For oysters: Heat oil in deep fryer or large skillet to 375°F. Combine masa mix, flour and 2½ tablespoons Cajun Seasoning Mix in medium bowl. Dredge oysters in mixture. Add oysters to oil in batches and fry until golden brown, about 1 minute. Transfer to paper towels using slotted spoon and let drain. Serve oysters, passing chili corn sauce separately.

*Poblano chili, a fresh green chili sometimes called a *pasilla,* and instant masa mix are available at Latin American markets and some supermarkets.

Cajun Seasoning Mix

Makes about ⅓ cup

- 4 teaspoons salt
- 4 teaspoons paprika
- 3 teaspoons garlic powder
- 3 teaspoons pepper
- 2½ teaspoons onion powder
- 1½ teaspoons cayenne pepper
- 1½ teaspoons dried thyme, crumbled
- 1½ teaspoons dried oregano, crumbled

Combine all ingredients in small bowl and mix thoroughly. (*Can be prepared 1 month ahead. Store in airtight container.*)

Spiced Tuna with Roasted Tomato Butter Sauce

A terrific, spicy dish that's both elegant and fun.

4 servings

Sauce
- 4 ripe plum tomatoes (about 14 ounces total), cored
- 2 shallots, peeled
- 2 small serrano chilies*
- ¼ small yellow onion, chopped
- 2 garlic cloves, peeled

- 1 cup chicken stock or canned broth
- ¼ cup chopped fresh cilantro
- 1 tablespoon fresh lime juice
- 4 tablespoons (½ stick) butter, cut into small pieces
- Salt and pepper

Tuna
- 4 teaspoons Chili Spice Mix (see recipe)
- 4 7-ounce ¾-inch-thick tuna steaks
- 1 tablespoon olive oil

- 2 ripe mangoes, peeled, seeded and chopped
- Fresh cilantro sprigs

For sauce: Preheat oven to 350°F. Place tomatoes, shallots, chilies, onion and garlic in heavy small roasting pan. Roast until tomatoes blister, turning occasionally, about 1 hour. Transfer vegetables along with any liquid to food processor and process until coarsely pureed. Transfer to heavy medium saucepan. (*Can be prepared 1 day ahead. Cover and refrigerate.*)

Add chicken stock to puree and bring to boil. Reduce heat to low. Add chopped cilantro and lime juice. Whisk in butter 1 piece at a time. Season with salt and pepper. Remove sauce from heat.

For tuna: Rub ½ teaspoon spice mix into each side of each tuna steak. Heat oil in heavy large skillet over high heat. Add tuna steaks and cook about 2 minutes per side for medium-rare.

Spoon tomato butter sauce onto each dinner plate. Sprinkle chopped mango over sauce. Top with tuna. Garnish with cilantro and serve.

*A very hot, small fresh green chili, available at Latin American markets and some supermarkets.

Chili Spice Mix

Try this with fish and poultry dishes.

Makes about ¾ cup

- 8 dried ancho chilies,* stemmed and seeded
- 1 tablespoon cumin seeds
- 1 teaspoon coriander seeds

- 2 tablespoons coarse salt
- 2 tablespoons brown sugar
- 1 teaspoon ground cinnamon

Preheat oven to 350°F. Place chilies on cookie sheet and bake until lightly roasted, 10 to 15 minutes. Halve chilies. Transfer to food processor. Cook cumin and coriander seeds in heavy small skillet over medium-low heat until aromatic, about 2 minutes. Add to processor. Add all remaining ingredients. Process to coarse powder. (*Can be prepared 1 month ahead. Store airtight.*)

*Available at Latin American markets and specialty foods stores.

Seafood, Sausage and Bell Pepper Paella

8 servings

¼ cup finely chopped fresh oregano
¼ cup finely chopped fresh thyme
¼ cup finely chopped fresh Italian parsley
¾ cup olive oil
8 tablespoons dry red wine
1 tablespoon cracked black peppercorns
1 tablespoon ground coriander
8 garlic cloves, minced
1 tablespoon cayenne pepper
2 teaspoons salt
1 teaspoon red wine vinegar
8 chicken legs

1½ pounds Spanish chorizo or linguiça sausage,* casings removed
4 large onions, coarsely chopped
½ pound tomatoes, cut into wedges
8 ounces ¼-inch-thick ham slices, cut into 2 × ¼-inch strips
2 tablespoons diced salt pork

1 pound hot Italian sausages

3½ cups chicken stock or canned broth

3 cups bottled clam juice
1 teaspoon saffron threads, crushed

4 cups short-grain rice
1½ pounds uncooked large shrimp, peeled, deveined, tails intact
16 littleneck clams, scrubbed
16 mussels, scrubbed and debearded
1 pound 1-inch-thick halibut or sea bass fillets or shark steaks, cut into 1-inch pieces
2 bay leaves

4 8-ounce frozen uncooked lobster tails (optional), thawed and split lengthwise
Vegetable oil
3 large yellow bell peppers, quartered
3 large red bell peppers, quartered
3 large green bell peppers, quartered

1 10-ounce package frozen peas, thawed
Limes, quartered
Lemons, quartered

Combine oregano, thyme and parsley in small bowl. Transfer half of chopped herbs to processor. Add ¼ cup olive oil, 1 tablespoon red wine, peppercorns, coriander, 3 minced garlic cloves, cayenne, salt and vinegar. Blend until coarse paste forms. Place chicken on large plate. Rub all but 2 tablespoons paste mixture over chicken. Cover and chill until ready to use.

Divide ¼ cup olive oil between 2 large Dutch ovens or heavy large deep skillets over medium heat. Divide chorizo, onions, tomatoes, ham, salt pork, remaining chopped herbs and remaining 5 minced garlic cloves between Dutch ovens. Cook until onions are soft but not brown, crumbling sausage with fork and stirring frequently, about 15 minutes. Transfer chorizo mixture to large bowl. (*Can be prepared 1 day ahead. Cover and refrigerate remaining 2 tablespoons herb paste, chicken legs and chorizo mixture separately.*)

Divide remaining ¼ cup oil between Dutch ovens. Add half of chicken and Italian sausages to each Dutch oven and cook until brown and partially cooked, turning frequently, about 8 minutes for sausage and 12 minutes for chicken. Transfer to plate. Return half of chorizo mixture to each Dutch oven.

Meanwhile, bring stock and clam juice to simmer in heavy medium saucepan. Add saffron and mix well.

Add half of rice to each Dutch oven. Cook over high heat until opaque, stirring frequently, about 5 minutes. Divide remaining herb paste and remaining 7 tablespoons wine between Dutch ovens. Bring to simmer, scraping up any bits. Stir half of stock mixture into each Dutch oven. Divide shrimp, clams, mussels, fish and bay leaves between Dutch ovens. Bring to boil. Reduce heat, cover and simmer until rice is very tender, stirring occasionally, about 25 minutes. Discard any clams or mussels that do not open.

Meanwhile, prepare barbecue (medium-high heat). Brush grill and lobster with vegetable oil. Place lobsters on grill shell side down. Add chicken and grill until lobster and chicken are cooked through, turning occasionally, about 15 minutes. Transfer to large plate. Tent with foil to keep warm. Add Italian sausage and bell peppers to grill and cook until sausage is cooked through and peppers are brown in spots, turning frequently, about 10 minutes. Transfer sausages and peppers to another plate. Cut sausages into 2-inch-long pieces. Cut bell peppers into ½-inch-wide strips.

Divide chicken, lobster, sausage, peppers and peas between Dutch ovens. Cover, remove from heat and let stand 15 minutes. Rearrange shellfish and peppers decoratively atop rice. Serve with lime and lemon wedges.

*Spanish chorizo, a fresh, garlic-flavored pork link sausage that is milder than Mexican chorizo, is available at Spanish markets. *Linguiça,* a similar Portuguese sausage, is available at Spanish markets and also at Latin American markets.

Tuna with Eggplant Puree and Curry Coulis

4 servings

Curry Butter
- 1 cup water
- ⅓ cup ⅛-inch cubes peeled tart green apple
- ½ cup plus 1 tablespoon butter, room temperature
- 1 tablespoon curry powder

Eggplant Puree
- 2 tablespoons olive oil
- ⅓ cup finely chopped onion
- 2 tablespoons minced shallot
- 1 tablespoon snipped fresh chives
- 2 small garlic cloves, crushed
- 1 medium eggplant, peeled, diced
- 1 medium red bell pepper, diced
- 2 small tomatoes, diced
- 8 large fresh basil leaves
- 7 fresh thyme branches

Tuna
- 2 tablespoons olive oil
- 4 6-ounce tuna steaks (about ½ inch thick)
- Salt and pepper

For butter: Bring water to boil in heavy small saucepan. Add apple and cook 3 minutes. Drain, reserving 1 tablespoon cooking liquid for sauce. Transfer apple to processor. Heat 1 tablespoon butter in heavy small skillet over medium heat. Add curry powder and stir 1 minute. Add to processor with apple. Add remaining ½ cup butter and mix until creamy. Cover and refrigerate butter until firm, about 1 hour. (*Can be prepared up to 1 day ahead. Bring butter to room temperature before using.*)

For puree: Heat olive oil in heavy large saucepan over high heat. Add onion, shallot, chives and garlic and stir 1 minute. Add eggplant, bell pepper, tomatoes, basil and thyme. Reduce heat and cook until vegetables are very tender, stirring occasionally, about 35 minutes. Cool slightly. Discard thyme. Transfer mixture to processor and puree until smooth. (*Can be prepared 1 day ahead. Refrigerate.*)

Bring 1 tablespoon reserved apple cooking liquid to boil in heavy small saucepan. Reduce heat to very low. Gradually whisk in curry butter. Set over pan of hot water to keep warm.

For tuna: Heat oil in heavy large skillet (preferably nonstick) over high heat. Pat tuna dry. Season with salt and pepper. Add to skillet. Reduce heat to medium and cook about 3 minutes per side for medium-rare.

Reheat eggplant puree if necessary. Place 2 tablespoons eggplant puree in center of each plate. Top with tuna. Spoon 2 tablespoons sauce around tuna.

Salmon with Peas, Fava Beans and Pearl Onions

4 servings

1 10-ounce basket pearl onions

12 cherry tomatoes

2 cups shelled fresh fava beans (about 1¾ pounds unshelled) or frozen lima beans
Salt

1½ cups shelled fresh peas (about 1¾ pounds unshelled) or frozen peas

6 tablespoons olive oil

¼ cup white wine

2 cups chicken stock or canned unsalted broth

4 ¾-inch-thick salmon fillets (about 6 ounces each)
Pepper

1 bunch parsley, minced

Bring heavy small saucepan of water to boil. Add pearl onions and boil 5 minutes. Drain. Rinse under cold water; drain. Using small sharp knife, cut off root end of pearl onions. Pinch pointed end of onions between thumb and finger to slip off peel. Set onions aside.

Bring another heavy small saucepan of water to boil. Add cherry tomatoes and boil 30 seconds. Using slotted spoon, remove tomatoes from water. Rinse under cold water; drain. Carefully peel tomatoes, leaving stem attached. Return water to boil. Add fresh fava beans and a pinch of salt and simmer until beans are tender, about 20 minutes. (Or cook frozen lima beans according to package directions.) Drain. Rinse under cold water to cool. Carefully peel tough outer skin off fava beans, leaving bean intact.

Place fresh peas and pinch of salt in same saucepan. Cover with water. Brings peas and water to simmer. Continue simmering until peas are tender, about 10 minutes. (Or cook frozen peas according to package directions.) Drain. Rinse peas under cold water; drain. (*Vegetables can be prepared 8 hours ahead. Cover each vegetable separately and refrigerate.*)

Heat 2 tablespoons oil in heavy large skillet over medium-high heat. Add pearl onions and sauté until golden brown, about 5 minutes. Add wine to skillet and simmer until wine is reduced to glaze, about 8 minutes. Add stock. Simmer until onions are tender, about 20 minutes. Using slotted spoon, transfer onions to plate. Continue to boil stock mixture until reduced to ⅔ cup, about 10 minutes. (*Can be prepared 2 hours ahead. Let onions stand at room temperature. Cover and refrigerate stock.*)

Season salmon fillets with salt and pepper. Bring water to boil in base of steamer. Arrange salmon on steamer rack, cover and steam until just opaque, about 7 minutes. Transfer to heated plates; keep salmon warm.

Bring stock to boil in heavy large skillet. Whisk in remaining 4 tablespoons olive oil and minced parsley. Add onions, tomatoes, fava beans and peas. Cook over medium heat until vegetables are just heated through, stirring gently, about 2 minutes. Season with salt and pepper. Spoon vegetables and sauce around salmon and serve immediately.

Eggs, Cheese and Vegetables

Pine Nut Pancakes

Makes about 16

1½ cups buttermilk
1 cup all purpose flour
1 egg
2 tablespoons (¼ stick) butter, melted
1 tablespoon golden brown sugar
1 teaspoon baking powder

½ teaspoon baking soda
Pinch of salt
¾ cup pine nuts, toasted, chopped
Melted butter
Warm maple syrup

Preheat oven to 250°F. Combine first 8 ingredients in large bowl. Stir in pine nuts. Heat griddle or heavy large skillet over medium-high heat; brush lightly with melted butter. Ladle batter onto griddle by 3 tablespoonfuls. Cook until bubbles begin to appear on surface, about 2 minutes. Turn and cook until second sides are golden brown, 1 to 2 minutes. Keep warm in oven. Repeat with remaining batter, adding more butter as necessary. Serve with syrup.

Chili Soufflé Roll with Chunky Tomato and Green Onion Sauce

Try this easy-to-make soufflé with fillings of your own design.

6 servings

2 tablespoons vegetable oil
5 medium-size fresh Anaheim chilies* or canned green chilies (about 6 ounces), chopped
2 onions, thinly sliced
1 garlic clove, minced

½ cup all purpose flour
½ teaspoon ground cumin
¼ teaspoon chili powder

2 cups milk
4 large eggs, separated
Salt and pepper
1½ cups grated Monterey Jack cheese (about 5½ ounces)

1 tablespoon chopped fresh cilantro

Chunky Tomato and Green Onion Sauce (see recipe)
Cilantro sprigs

Preheat oven to 325°F. Line 10 × 15-inch jelly roll pan with foil. Butter foil and lightly dust with flour. Set aside.

Heat oil in heavy large skillet over medium-low heat. Add chilies, onions and garlic. Sauté until chilies and onions are tender, stirring occasionally, about 20 minutes. Transfer chili mixture to bowl.

Place flour, cumin and chili powder in heavy medium saucepan. Gradually add milk, whisking until smooth. Cook over medium heat until thickened, stirring constantly, about 4 minutes. Beat egg yolks in medium bowl. Gradually whisk half of milk mixture into yolks. Return to remaining milk mixture in saucepan. Season with salt and pepper. Add ½ cup cheese and stir until melted.

Place egg whites in large bowl and beat until stiff but not dry. Fold ¼ of whites into yolk mixture to lighten. Add chopped cilantro and fold in remaining whites. Pour soufflé mixture into prepared jelly roll pan, spreading evenly. Bake until puffed and golden brown, about 45 minutes.

Slide soufflé and foil onto work surface. Sprinkle soufflé with remaining 1 cup cheese. Spread chili mixture evenly over cheese, leaving ½-inch border on all sides. Starting from one long side, roll soufflé into tight cylinder using foil as aid. Cut into 1½-inch slices. Transfer to plates. Spoon warm Chunky Tomato and Green Onion Sauce over. Garnish with cilantro sprigs and serve.

*Also known as California chilies, and available at Latin markets as well as specialty foods stores.

Chunky Tomato and Green Onion Sauce

Makes about 1½ cups

2 tablespoons corn oil
2 garlic cloves, finely chopped
1½ pounds plum tomatoes, cored, peeled, seeded, coarsely chopped

Salt and pepper
Cayenne pepper
3 green onions, halved lengthwise, thinly sliced
2 tablespoons chopped fresh cilantro

Heat oil in heavy medium skillet over medium heat. Add garlic and cook until translucent, about 1 minute. Stir in tomatoes. Season with salt, pepper and cayenne pepper. Cook until slightly thickened and most of liquid evaporates, stirring occasionally, about 10 minutes. (*Can be prepared 1 day ahead. Chill. Reheat before continuing.*) Stir in green onions and cilantro.

Cheesy Eggs Benedict

4 servings

¼ cup (½ stick) unsalted butter
3 tablespoons all purpose flour
2 cups milk (do not use lowfat or nonfat)
1½ cups grated cheddar

8 slices Canadian bacon

1 tablespoon white wine vinegar
8 eggs
4 English muffins, halved, lightly toasted
Chopped fresh parsley

Melt butter in heavy medium saucepan over medium heat. Add flour and stir 2 minutes. Whisk in milk and cook until thickened, stirring constantly, about 4 minutes. Add cheese and stir until melted and well blended. Keep warm. (*Can be prepared 1 day ahead. Refrigerate. Rewarm over low heat before using.*)

Preheat oven to 300°F. Place Canadian bacon in single layer in baking pan. Bake until brown, about 10 minutes.

Place 2 inches salted water in large skillet. Add vinegar and bring to simmer. Break eggs 1 at a time into cup and slide into water. Poach until whites are set but yolks are still runny, about 4 minutes. Place 2 muffin halves on each of 4 plates. Top each muffin half with 1 slice Canadian bacon and 1 egg. Spoon some of sauce over. Sprinkle with parsley and serve.

Cabbage-Caraway Quiche

4 servings

4 bacon slices, chopped
½ large onion, chopped
3½ cups chopped cabbage

1 cup half and half
3 eggs
1 cup grated Gruyère cheese

1 teaspoon salt
¾ teaspoon caraway seeds
Pepper
1 9-inch frozen deep-dish pie crust, baked according to package directions

Preheat oven to 375°F. Cook bacon in heavy large skillet over medium heat 5 minutes to render fat. Add onion and sauté until tender, about 5 minutes. Add cabbage and cook until all liquid evaporates, stirring frequently, about 16 minutes. Set cabbage mixture aside.

Combine half and half, eggs, cheese, salt, caraway and generous amount of pepper in large bowl. Stir in cabbage mixture. Pour into crust. Bake until filling puffs and begins to brown, about 40 minutes.

Cannelloni with Spinach and Mushrooms

This lightened version of a classic dish has only 280 calories per serving.

6 servings

Crepes
- ½ cup milk
- ½ cup water
- ½ cup whole wheat flour
- ¼ cup all purpose flour
- 3 large eggs

Filling
- 2 bunches spinach, stemmed
- 3 cups part skim ricotta cheese
- ⅓ cup freshly grated Parmesan cheese (about 1 ounce)
- 2 tablespoons pine nuts, toasted
- ½ teaspoon pepper
- ⅛ teaspoon ground nutmeg

Mushrooms
- 1 tablespoon olive oil
- 6 ounces mushrooms, sliced

  Low-Calorie Tomato Sauce (see recipe)
- ¼ teaspoon cayenne pepper
- 3 tablespoons freshly grated Parmesan cheese
  Minced fresh parsley

For crepes: Whisk first 5 ingredients in bowl until smooth. Chill 2 hours.

Heat 7-inch-diameter nonstick skillet over medium-high heat. Spray with nonstick vegetable oil spray. Working quickly, ladle 2 tablespoons crepe batter into pan, tilting so batter just coats bottom. Immediately return any excess batter to bowl. Cook crepe until bottom is brown, about 45 seconds. Loosen edges with spatula. Turn crepe and cook until second side is speckled brown, about 15 seconds. Slide crepe out onto plate and cover with waxed paper. Repeat with remaining batter, stirring occasionally (if batter thickens, thin with a little additional milk). Adjust heat and spray pan with vegetable oil spray as necessary. (*Crepes can be prepared 3 days ahead; refrigerate.*)

For filling: Cook spinach in large pot of boiling salted water until just wilted, about 3 seconds. Drain well. Squeeze out excess liquid. Chop spinach. Transfer to bowl. Add ricotta, Parmesan, pine nuts, pepper and nutmeg. (*Can be prepared 1 day ahead. Cover and refrigerate. Bring to room temperature.*)

Preheat oven to 375°F. Arrange 1 crepe on work surface. Spoon ½ cup filling into center. Roll crepe over filling into cylinder. Arrange seam side down on nonstick cookie sheet. Repeat with 5 more crepes and remaining filling. Bake until crepes are heated through, about 15 minutes.

Meanwhile, prepare mushrooms: Heat oil in heavy large nonstick skillet over high heat. Add mushrooms and sauté until golden, about 5 minutes.

Spoon ⅓ cup tomato sauce into center of each plate. Transfer crepes to plates. Spoon remaining sauce over. Surround crepes with mushrooms. Sprinkle cayenne, Parmesan and parsley over crepes and serve.

Low-Calorie Tomato Sauce

Makes 3 cups

1 tablespoon olive oil
⅔ cup chopped green onions (white part only)
1 tablespoon chopped garlic
3½ cups canned tomato puree

1 cup dry red wine
1 tablespoon chopped fresh basil or ½ teaspoon dried, crumbled
Pinch of sugar
Salt

Heat oil in heavy medium saucepan over medium heat. Add onions and garlic and sauté 1 minute. Add tomato puree and wine. Reduce heat to medium-low. Simmer sauce until reduced to 3 cups, stirring occasionally, about 45 minutes. Mix in basil and sugar. Season with salt. (*Can be prepared 2 days ahead. Cover and refrigerate. Rewarm over low heat before using.*)

Mixed Mushroom and Potato Charlotte

An attractive, satisfying main course, delicious as well as healthful.

4 servings

1 tablespoon unsalted butter
4 ounces fresh shiitake mushrooms, stems removed, chopped
4 ounces fresh oyster mushrooms, chopped
4 ounces fresh chanterelle mushrooms, chopped
1 tablespoon chopped fresh chives
Salt and pepper

3 cups ¼-inch-thick slices peeled russet potatoes (about 2 pounds)

Olive oil
6 tablespoons freshly grated Parmesan cheese
2 tablespoons olive oil

Melt butter in heavy large skillet over medium heat. Add all mushrooms and sauté until tender and liquid has evaporated, about 15 minutes. Stir in chives. Season mushrooms with salt and pepper.

Blanch potatoes in pot of boiling salted water 3 minutes. Drain. Arrange in single layer on paper towels and pat dry.

Brush 5-cup charlotte mold or soufflé dish with olive oil. Line bottom of mold with foil. Cover bottom of mold with ⅛ of potato slices, arranging in concentric circles, overlapping slightly. Sprinkle 1 rounded tablespoon mushroom mixture and 2 rounded teaspoons Parmesan over potatoes. Drizzle with ¾ teaspoon olive oil and season with salt and pepper. Repeat layering with remaining potato slices, mushroom mixture, cheese and olive oil, ending with potatoes and making 8 potato layers total. Drizzle potatoes with oil. (*Can be made 4 hours ahead. Cover; let stand at room temperature.*)

Preheat oven to 400°F. Bake charlotte until golden brown and potatoes are tender, pressing down with wide metal spatula every 15 minutes, about 1 hour. Let charlotte cool 10 minutes on rack. Run small sharp knife around edge of charlotte if necessary to loosen sides. Turn out onto platter. Carefully peel off foil and serve charlotte immediately.

Potato and Mushroom Lasagnes with Celery-Herb Sauce

4 servings

¼ cup (½ stick) unsalted butter, melted
3 large russet potatoes, peeled
Salt and pepper

5 tablespoons unsalted butter
2 cups chopped oyster mushrooms (about 6 ounces)

1 cup chopped fresh shiitake mushrooms* (about 3 ounces)
1 cup chopped button mushrooms (about 3 ounces)
1 large shallot or green onion, finely chopped

Celery-Herb Sauce (see recipe)

Preheat oven to 400°F. Brush two large cookie sheets with melted butter. Line cookie sheets with parchment paper. Brush parchment with butter. Trim each potato into 3 × 2-inch rectangle. Slice each rectangle lengthwise into ⅛-inch-thick slices, forming twenty 3 × 2-inch slices. Arrange potato slices in single layer on parchment. Brush potato slices with butter and season with salt and pepper. Bake until tender, about 12 minutes. Cool.

Melt 5 tablespoons butter in heavy large skillet over medium-high heat. Add all mushrooms and cook until mushrooms are dry, stirring occasionally, about 8 minutes. Add shallot and continue cooking until mushrooms are brown, about 4 minutes. Season with salt and pepper. Cool slightly.

Brush small cookie sheet with melted butter. Carefully transfer 1 potato slice to sheet. Spoon 1 scant tablespoon mushroom mixture onto potato slice. Top with second potato slice. Continue layering with 3 more scant tablespoons mushroom mixture and 3 more potato slices, ending with potato slice. Repeat process with remaining potato slices and mushroom mixture forming 3 more "lasagnes." (*Can be prepared 2 hours ahead. Cover loosely.*)

Preheat oven to 350°F. Bake lasagnes until heated through, about 15 minutes. Remove from oven; preheat broiler. Broil lasagnes until just golden, about 1 minute. Transfer to 4 plates. Surround lasagnes with sauce.

*If unavailable, ¾ ounce dried shiitake mushrooms can be substituted. Soak in hot water to cover 30 minutes. Drain thoroughly; squeeze mushrooms dry.

Celery-Herb Sauce

Makes about 1½ cups

16 tablespoons (2 sticks) unsalted butter, room temperature
1 1-pound bunch celery, leaves and stalks chopped
3 medium leeks (white and pale green parts only), chopped
1 large onion, chopped

4 fresh parsley sprigs
2 fresh thyme sprigs or 1 pinch dried, crumbled
1 teaspoon whole white peppercorns
2½ cups dry white wine
3 cups water

Melt 4 tablespoons butter in heavy 3-quart saucepan over medium-low heat. Add celery, leeks, onion, parsley, thyme and peppercorns. Sauté until vegetables are tender, stirring occasionally, about 15 minutes. Add wine, increase heat and boil until liquid is reduced by half, about 20 minutes. Add water and continue boiling until liquid is reduced to 1½ cups, about 30 minutes. Strain, pressing on solids to extract as much liquid as possible. Boil celery liquid until reduced to ¾ cup, about 15 minutes. (*Can be prepared up to 1 day ahead; refrigerate.*)

Return celery liquid to boil. Add 6 tablespoons butter and continue boiling 1 minute. Transfer mixture to blender. Add remaining 6 tablespoons butter and blend until sauce is thickened and emulsified. Use immediately.

5 ❦ Vegetables, Grains and Breads

If you are like a lot of cooks, you're of two minds about side dishes: On the one hand, you want something simple, speedy and nutritious; on the other, you want something that will really impress your guests. Of course this probably depends on whether you're cooking for company on a Saturday night or whipping up a fast supper after work. Whichever, you'll find both kinds of recipes here—the quick and easy and the show-stopping, and everything in between as well.

If dinner's as simple as steak and potatoes, simplify it even further by serving Panfried Garlic Potatoes or Mashed Potatoes with Green Onions and Parmesan. Sauté of Peas with Tarragon is a pretty mix of fresh peas and snow peas that cooks up in less than five minutes. For that special evening, try Potato Baskets with Glazed Onions (made by scooping the potato pulp out of the skins, then deep-frying them until golden) or Braised Brussels Sprouts, Pearl Onions and Chestnuts, both of which include do-ahead steps. Risotto with Prosciutto and Lemon is another elegant accompaniment your guests will love.

Most everyone, however, is of one mind about breads: Who can resist the sweet smell of muffins, rolls and loaves fresh from the oven? You'll find plenty of recipes to tempt you here, many of them surprisingly easy, a good number of them do-ahead, including Braided Butter Bread and Herbed Onion Rolls. If it's fresh and fast you had in mind, try Blue Cheese Corn Bread or Spicy Pear Muffins.

 *Vegetables*

Panfried Garlic Potatoes

10 servings

2½ **pounds small new potatoes (unpeeled)**

2 **tablespoons (¼ stick) unsalted butter**

3 **tablespoons corn oil**

2 **tablespoons olive oil**

4 **large garlic cloves, coarsely chopped**
 Salt and pepper

Cook unpeeled potatoes in large pot of boiling salted water until just tender, about 15 minutes. Drain and cool. Quarter potatoes and set aside.

Melt butter with both oils in heavy large skillet over medium heat. Add potatoes and cook 5 minutes, stirring frequently. Increase heat to high. Cook potatoes until deep golden brown, turning frequently, about 20 minutes. Add garlic, salt and pepper and sauté 3 minutes. Transfer to bowl and serve.

Mashed Potatoes with Green Onions and Parmesan

Pressing potatoes through a food mill or ricer gives them a fabulous texture. But they're just as delicious when simply mashed.

2 servings

2 **large russet potatoes (about 1¼ pounds), peeled, cut into chunks**

2 **tablespoons milk**

2 **tablespoons (¼ stick) butter**

1 **bunch green onions, chopped**

⅔ **cup freshly grated Parmesan cheese**
 Salt and pepper

Cook potatoes in large pot of boiling water until tender. Drain well. Press through food mill or ricer into same pot or return to pot and mash. Mix in milk and 1½ tablespoons butter. Keep warm.

Melt remaining ½ tablespoon butter in heavy small skillet. Add green onions and sauté until wilted, about 1 minute. Add to potatoes. Add Parmesan and mix gently. Season with salt and pepper and serve.

Braised Brussels Sprouts, Pearl Onions and Chestnuts

12 servings

¼ **cup (½ stick) butter**

2 **pounds pearl onions, blanched 1 minute in boiling water, peeled**

1½ **cups turkey broth or canned chicken broth**

2 **bay leaves**

2 **pounds fresh brussels sprouts, trimmed or 2 pounds frozen**

16 **ounces whole roasted chestnuts in jars**
 Salt and pepper

Melt butter in heavy large skillet over medium-high heat. Add onions and cook until golden brown, stirring occasionally, about 15 minutes. Add broth and bay leaves. Reduce heat to medium-low. Cover and simmer until onions are just tender, approximately 25 minutes.

Meanwhile, cook fresh brussels sprouts in large pot of boiling salted water until just crisp-tender, about 8 minutes. Drain. (Or cook frozen brussels sprouts according to package directions.) Rinse with cold water. Drain.

Add chestnuts to onions, cover and simmer until chestnuts are tender, about 4 minutes. (*Can be prepared 1 day ahead. Cover onion mixture and brussels sprouts separately and refrigerate. Reheat onion mixture before continuing.*) Add brussels sprouts to onions. Boil until brussels sprouts are heated through and liquid is syrupy, about 4 minutes. Season vegetables with salt and pepper to taste and serve immediately.

Sauté of Peas with Tarragon

For a pretty decorative touch, snip a V at one end of each snow pea.

8 servings

3 tablespoons unsalted butter
1½ pounds fresh peas, shelled or 1¾ cups frozen, thawed
8 ounces snow peas, trimmed

3 tablespoons fresh whole tarragon leaves
Salt and pepper

Melt butter in heavy large skillet over medium heat. Add peas and snow peas. Stir to coat. Cook until just tender, stirring occasionally, about 3 minutes. Stir in tarragon. Season with salt and pepper. Serve immediately.

Potato Baskets with Glazed Onions

Delicious with any roast meat or poultry dish.

4 servings

30 pearl onions

1½ teaspoons sugar
1 tablespoon Sherry wine vinegar
¾ cup chicken stock or canned low-salt chicken broth
2 tablespoons (¼ stick) butter

Salt and pepper

4 large white-skinned boiling potatoes, peeled
Vegetable oil (for deep frying)

½ cup chilled whipping cream
1 egg yolk

Cut X in root end of each onion. Bring saucepan of water to boil. Add onions and boil 3 minutes. Drain; peel onions. Set aside.

Heat heavy small skillet over medium heat. Add sugar and cook until golden brown, swirling skillet occasionally, about 4 minutes. Remove from heat and stir in vinegar. Add onions, stock and butter. Season with salt and pepper. Cook over medium heat until onions are tender and sauce is thickened, stirring occasionally, about 20 minutes. (*Can be prepared 2 hours ahead. Let stand at room temperature. Reheat over medium-low heat.*)

To form potato baskets, cut lengthwise slice off top and bottom of each potato to flatten surfaces. Using melon baller, scoop out inside of potatoes, leaving ¼-inch-thick shells. Heat oil in deep fryer or heavy large saucepan to 375°F. Add potato baskets and fry until golden brown, 3 to 5 minutes. Remove using slotted spoon and drain on paper towels. (*Can be prepared 2 hours ahead. Let stand at room temperature. Refry in 375°F oil until heated through.*)

Preheat broiler. Whip cream until stiff peaks form. Fold in egg yolk. Divide warm onions among potato baskets. Spoon cream mixture over. Broil until glazed. Serve potato baskets immediately.

Potato Gratin with Thyme

White wine adds a tangy flavor to this rich, easy and satisfying side dish.

6 servings

1½ cups whipping cream
1 cup dry white wine
1 cup milk (do not use lowfat or nonfat)
2 garlic cloves, finely chopped

3 pounds russet potatoes, peeled, cut into ⅛-inch-thick slices
Salt and pepper
1 tablespoon minced fresh thyme or 1 teaspoon dried, crumbled

Preheat oven to 400°F. Mix cream, wine, milk and garlic in bowl. Arrange half of potatoes in 12-cup baking dish. Season generously with salt and pepper. Sprinkle with half of thyme. Pour half of cream mixture over. Repeat layering with remaining ingredients. Bake until potatoes are tender and top is light golden brown, about 1 hour. Serve immediately.

Shiitake Mushroom and Potato Galette

6 servings

2 tablespoons (¼ stick) unsalted butter
¾ pound fresh shiitake mushrooms, stemmed and sliced
⅓ cup freshly grated Parmesan cheese

1 tablespoon chopped fresh basil or 1 teaspoon dried, crumbled

2 large russet potatoes, peeled, very thinly sliced crosswise
Salt and pepper

Preheat oven to 350°F. Line cookie sheet with buttered foil. Melt 2 tablespoons butter in heavy large skillet over medium heat. Add mushrooms and sauté until tender, about 10 minutes. Add Parmesan and basil.

Arrange half of potato slices in solid 9-inch round on buttered foil, overlapping slices. Cover with mushroom mixture, pressing as flat as possible. Season with salt and pepper. Top with another layer of potato slices. Cover with buttered foil and another cookie sheet. Place brick atop cookie sheet. Bake until potatoes are tender, about 1 hour 10 minutes. Cool, leaving brick and cookie sheet in place. (*Can be made 2 hours ahead. Store at room temperature.*)

Preheat broiler. Remove brick, top cookie sheet and top piece of foil. Broil galette until crisp and brown, about 2 minutes per side. Cut into 6 wedges.

Whipped Sweet Potatoes with Nutmeg and Lemon

12 servings

5 pounds deep orange sweet potatoes (yams), peeled and cut into 2-inch pieces
½ cup (1 stick) butter, room temperature
3 tablespoons unsulfured molasses
2 teaspoons grated lemon peel

1½ teaspoons ground nutmeg
Salt and pepper

Minced fresh parsley
Grated lemon peel
Ground nutmeg

Cook sweet potatoes in large pot of boiling salted water until tender, about 15 minutes. Drain well. Transfer to large bowl and puree in mixer or processor in batches. Return to pot. Mix in butter, molasses, 2 teaspoons grated lemon peel and 1½ teaspoons ground nutmeg. Season with salt and pepper. (*Can be prepared 1 day ahead. Cover and refrigerate.*) Stir potato mixture over medium heat to rewarm and thicken slightly.

Transfer potatoes to serving bowl. Top with parsley, lemon and nutmeg.

Mashed Potatoes with Sautéed Leeks

2 servings

2 russet potatoes, peeled, cut into
¾-inch pieces

2 tablespoons (¼ stick) butter
2 large leeks, sliced (white and light
green parts)

¼ cup milk
Salt and pepper

Cook potato pieces in large pot of boiling water until tender.

Meanwhile, melt 2 tablespoons butter in heavy medium skillet over medium-low heat. Add leeks and cook until tender and beginning to color, stirring frequently, about 10 minutes.

Drain potatoes and return to pot. Mash. Mix in milk. Stir in leek mixture. Season with salt and pepper and serve.

Creamy Baby Lima Beans with Sausage and Gruyère Cheese

Makes about 8 cups

7 cups frozen baby lima beans
(about 3½ 10-ounce packages)

½ pound hot Italian sausages,
casings removed
¼ cup finely chopped shallots

2 cups half and half
1 cup grated Gruyère cheese (about
4 ounces)
Salt and pepper
Minced fresh parsley

Cook baby lima beans in large saucepan according to package directions. Drain. (*Can be prepared 1 day ahead. Cool. Cover and refrigerate.*)

Cook sausages and shallots in heavy 3-quart saucepan over medium heat until sausages are cooked through, crumbling with fork, about 10 minutes. Pour off drippings from skillet. Add half and half and cheese to sausage. Simmer 2 minutes, stirring constantly. Add beans. Season with salt and pepper. Cook over low heat until sauce thickens slightly and beans are heated through, stirring mixture gently, about 8 minutes. Transfer to bowl. Sprinkle with parsley.

Sauté of Zucchini and Bell Peppers

A light and colorful dish.

6 servings

¼ cup (½ stick) unsalted butter or
olive oil
1 large garlic clove, minced
1 large green bell pepper, cut into
matchstick-size strips
1 large yellow bell pepper, cut into
matchstick-size strips

1 pound zucchini, cut into
matchstick-size strips
1 tablespoon fresh lemon juice
Salt and pepper

Melt butter in heavy large skillet over medium-high heat. Add garlic, then bell peppers and sauté until peppers begin to soften, about 5 minutes. Add zucchini and sauté until crisp-tender, about 4 minutes. Add lemon juice. Season with salt and pepper. Transfer vegetables to bowl and serve.

 Grains

Lemon-scented Saffron Rice

This creamy rice is fragrant with lemon. If you like, pack it into half-cup custard cups and unmold onto serving plates. Garnish with snipped chives, if desired.

8 servings

3 tablespoons unsalted butter
3 large shallots, thinly sliced
Pinch (generous) of saffron threads
1½ cups Arborio* or other short-grain rice
3 cups chicken stock or canned low-salt broth

3 tablespoons fresh lemon juice
2 tablespoons chopped lemon peel
1 large bunch chives, chopped (about ½ cup)
Salt and cracked white pepper

Melt butter in heavy large saucepan over medium heat. Add shallots and saffron and cook 3 minutes, stirring occasionally. Add rice and stir to coat. Add stock and lemon juice; bring to boil. Reduce heat to low, stir and cover. Let simmer until creamy and tender, stirring vigorously every 10 minutes, 20 to 25 minutes. Add lemon peel and chives. Season with salt and pepper. Stir vigorously until well combined. Serve immediately.

*Arborio, an Italian short-grain rice, is available at Italian markets and specialty foods stores.

Rice Pilaf with Basil and Pine Nuts

2 servings

1 14½-ounce can chicken broth
1½ tablespoons olive oil
½ large onion, chopped
1 cup long-grain rice

⅓ cup chopped fresh basil or 1½ teaspoons dried, crumbled
¼ cup toasted pine nuts
Salt and pepper

Bring broth to simmer in small saucepan. Reduce heat to low and keep warm. Meanwhile, heat oil in another heavy small saucepan over medium heat. Add onion and sauté until translucent, about 6 minutes. Add rice and stir 1 minute. Add broth and bring to boil. Reduce heat to low. Cover and cook until broth is absorbed and rice is tender, about 20 minutes. Stir basil and pine nuts into rice. Season pilaf with salt and pepper and serve hot.

Arborio Rice with Wild Mushrooms

4 servings

¾ cup hot water
½ ounce dried porcini mushrooms*

1½ tablespoons olive oil
3½ tablespoons minced fresh parsley
1 shallot or green onion, minced
1¼ cups Arborio rice*
3 tablespoons dry white wine

3 cups chicken stock or canned low-salt broth
⅓ cup freshly grated Parmesan cheese (about 1 ounce)
2 tablespoons (¼ stick) unsalted butter
Pepper

Pour hot water over mushrooms in small bowl. Let stand 30 minutes to soften. Remove mushrooms from liquid. Strain soaking liquid through fine sieve and reserve. Rinse mushrooms; chop finely. Set aside.

Heat oil in heavy medium saucepan over medium heat. Add parsley and shallot and sauté 3 minutes. Add mushrooms and sauté 5 minutes. Add rice and stir until opaque. Add wine and stir until almost no liquid remains in pan. Add reserved mushroom soaking liquid and 1½ cups stock and bring to boil, stirring occasionally. Add remaining 1½ cups stock and return to boil. Cook over medium heat until rice is just tender, stirring frequently, about 15 minutes. Remove from heat. Mix in cheese and butter. Season with pepper. Cover and let stand 3 minutes. Divide rice among plates and serve.

*Dried *porcini* and Arborio rice are available at Italian markets and specialty foods stores.

Risotto with Prosciutto and Lemon

This would be excellent with roast chicken.

4 servings

2 tablespoons matchstick-size strips lemon peel
4 tablespoons (½ stick) unsalted butter
¾ cup chopped onion
1 garlic clove, bruised
2 ounces paper-thin slices prosciutto, chopped

1 cup plus 2 tablespoons Arborio rice*
½ cup sparkling or dry white wine
3½ cups (about) chicken stock or canned broth
½ cup freshly grated Parmesan cheese (about 2 ounces)

Blanch lemon peel in small saucepan of boiling water 15 seconds. Drain. Repeat blanching process twice using fresh water each time.

Melt 2 tablespoons butter in heavy large saucepan over medium heat. Add onion and sauté until translucent, about 5 minutes. Add garlic and half of prosciutto and sauté 2 minutes. Discard garlic. Add rice and stir 1 minute. Add ½ cup wine and cook until no liquid remains, stirring constantly, 5 minutes.

Meanwhile, bring 3½ cups stock to simmer in small saucepan. Reduce heat to low. Cover stock and keep warm.

Add ½ cup stock to rice, reduce heat and simmer until liquid is absorbed, stirring frequently. Continue adding enough of remaining stock ½ cup at a time until rice is just tender but still firm to bite, stirring frequently and allowing each addition to be absorbed before adding next, about 25 minutes. Remove from heat. Mix in remaining 2 tablespoons butter, then Parmesan, lemon peel and remaining prosciutto. Divide among plates and serve.

*Arborio, an Italian short-grain rice, is available at Italian markets and specialty foods stores.

Microwave Polenta

Offer this Italian cornmeal side dish in place of potatoes or rice. It's best served immediately.

Microwave

2 servings

2 13¾-ounce cans low-salt chicken broth
¾ cup yellow cornmeal
5 strips bacon, cooked, crumbled (optional)

¼ cup plus 2 tablespoons freshly grated Romano
3 tablespoons butter
½ teaspoon pepper

Whisk together broth and cornmeal in large bowl. Cook in microwave on High until thickened, about 15 minutes, whisking every 5 minutes to combine. Stir in bacon, Romano, butter and pepper and serve.

 Breads

Traditional English Scones

Makes about 10

2½ cups all purpose flour
½ cup bread flour
6 tablespoons sugar
1½ tablespoons baking powder
¾ teaspoon salt
4½ tablespoons chilled unsalted butter, cut into pieces

1 cup whole milk
2 large eggs
1 large egg yolk
1 cup raisins (optional)

1 egg yolk beaten with 2 tablespoons water (glaze)
Strawberry preserves

Preheat oven to 375°F. Butter and flour heavy large cookie sheet. Mix first 5 ingredients in large bowl. Add butter and cut in until mixture resembles fine meal. Add milk, eggs and yolk, then raisins, and mix until thoroughly incorporated. Turn dough out onto lightly floured surface. Press dough into 1-inch-thick round. Cut out rounds using floured 3-inch round cookie cutter. Gather scraps and re-form into 1-inch-thick round. Cut out more rounds.

Transfer rounds to prepared cookie sheet, spacing evenly. Brush with glaze. Refrigerate 15 minutes. Bake until golden brown, about 25 minutes. Serve scones warm with berry preserves.

Braided Butter Bread

There's nothing like home-made bread to turn a meal into a celebration. This dough requires only two minutes of kneading. You can make the pretty loaves up to a week ahead and then freeze them.

Makes 2 loaves

1 cup milk
½ cup (1 stick) butter, cut into pieces
½ cup sugar
½ teaspoon salt
1 envelope dry yeast
¼ cup warm water (105°F to 115°F)

1 large egg, beaten to blend, room temperature
4 cups (about) unbleached all purpose flour

1 large egg, beaten with 2 tablespoons water (glaze)

Scald milk in heavy medium saucepan. Add butter, sugar and salt. Let stand until butter melts. Pour mixture into large bowl. Cool to 105°F to 115°F. Sprinkle yeast over ¼ cup warm water in small bowl; stir to dissolve. Let yeast mixture stand 10 minutes at room temperature.

Add yeast mixture and 1 beaten egg to milk mixture. Stir in enough flour ½ cup at a time to form soft, slightly sticky dough. Lightly grease large bowl. Add dough, turning to coat. Cover bowl with kitchen towel and let dough rise in warm draft-free area until doubled in volume, about 2 hours.

Grease two heavy large cookie sheets. Turn dough out onto lightly floured work surface and knead until smooth, 2 minutes. Divide dough in half. Divide each half into 3 pieces. Roll each dough piece out between hands and floured work surface to 18-inch-long rope.

Arrange 3 ropes side by side on 1 prepared cookie sheet. Braid ropes. Pinch ends together and tuck under loaf. Repeat process with remaining 3 ropes on second cookie sheet for second loaf. Cover each loaf with kitchen towel and let rise in warm draft-free area until almost doubled in volume, about 1 hour.

Preheat oven to 350°F. Brush egg glaze over loaves. Bake until loaves are golden brown and sound hollow when tapped on bottom, about 25 minutes. Transfer loaves to racks and cool. (*Can be prepared 1 week ahead. Wrap tightly in foil and freeze. Thaw. Place foil-wrapped bread on cookie sheet and rewarm in 350°F oven for about 15 minutes.*)

Killer Bread

12 servings

1 cup mayonnaise
1 cup freshly grated Parmesan cheese (about 3 ounces)
1½ teaspoons minced garlic
1 1-pound round sourdough bread, halved horizontally

Butter
2 tablespoons finely chopped fresh basil or 2 teaspoons dried, crumbled

Preheat broiler. Mix mayonnaise, Parmesan and garlic in large bowl to blend. Arrange bread cut side up on large cookie sheet. Butter bread. Broil until crisp and brown. Spread Parmesan mixture over cut sides of bread. Broil until top is puffed and golden brown. Sprinkle with chopped basil. Cut bread into wedges.

Herbed Onion Rolls

Makes 24

3 tablespoons butter
2 tablespoons finely chopped onion
½ teaspoon minced garlic
½ teaspoon dried oregano, crumbled
½ teaspoon dried tarragon, crumbled
½ teaspoon dried basil, crumbled

¾ cup warm water (105°F to 115°F)
1 envelope dry yeast
1 teaspoon sugar
1 teaspoon salt
2 cups all purpose flour

1 egg, beaten to blend (glaze)
Melted butter

Melt 3 tablespoons butter in heavy medium skillet over medium heat. Add onion, garlic, oregano, tarragon and basil and sauté until onion is translucent, about 5 minutes. Cool onion mixture.

Pour warm water into bowl of heavy-duty mixer fitted with dough hook. Sprinkle yeast and sugar over; stir to dissolve. Let stand until foamy, about 5 minutes. Mix in salt, then cooled onion mixture. Add 1¾ cups flour and mix until smooth. Mix in enough remaining flour by tablespoonfuls to form soft, smooth dough. Turn dough out onto lightly floured surface and knead until smooth and elastic (dough will be slightly sticky), about 5 minutes.

Lightly grease large bowl. Add dough, turning to coat. Cover bowl with clean, dry kitchen towel and let dough rise in warm draft-free area until doubled in volume, approximately 1 hour.

Grease 2 large cookie sheets. Punch dough down. Cut into 24 pieces. Roll each piece on lightly floured surface into smooth ball. Transfer to prepared sheets, spacing 1½ inches apart. Cover with clean, dry kitchen towel and let dough rise in warm draft-free area until doubled in volume, about 1 hour.

Preheat oven to 350°F. Gently brush egg glaze over rolls. Bake until golden brown, about 20 minutes. Brush melted butter over rolls. (*Can be prepared 1 day ahead. Cool completely. Wrap tightly and store at room temperature. Rewarm in 350°F oven before serving.*) Serve onion rolls warm.

Berry Streusel Muffins

Makes 1 dozen

Streusel Topping
- ½ cup firmly packed golden brown sugar
- ¼ cup unbleached all purpose flour
- 1½ teaspoons grated lemon peel
- ½ cup chopped toasted pecans
- 2 tablespoons (¼ stick) unsalted butter, melted and cooled

Batter
- 1½ cups unbleached all purpose flour
- ½ cup firmly packed golden brown sugar
- ¼ cup plus 1½ teaspoons sugar
- 2 teaspoons baking powder
- 1½ teaspoons grated lemon peel
- 1 teaspoon ground cinnamon
- ¼ teaspoon salt
- ½ cup milk
- ½ cup (1 stick) unsalted butter, melted and cooled
- 1 egg
- ¾ cup fresh blackberries
- ¾ cup fresh raspberries

For streusel: Mix brown sugar, flour and lemon peel in bowl. Stir in pecans and melted butter. Set streusel aside.

For batter: Preheat oven to 350°F. Grease 12-cup muffin tin or line with 2½-inch paper baking cups. Combine flour, sugars, baking powder, lemon peel, cinnamon and salt in large bowl. Make well in center. Add milk, butter and egg to well and mix until smooth. Fold in berries. Spoon batter into prepared tin, filling cups ⅔ full. Top each with 1 heaping tablespoon streusel. Bake muffins until tester inserted in centers comes out clean, 20 to 25 minutes. Cool 5 minutes in tin on rack. Remove from tin. Serve warm or at room temperature.

Spicy Pear Muffins

These fruit-studded muffins are hard to resist.

Makes 18

- 4 large pears (about 2 pounds), peeled, cored, diced
- 1 cup sugar
- ½ cup vegetable oil
- 2 large eggs, beaten to blend
- 2 teaspoons vanilla extract
- 2 cups all purpose flour
- 2 teaspoons baking soda
- 2 teaspoons ground cinnamon
- 1 teaspoon ground nutmeg
- 1 teaspoon salt
- 1 cup raisins
- 1 cup chopped walnuts (about 3½ ounces)

Preheat oven to 325°F. Butter 18 muffin cups. Mix pears and sugar in medium bowl. Blend oil, eggs and vanilla in large bowl. Combine flour, baking soda, cinnamon, nutmeg and salt in another medium bowl. Stir pear mixture into egg mixture. Mix in dry ingredients. Fold in raisins and walnuts; do not overmix. Divide batter among prepared cups. Bake until tester inserted in centers comes out clean, about 30 minutes. Serve warm or at room temperature.

Onion-Fennel Breadsticks

This recipe is a fast version of an old favorite.

Makes about 4 dozen

- 1 tablespoon fennel seeds
- ¼ cup (½ stick) unsalted butter
- 1 large onion, minced
- 3¾ cups (about) unbleached all purpose flour
- 1 package fast-rising dry yeast
- 1 tablespoon sugar
- 1½ teaspoons salt
- 1¼ cups hot water (125°F to 130°F)

Coarse salt

Heat heavy medium skillet over high heat. Add fennel seeds and stir until just golden brown and aromatic, about 1 minute. Transfer to large bowl. Reduce heat to medium. Add butter and onion to same skillet. Sauté until onion is golden brown, about 20 minutes. Cool slightly.

Preheat oven to 400°F. Add 2 cups flour, yeast, sugar and salt to fennel seeds in large bowl. Stir in hot water and onion mixture. Mix in enough of remaining flour, ¼ cup at a time, to form soft dough. Knead dough on lightly floured surface until smooth, adding more flour if sticky, about 8 minutes.

Form dough into ball. Place on floured surface. Cover with clean, dry towel. Let dough stand for 10 minutes.

Dust 4 cookie sheets with flour. Divide dough in half. Roll each half out on floured surface to 12-inch square. Dust well with flour. Fold each square in thirds and cut crosswise into ½-inch-wide strips. Unfold strips. Let dough rest 5 minutes. Stretch each strip to 14 inches. Place strips ½ inch apart on prepared cookie sheets. Let breadsticks rest 10 minutes.

Brush breadsticks lightly with water. Sprinkle lightly with coarse salt. Bake breadsticks until golden brown, about 20 minutes. Cool 15 minutes.

Reduce oven temperature to 300°F. Return breadsticks to oven and bake until crisp, about 12 minutes. Cool completely. (*Can be prepared 2 days ahead. Store breadsticks in airtight container.*)

Blue Cheese Corn Bread

4 to 6 servings

1 8½-ounce package Jiffy corn
  muffin mix
1 egg
⅓ cup milk

½ cup crumbled blue cheese
  (about 2 ounces)
2 green onions, chopped
1 tablespoon pepper

Preheat oven to 350°F. Grease 8-inch square baking pan. Combine all ingredients in medium bowl and mix until blended. Spread batter in prepared pan. Bake until firm to touch and golden brown, about 30 minutes. Cool slightly. Cut corn bread into squares and serve hot.

Red and Green Toasts

A festive hors d'oeuvre during the holiday season.

12 servings

1 French bread baguette, cut into
  24 ½-inch-thick rounds
½ pound St. André or other triple
  cream cheese, room temperature
½ pound Saga or other soft ripened
  blue cheese, room temperature

2 radish bunches, trimmed and
  thinly sliced
3 celery stalks, thinly sliced

Preheat broiler. Arrange bread on baking pan. Broil until lightly colored on both sides. Cool very slightly. Spread 12 bread rounds with St. André and 12 with Saga. Arrange radish slices in circle atop St. André toasts and celery slices in circle atop blue cheese toasts. Serve toasts immediately.

Shallot Bruschetta

2 servings

3 tablespoons olive oil
5 large shallots or green onions,
   thinly sliced

4 3 × 5-inch slices French bread
  Pepper
  Freshly grated Romano cheese

Preheat broiler. Heat oil in heavy small skillet over medium heat. Add shallots and sauté until tender, stirring frequently, about 5 minutes.

Broil 1 side of bread until toasted. Spread shallot mixture on second side of bread. Sprinkle generously with pepper and cheese. Broil until beginning to brown. Serve bruschetta immediately.

6 ❦ Desserts

Cookbooks can be fun to read backwards, especially when that means you get to see the sort of irresistible, gorgeous, downright delicious desserts you'll find right here. And whether you're just sneaking a peek at what's to come or planning your menu around dessert, you're bound to be tempted by almost everything that follows.

If it's something light you have in mind, turn to the fruit desserts, where you'll find luscious Strawberries with Orange Champagne Sabayon. If custards and puddings are your weakness, try Deep-Chocolate Custard Pudding or the innovative Corn Crème Brûlée. And if it's ice cream you fancy, there are some terrific ones here, including a homemade version of the ice cream sandwich, Chocolate Chip 'Wiches.

For all you bakers out there, the section on pies, tarts and pastries offers Apple Strudel Tartlets (made simple with purchased phyllo pastry) and kid-pleasing Peanut Butter Pie with Fudge Topping. Among the cakes here are easy-to-make Mixed Berry and Pecan Shortcakes and a wonderfully decadent Double Chocolate Cheesecake.

We finish up the chapter with a selection of cookies and brownies—among them S'More Brownies and Cran-Raspberry Star Cookies—all perfect for lunch boxes, snacks or midnight treats.

❦ Fruit Desserts

Fig and Pear Crumble

Crumble is traditionally an English dessert. This one can be served with scoops of vanilla ice cream.

6 servings

Filling
1 cup (about 7½ ounces) dried figs, stemmed and cut into quarters
  Hot water

3 large pears, peeled, cored, cut into eighths
⅓ cup sugar
2 tablespoons (¼ stick) unsalted butter, melted
1 tablespoon all purpose flour
¼ teaspoon ground cinnamon

Topping
1 cup all purpose flour
½ cup firmly packed golden brown sugar
¼ cup sugar
¼ teaspoon ground cinnamon
¼ teaspoon salt
½ cup (1 stick) chilled unsalted butter, cut into ½-inch pieces

For filling: Place figs in small bowl. Add enough hot water to cover and let stand until softened, about 20 minutes. Drain figs thoroughly.

Preheat oven to 350°F. Butter 8-inch square baking dish with 2-inch-high sides. Mix pear slices with sugar, melted butter, flour and cinnamon in large bowl. Transfer pears to prepared dish. Arrange figs evenly over pears.

For topping: Combine flour, both sugars, cinnamon and salt in large bowl. Add butter and cut in until mixture resembles coarse meal. Sprinkle topping over apples. Bake until topping is golden brown and pears are tender, about 45 minutes. Cool slightly. Serve crumble warm.

Strawberries with Orange Champagne Sabayon

4 servings

¼ cup plus 1 tablespoon sugar
3 egg yolks
1½ teaspoons grated orange peel
½ cup Champagne or sparkling wine

¼ cup plus 2 tablespoons chilled whipping cream

1½ teaspoons Grand Marnier or other orange liqueur

1½ 1-pint baskets fresh strawberries, hulled, halved
  Fresh mint leaves

Whisk first 3 ingredients in medium metal bowl until pale yellow and thick, about 3 minutes. Set bowl over saucepan of simmering water. Add Champagne to yolk mixture and whisk until mixture is doubled in volume and holds shape on spoon, about 5 minutes. Remove bowl from over water. Set over another bowl filled with ice. Cool completely, whisking occasionally.

Using electric mixer, beat cream with Grand Marnier in small bowl until almost stiff. Fold cream and Grand Marnier into sabayon. (*Can be prepared 8 hours ahead. Cover with plastic wrap and refrigerate.*)

Preheat broiler. Divide strawberries among 4 shallow broilerproof bowls or gratin dishes. Spoon sabayon over. Broil until light brown, about 2 minutes. Garnish with mint and serve immediately.

Dried Fruit Stewed with Brown Sugar and Vanilla

This fruit keeps for several days in the refrigerator and is delicious for breakfast, too. Any dried fruit will work well.

4 servings

4 cups water
½ cup firmly packed brown sugar
1 8-ounce package mixed dried fruit
4 orange slices
1 cinnamon stick

1 1½-inch piece vanilla bean, split lengthwise
Plain yogurt or sour cream
Ground cinnamon

Combine all ingredients except yogurt and ground cinnamon in heavy medium saucepan. Bring to boil, stirring until sugar dissolves. Reduce heat and simmer until fruit softens, stirring occasionally, about 20 minutes. Transfer fruit only to glass bowl, using slotted spoon. Boil liquid until reduced to 1 cup, returning liquid exuded from fruit to saucepan, about 10 minutes. Pour liquid over fruit, discarding orange slices. Serve warm, room temperature or chilled, with dollop of yogurt and dusting of cinnamon.

Apple-Cranberry Crisp with Maple Whipped Cream

A hearty, down-home dessert that will appeal to most everyone.

6 servings

1 cup rolled oats
¾ cup unbleached all purpose flour
¾ cup firmly packed dark brown sugar
1 teaspoon ground cinnamon
½ teaspoon salt
¼ teaspoon ground nutmeg
½ cup (1 stick) unsalted butter, cut into pieces

¾ cup chopped toasted walnuts
10 large tart green apples, peeled, cored, cut into ¼-inch-thick slices
1⅓ cups cranberries
⅓ cup sugar
2 tablespoons fresh lemon juice
Maple Whipped Cream (see recipe)

Mix first 6 ingredients in small bowl. Add butter and cut in until mixture resembles coarse meal. Mix in walnuts. (*Crumb topping can be prepared 1 day ahead. Cover tightly and refrigerate.*)

Preheat oven to 375°F. Butter 12-cup baking dish. Combine apples, cranberries, ⅓ cup sugar and lemon juice in large bowl; toss gently. Transfer fruit to prepared dish. Sprinkle rolled-oats topping over. Cover with foil and bake 20 minutes. Uncover and continue baking until apples are tender and topping browns, about 40 minutes. Cool slightly. Spoon crisp into bowls. Top each with dollop of Maple Whipped Cream and serve.

Maple Whipped Cream

Makes about 2 cups

1 cup chilled whipping cream
1 tablespoon (or more) pure maple syrup

Whip cream in large bowl to soft peaks. Beat in 1 tablespoon syrup. Taste, adding more maple syrup if sweeter flavor is desired. Continue whipping to firm peaks. (*Can be prepared 1 day ahead. Refrigerate.*)

Custards, Puddings and Mousses

Vanilla Crème Caramel

Simple and soothing, this crème caramel is flavored with vanilla bean sugar. Serve it plain or garnish it with fresh berries.

6 to 8 servings

1½ cups sugar
¼ cup water

1 3-inch vanilla bean, cut into small pieces
4 large eggs
⅛ teaspoon salt

1½ cups whipping cream
1 cup milk (do not use lowfat or nonfat)

1½ 1-pint baskets fresh strawberries, hulled

Position rack in center of oven and preheat to 300°F. Cook 1 cup sugar and water in heavy small saucepan over low heat, stirring until sugar dissolves. Increase heat and boil without stirring until deep golden brown, washing down sugar crystals from sides of pan with wet pastry brush and swirling occasionally, about 8 minutes. Immediately pour caramel into 6-cup ring mold. Using pot holders, swirl mold so caramel coats sides and bottom.

Process vanilla bean with remaining ½ cup sugar in processor until finely minced, about 2 minutes. Strain sugar through fine sieve. Return sugar to work bowl. Add eggs and salt. Process until smooth, 1 minute. Add cream and milk. Mix custard, using 3 on/off turns.

Pour custard into prepared ring mold. Set mold in large baking pan. Add enough boiling water to baking pan to come halfway up sides of ring mold. Bake until custard is softly set in center, about 1 hour. Remove custard from water. Cool. Refrigerate overnight.

Run small sharp knife between pan and edge of pudding. Place serving platter over ring mold. Invert. Place hot towel over ring mold. Shake mold gently to release pudding. Lift ring mold off carefully, letting caramel syrup drizzle onto platter. Fill center of pudding with fresh strawberries and serve.

Chocolate Mascarpone with Vanilla Custard and Praline

6 servings

Praline
½ cup sugar
3 tablespoons water
½ cup chopped toasted hazelnuts or pecans (about 3 ounces)

Custard
1¼ cups whipping cream
1 vanilla bean, split lengthwise

4 egg yolks
¼ cup sugar

Chocolate Mascarpone
6 ounces bittersweet (not unsweetened) or semisweet chocolate, chopped
1¼ cups chilled whipping cream
1 cup mascarpone cheese*

Additional whipped cream
Fresh mint leaves

For praline: Butter small cookie sheet. Cook sugar and water in heavy small saucepan over low heat, stirring until sugar dissolves. Increase heat and boil without stirring until syrup turns deep golden brown. Mix in nuts. Immediately pour onto prepared sheet. Cool completely. Break praline into 2-inch pieces. Chop coarsely using heavy large knife. (*Can be prepared 2 weeks ahead. Refrigerate praline in airtight container.*)

For custard: Place cream in heavy medium saucepan over medium heat. Scrape in seeds from vanilla bean; add pod. Bring to simmer. Remove from heat. Cover cream mixture and let stand 1 hour.

Whisk yolks and sugar in medium bowl to blend. Bring cream mixture to simmer over medium-low heat. Gradually whisk hot cream into yolks. Return mixture to saucepan and stir until custard thickens and leaves path on back of spoon when finger is drawn across, about 4 minutes; do not boil. Strain into bowl. Cover custard with plastic wrap and refrigerate until well chilled.

For chocolate mascarpone: Melt chocolate in top of double boiler over simmering water, stirring until smooth. Pour chocolate into large bowl. Cool until just barely lukewarm. Using electric mixer, whip cream to soft peaks in medium bowl. Fold mascarpone into chocolate, then fold in whipped cream.

Divide mascarpone mixture among six balloon-shaped wineglasses or goblet-shaped dishes. Top each with 3 tablespoons praline. Pour custard over praline. Cover and refrigerate at least 1 hour. (*Can be prepared 1 day ahead.*) Top each dessert with dollop of whipped cream. Garnish with mint.

*Italian cream cheese available at Italian markets and some specialty foods stores. If unavailable, blend ½ pound cream cheese with 3 tablespoons whipping cream and 2 tablespoons sour cream. Use 1 cup mixture for recipe. Refrigerate remainder.

Deep-Chocolate Custard Pudding

Blending hot cream with minced chocolate in the food processor simplifies the melting technique.

4 servings

8 tablespoons sugar
⅓ cup water
¼ cup unsweetened cocoa powder

4 ounces semisweet chocolate, cut into large pieces
1 cup half and half

2 tablespoons (¼ stick) unsalted butter, cut into small pieces
1 teaspoon vanilla extract
Pinch of salt
2 large eggs
2 egg yolks

Position rack in center of oven and preheat to 325°F. Mix 1 tablespoon sugar, water and cocoa in small bowl. Set aside.

Process semisweet chocolate with remaining 7 tablespoons sugar in processor until chocolate is finely minced, about 2 minutes. Scrape down sides of work bowl. Bring half and half and butter to boil in heavy small saucepan. With processor running, pour boiling half and half mixture gradually through feed tube. Process until chocolate melts and is smooth and mixture cools slightly, about 1 minute. Scrape down sides of work bowl. Mix in cocoa mixture, vanilla and salt. Add eggs and egg yolks and blend well, 15 seconds.

Divide chocolate mixture evenly among four 6- to 8-ounce custard cups. Arrange cups in large baking pan. Pour enough boiling water into baking pan to come halfway up sides of custard cups. Bake until centers are gently set, about 25 minutes. Transfer chocolate puddings to rack and cool completely. Cover and refrigerate until well chilled, at least 6 hours or overnight.

Corn Crème Brûlée

Sweet corn combines with a rich vanilla custard for a luscious dessert.

6 servings

1 ear corn
2 cups water
8 tablespoons sugar

8 large egg yolks

1 vanilla bean, split lengthwise
2¼ cups whipping cream

6 scant teaspoons raw sugar

Preheat oven to 250°F. Using large knife, cut corn kernels from cob. Bring water and 2 tablespoons sugar to boil in small saucepan. Add corn kernels and cook until just tender, about 3 minutes. Drain. Divide kernels among six ½-cup ramekins or soufflé dishes. Set aside.

Beat egg yolks and remaining 6 tablespoons sugar in large bowl to blend. Using small sharp knife, scrape seeds from vanilla bean into yolk mixture. Whisk in cream. Ladle cream mixture over corn. Place ramekins in large baking pan. Add enough hot water to baking pan to come halfway up sides of ramekins. Bake until centers no longer move when ramekins are gently shaken, approximately 1 hour 50 minutes.

Cover and refrigerate custards overnight. (*Can be prepared 1 day ahead.*)

Preheat broiler. Sprinkle each custard with 1 scant teaspoon raw sugar. Broil until sugar melts, browns and bubbles, watching carefully, about 1 minute. Refrigerate custards until well chilled, about 1 hour. (*Can be prepared up to 4 hours ahead.*) Serve custards cold.

Scotch Whisky Trifle

12 servings

Coffee-Caramel Custard
2⅔ cups half and half
 6 egg yolks
 ¾ cup firmly packed dark brown sugar
 3 tablespoons all purpose flour
1½ teaspoons vanilla extract

 1 cup plus 2 tablespoons chilled whipping cream
1¼ teaspoons instant espresso powder or instant coffee powder
 3 tablespoons Scotch whisky

Trifle
 1 1-pound frozen pound cake, thawed, cut into ¾-inch cubes
 6 tablespoons Scotch whisky
 1 cup raspberry jam (about 10½ ounces)
 2 ½-pint baskets fresh raspberries or two 12-ounce bags frozen unsweetened raspberries, thawed
 2 large bananas, peeled, halved lengthwise, sliced

 2 cups chilled whipping cream
 3 tablespoons sugar
 3 tablespoons Scotch whisky
 1 ½-pint basket fresh raspberries
   Semisweet chocolate, curled or grated

For custard: Scald half and half in heavy medium saucepan. Whisk yolks, sugar and flour in top of double boiler until smooth. Gradually whisk in hot half and half. Set over boiling water and stir until custard is very thick and mounds when dropped from spoon, about 6 minutes. Set top of double boiler over ice and chill custard, whisking occasionally. Mix in vanilla.

Combine whipping cream and espresso powder in large bowl and stir until powder dissolves. Beat to firm peaks. Add Scotch and beat until firm. Fold cream mixture into cold custard in 2 additions. (*Can be prepared up to 1 day ahead. Cover custard and refrigerate.*)

For trifle: Place half of pound cake cubes in 3-quart trifle bowl or glass bowl. Sprinkle with 3 tablespoons Scotch and toss. Heat jam in heavy small saucepan until just pourable. Spoon half of jam over cake and spread. Top with half of custard. Top with 1 basket or 1 package raspberries, making sure some berries show at sides of bowl. Top with half of bananas. Place remaining pound cake cubes in another bowl. Sprinkle with 3 tablespoons Scotch and toss. Place atop bananas in trifle bowl. Layer fruit over. Spoon remaining jam over and spread. Top with remaining custard, then with 1 basket or package of raspberries and remaining banana. Cover and refrigerate until set, at least 3 hours. (*Can be prepared up to 1 day ahead.*)

Whip cream and sugar in large bowl to stiff peaks. Add 3 tablespoons Scotch and beat to firm peaks. Mound whipped cream atop trifle. Garnish trifle with fresh raspberries and chocolate.

Chocolate Passion

An irresistible mix of brownies, chocolate pudding, crumbled candy bars and raspberries.

10 servings

Brownies
- 8 ounces semisweet chocolate, chopped
- 1 cup firmly packed golden brown sugar
- ¼ cup (½ stick) unsalted butter
- 1 egg
- 1 teaspoon vanilla extract
- ½ cup sifted all purpose flour
- 1 teaspoon baking powder
- ½ teaspoon salt
- 1 cup finely chopped toasted pecans (about 4 ounces)

- 4 teaspoons Kahlúa or other coffee liqueur

Pudding
- 16 ounces semisweet chocolate, chopped
- ½ cup whipping cream
- ¼ cup (½ stick) unsalted butter
- 10 large eggs, separated, room temperature
- 2 tablespoons Kahlúa or other coffee liqueur

- 2 cups chilled whipping cream
- 3 tablespoons sugar
- ¾ cup seedless raspberry jam
- 1 ½-pint basket fresh raspberries
- 6 1.2-ounce packages Heath Bars, chopped, or 1½ cups chopped Almond Roca
- 12 Oreo cookies, crumbled (optional)
- 1 cup toasted walnuts, chopped (about 4 ounces)
  Additional fresh raspberries

For brownies: Preheat oven to 350°F. Grease 9-inch square baking pan with 2-inch-high sides. Melt chocolate, sugar and butter in heavy medium saucepan over low heat, stirring until chocolate melts (mixture will be grainy). Pour into large bowl and cool slightly. Add egg and vanilla and stir to blend. Sift flour, baking powder and salt into chocolate mixture; stir together. Mix in pecans.

Pour batter into prepared pan. Bake until top is dry and cracked and tester inserted in center comes out with some wet batter still attached, about 27 minutes. Cool slightly. Run small sharp knife around pan sides to loosen. While still warm, cut brownie into bite-size pieces. Drizzle Kahlúa over brownie pieces. (*Can be prepared 1 day ahead. Cool. Cover; let stand at room temperature.*)

For pudding: Combine chocolate, cream and butter in heavy large saucepan. Stir over low heat until chocolate and butter melt and mixture is smooth. Remove from heat. Mix in yolks 1 at a time. Add Kahlúa. Pour into large bowl. Cool to lukewarm. Using electric mixer, beat whites in large bowl until stiff but not dry. Fold ½ of whites into chocolate mixture. Gently fold in remaining whites. Chill until set, about 4 hours. (*Can be prepared 1 day ahead.*)

Using electric mixer, whip cream in large bowl until soft peaks form. Gradually add 3 tablespoons sugar and beat until stiff. Sprinkle ⅓ of brownie pieces over bottom of 16-cup glass bowl. Spread ⅓ of jam over. Sprinkle ⅓ of raspberries over. Spread ⅓ of pudding over. Top with ⅓ of Heath Bars, ⅓ of crumbled cookies, ⅓ of walnuts and ⅓ of whipped cream. Repeat layering process 2 more times. Cover and refrigerate until well chilled, about 4 hours. (*Can be prepared 8 hours ahead.*) Top dessert with raspberries and serve.

Bread Pudding with Apple, Raisins and Figs

6 servings

⅔ cup raisins
⅓ cup chopped dried figs
¼ cup Marsala or brandy

9 white sandwich bread slices
5 tablespoons butter, room temperature
½ cup sugar
3 large eggs

1 egg yolk
1½ cups whipping cream
1½ cups milk (do not use lowfat or nonfat)
2 tablespoons lemon juice
2 teaspoons grated lemon peel
1 teaspoon vanilla
1 apple, peeled, cored, chopped

Combine raisins, figs and Marsala in small bowl. Let stand 30 minutes.

Preheat oven to 350°F. Generously butter 8-cup soufflé dish. Spread 1 side of each bread slice generously with butter. Cut bread into 1-inch cubes. Transfer to prepared dish. Mix sugar, eggs and egg yolk in large bowl. Whisk in cream and next 4 ingredients. Stir in apple, raisins and figs with Marsala. Pour over bread and stir to combine. Let stand 15 minutes.

Set soufflé dish in large baking pan. Add enough hot water to large pan to come 1 inch up sides of soufflé dish. Bake until custard is set and top is golden and puffed slightly in center, about 1¾ hours. Serve warm.

Chocolate Coconut Mousse with Caramel Sauce

A rich frozen chocolate and coconut mousse complemented by a warm, sweet caramel sauce.

8 to 10 servings

1 fresh coconut or 1 cup sweetened shredded coconut

Mousse
3 cups semisweet chocolate chips (about 1¼ pounds)
1 cup whipping cream

4 extra-large egg yolks
1 cup chilled whipping cream
8 extra-large egg whites, room temperature

Sauce
1¼ cups sugar
¼ cup water
1 cup whipping cream
½ cup (1 stick) unsalted butter, cut into pieces
1 teaspoon vanilla extract

Additional chocolate chips
Additional sweetened shredded coconut

If using fresh coconut: Preheat oven to 400°F. Pierce holes through coconut at three soft spots on one end, using hammer and nail. Drain liquid and reserve for another use. Bake coconut until shell cracks, about 20 minutes. Cool slightly. Wrap in towel. Sharply pound center of coconut with hammer to crack open. Separate meat from shell. Remove brown skin using vegetable peeler. Grate enough coconut to measure 1 cup. Set aside.

For mousse: Melt chocolate chips in heavy medium saucepan over very low heat, stirring until smooth. Add 1 cup cream and grated coconut or 1 cup sweetened shredded coconut and stir until smooth. Pour into large bowl. Cool chocolate mixture to room temperature.

Whisk yolks into chocolate mixture. Using electric mixer, whip 1 cup chilled cream in medium bowl until soft peaks form. Using electric mixer fitted with clean dry beaters, beat whites in another large bowl until stiff but not dry. Fold whipped cream into chocolate mixture. Gently fold in whites. Pour mixture into 10-inch-diameter springform pan with 2-inch-high sides. Cover and freeze at least 6 hours or overnight. (*Can be prepared 2 days ahead.*)

For sauce: Cook sugar and water in heavy medium saucepan over low heat, stirring until sugar dissolves. Increase heat and boil without stirring until syrup turns caramel color. Add cream (mixture will bubble vigorously) and stir until smooth. Remove from heat. Add butter and vanilla and stir until smooth. (*Can be prepared 1 day ahead. Cover and refrigerate. Rewarm caramel sauce over low heat before using, stirring frequently.*)

Place mousse in refrigerator for 30 minutes to soften slightly. Run small sharp knife around cake pan sides to loosen. Release pan sides. Cut mousse into wedges. Ladle warm caramel sauce onto plates. Place mousse wedges atop sauce. Sprinkle additional chocolate chips over sauce. Sprinkle shredded coconut over mousse and serve immediately.

White Chocolate and Fresh Raspberry Terrine

The trick to this gorgeous dessert is to use imported white chocolate and to melt it carefully, since white chocolate is extremely heat sensitive. Let the terrine mixture get only warm enough to melt the white chocolate and butter.

8 servings

Terrine

18 ounces imported white chocolate (such as Tobler or Lindt), finely chopped

½ cup whipping cream

6 tablespoons (¾ stick) unsalted butter, cut into small pieces, room temperature

2 tablespoons framboise eau-de-vie (clear raspberry brandy)

1 pint (2 baskets) raspberries

Sauce

1 10-ounce package frozen raspberries in syrup

1 7-ounce ripe pear, halved, cored, cut into eighths

Mint leaves

2 tablespoons framboise eau-de-vie

For terrine: Coat 7½ × 3¾ × 2-inch (3-cup) loaf pan with nonstick vegetable oil spray. Line with 3 × 12-inch strip of waxed paper, pressing gently to fit and overlapping ends of pan. Set aside.

Warm ⅓ of chocolate with cream in heavy small saucepan over low heat, stirring constantly with rubber spatula until melted and smooth. Add remaining chocolate in 2 batches, allowing second batch to melt completely before adding last third. Remove from heat occasionally to avoid overheating chocolate. Add 3 tablespoons butter and 1 tablespoon framboise. Stir until butter is just melted. Repeat with remaining butter and framboise. Remove from heat; let stand in warm area while assembling terrine layers.

Pour ⅔ cup chocolate mixture into prepared pan and freeze until set but not hard, about 15 minutes. Choose medium-size berries and arrange upside down in 9 crosswise rows of 3 berries each, spacing evenly and leaving border around edge of pan. Press gently into chocolate. Gently pour 1 cup chocolate mixture over berries in even layer. Freeze until set but not hard, about 20 minutes. Repeat layering with more berries to form second layer. Press gently into chocolate. Gently pour remaining chocolate mixture over. Smooth to form even layer. Refrigerate until firm. Cover and chill overnight. Reserve remaining berries for garnish. (*Can be prepared 2 days ahead.*)

For sauce: Combine raspberries with syrup and pear in heavy small saucepan. Stir to coat pear with syrup. Bring to simmer. Simmer until pear softens, about 10 minutes. Puree in blender until smooth. Strain puree through fine sieve. (*Can be prepared 2 days ahead. Cover tightly and refrigerate.*)

Run small sharp warm knife around top edge of terrine. If necessary dip bottom of terrine into warm water about 5 seconds. Using waxed paper as aid, gently unmold onto small cutting board. Peel off waxed paper. Use spatula to smooth surface of terrine if necessary.

Heat long thin knife under warm water. Dry knife and slice terrine into

⅛-inch-thick slices, cleaning and warming knife as necessary. Place 2 to 3 slices in center of each plate. Garnish one side of plate with reserved fresh berries and mint leaves. (*Can be prepared 2 hours ahead. Cover; chill.*)

Just before serving, mix framboise into sauce. Spoon 2 to 3 tablespoons sauce opposite berries. Let stand at room temperature 10 minutes.

❦ Frozen Desserts

Late Harvest Riesling Ice Cream

Late harvest wines are made from grapes affected by Botrytis cinerea, *a mold that sometimes occurs when the grapes are allowed to become overripe. Botrytis gives the resulting wine a honeylike flavor.*

Makes about 5 cups

½ cup half and half
6 tablespoons sugar
3 egg yolks

1½ cups chilled whipping cream
1 cup late harvest Riesling

Cook half and half with sugar in heavy medium saucepan over medium heat, stirring until sugar dissolves. Whisk yolks in medium bowl to blend. Gradually whisk hot half and half mixture into yolks. Return mixture to saucepan and stir over medium heat until custard thickens and leaves path on back of spoon when finger is drawn across, about 3 minutes; do not boil. Strain into bowl. Mix in cream and wine. Refrigerate custard until cold.

Transfer custard to ice cream maker and freeze according to manufacturer's instructions. Freeze in covered container. (*Can be prepared 3 days ahead.*) If ice cream is frozen solid, soften slightly in refrigerator before serving.

Chocolate-Peanut Butter "Pound Cake"

With flavors reminiscent of a popular candy bar, this whimsical dessert comprises side-by-side chocolate and peanut butter mousses frozen in a loaf or pound-cake pan. When unmolded, the "cake" is covered with chocolate glaze.

12 servings

Peanut Butter Mousse
2 cups powdered sugar, sifted
¾ cup plus 2 tablespoons creamy peanut butter (do not use freshly ground or old-fashioned style)
6 ounces cream cheese, room temperature
3 tablespoons whipping cream
2 large egg whites

Chocolate Mousse
1 cup whipping cream
⅓ cup sugar

8 ounces bittersweet (not unsweetened) or semisweet chocolate, chopped

1½ teaspoons instant espresso powder
2½ tablespoons hot water
3 egg yolks

Chocolate Glaze
⅔ cup whipping cream
5 tablespoons unsalted butter, diced
5 ounces semisweet chocolate, finely chopped

Raspberries
Fresh mint sprigs

For peanut butter mousse: Line 6-cup loaf pan with foil. Mix together 1⅓ cups sugar, peanut butter and cream cheese in large bowl until smooth. Mix in cream. Beat egg whites in medium bowl until soft peaks form. Gradually add remaining ⅔ cup sugar and beat until stiff and shiny. Fold whites into peanut butter mixture in 2 additions.

Tilt prepared pan lengthwise at 45° angle. Spoon in peanut butter mousse

Veal with Leek and Roquefort Sauce; Sauté of Peas with Tarragon; Lemon-scented Saffron Rice; White Chocolate and Fresh Raspberry Terrine

Brian Leatart

Clockwise from top left:
Blue Cheese Potato Salad;
Grilled Flank Steak, Onion
and Bell Pepper Sand-
wiches; Toffee Brownies;
Grilled French Bread Rolls;
White Bean Dip with Chips
and Sticks

Myron Beck

Lamb Shoulder Chops with Tomatoes and Marjoram and Mashed Potatoes with Green Onions and Parmesan

Umack.

Cheesy Eggs Benedict

Strawberry and Cream Tart

John Reed Forsman

*Boysenberry-Grand Marnier
Ice Cream Bonbons*

Double Chocolate Cheesecake

and smooth top. (Mousse will form triangle down length of pan.) Set pan in freezer, propping to hold angle. Freeze until mousse is firm, about 1 hour.

For chocolate mousse: Heat cream and sugar in heavy small pan over very low heat, stirring just until sugar dissolves. Transfer cream mixture to medium bowl and refrigerate until well chilled.

Meanwhile, melt chocolate in top of double boiler over simmering water, stirring until smooth. Cool 5 minutes. Dissolve espresso powder in hot water in small bowl. Whisk in yolks. Add mixture to warm chocolate and stir until mixture is smooth and slightly thickened. Let chocolate mixture stand until batter is cooled to room temperature, but not set.

Beat chilled cream to soft peaks. Fold cream into chocolate mixture in 2 additions. Set pan with frozen peanut butter mousse flat onto work surface. Spoon chocolate mousse over frozen peanut butter mousse. Smooth top. Cover pan. Freeze until chocolate is firm, about 6 hours or overnight.

For glaze: Heat cream and butter in medium saucapan over low heat until cream simmers and butter is melted. Turn off heat. Add chocolate and whisk until mixture is smooth. Let glaze cool until thickened but still of pouring consistency, approximately 1½ hours.

Turn loaf out onto cake rack. Remove pan; remove foil. Pour glaze over mousse and smooth all surfaces. Transfer mousse to serving platter. Freeze until glaze is set, about 1 hour. (*Mousse can be prepared up to 1 day ahead. Wrap loosely when chocolate glaze is frozen solid.*)

Cut mousse into ½-inch-thick slices. Center each portion on dessert plate. Garnish with berries and mint and serve.

Mocha Crunch Ice Cream Cake

A big, beautiful dessert that layers chocolate and coffee ice creams with mocha sauce in a macaroon cookie crust.

10 to 12 servings

Mocha Sauce
1½ cups water
½ cup sugar
2½ tablespoons instant espresso powder
12 ounces semisweet chocolate, chopped
6 tablespoons (¾ stick) unsalted butter

Crust
3 cups macaroon cookie crumbs (about 21 Mother's brand cookies)

¼ cup (½ stick) unsalted butter, melted

Filling
2 pints chocolate ice cream
2 pints coffee ice cream
¾ cup chopped Almond Roca or Heath Bars (about 14 Almond Roca or 12 miniature Heath Bars, about 5 ounces)

For sauce: Cook water, sugar and espresso in heavy medium saucepan over low heat, stirring until sugar dissolves. Add chocolate and butter. Stir until chocolate and butter are melted and sauce is smooth. Cool completely. (*Sauce can be prepared 3 days ahead. Cover and refrigerate. Bring sauce to room temperature.*)

For crust: Oil 9-inch springform pan. Mix 2 cups crumbs and butter in medium bowl. Press firmly into bottom of prepared pan. Freeze until firm.

For filling: Soften chocolate ice cream in refrigerator until spreadable but not melted. Spread in pan and smooth top. Freeze until firm.

Spoon ½ cup sauce over ice cream and sprinkle with remaining 1 cup cookie crumbs. Freeze until firm.

Soften coffee ice cream in refrigerator until spreadable but not melted. Spread in pan. Smooth surface and freeze until firm. Spread ½ cup sauce over coffee ice cream. Sprinkle with Almond Roca and freeze until firm. (*Can be prepared 3 days ahead. Cover tightly.*)

Soften cake slightly in refrigerator if necessary. Rewarm remaining sauce over low heat until lukewarm, stirring frequently. Remove pan sides. Cut cake into wedges. Serve, passing warm mocha sauce separately.

Boysenberry-Grand Marnier Ice Cream Bonbons

Pretty ice cream treats, decorated five different ways. Turn the freezer to the coldest setting for best results. Pack the leftover ice cream into a container and freeze it to enjoy after the bonbons are gone. Begin this recipe at least a day ahead (and you can start up to a week ahead). Once you've mastered the technique here, create bonbons of your own using other homemade ice creams or your favorite purchased ones.

Makes 30

Boysenberry Ice Cream
- 2/3 **cup sugar**
- 12 **ounces frozen unsweetened boysenberries or raspberries (about 2½ cups), thawed**
- 1⅓ **cups whipping cream**
- 3 **egg yolks**

Grand Marnier Ice Cream
- 2 **oranges**
- 2 **cups whipping cream**
- 1 **cup half and half**
- 3/4 **cup sugar**
- 6 **egg yolks**
- 1½ **teaspoons grated orange peel**

- 2 **tablespoons Grand Marnier or other orange liqueur**

Dipping
- 1¼ **pounds bittersweet (not unsweetened) or semisweet chocolate, chopped**
- 1/4 **cup plus 1 tablespoon solid vegetable shortening**

- 6 **ounces imported white chocolate (such as Lindt), chopped**

  Milk chocolate shavings

- 5 **walnut halves**
  Unsweetened cocoa powder

For boysenberry ice cream: Sprinkle sugar over berries in small bowl. Let stand 45 minutes at room temperature. Puree berries in processor. Strain through sieve into large bowl, pressing on solids with back of spoon. Bring cream to simmer in heavy medium saucepan. Whisk yolks in bowl to blend. Gradually whisk in hot cream. Return mixture to saucepan and stir over medium-low heat until custard thickens and leaves path on back of spoon when finger is drawn across, about 2 minutes. Strain into berry puree. Refrigerate until cold.

Place 9 × 13-inch baking dish in freezer. Transfer berry custard to ice cream maker and process according to manufacturer's instructions. Spread ice cream in bottom of chilled baking dish. Freeze.

For Grand Marnier ice cream: Remove peel (orange part only) from oranges in long wide strips, using vegetable peeler. Place in heavy medium saucepan. Add 1 cup cream, half and half and sugar. Bring to boil, stirring occasionally. Remove from heat. Cover and let steep 30 minutes.

Remove peel from cream using slotted spoon and discard. Bring cream mixture to simmer. Whisk yolks in medium bowl to blend. Gradually whisk in hot cream mixture. Return mixture to saucepan and stir over medium-low heat until custard thickens and leaves path on back of spoon when finger is drawn across, about 2 minutes. Strain into bowl. Mix in 1½ teaspoons grated orange peel, then remaining 1 cup cream. Cover and refrigerate custard until cold, about 2 hours. Mix Grand Marnier into custard.

Transfer custard to ice cream maker and process according to manufacturer's instructions. Spoon over boysenberry ice cream in dish; smooth top. Cover with waxed paper. Freeze until very firm, at least 6 hours or overnight.

For dipping: Line 4 small cookie sheets with foil. Place in freezer for

20 minutes. Remove 1 sheet. Dip 1½-inch-diameter ice cream scoop into cup of hot water. Working quickly, scoop up layered ice cream. Round off edges with index finger. Release ice cream ball onto frozen sheet. Repeat, forming 15 ice cream balls. Insert 1 toothpick into center of each ball. Return sheet to freezer. Remove second sheet from freezer. Repeat process to form 15 more ice cream balls. Return sheet to freezer. Pack remaining ice cream into container and freeze. Freeze ice cream balls until very firm, at least 6 hours or overnight. Using metal icing spatula, loosen ice cream balls from foil; refreeze.

Melt bittersweet chocolate with ¼ cup shortening in heavy medium saucepan over very low heat, stirring until smooth. Cool to lukewarm. Remove 1 sheet of ice cream balls and 1 foil-lined frozen sheet from freezer. Fill ¼-cup measuring cup with melted chocolate. Working quickly, hold 1 ice cream ball by toothpick over saucepan of chocolate; pour chocolate in cup over ball, turning to coat. Allow excess chocolate to drip off. Place bonbon on foil-lined sheet. Repeat with remaining balls. Twist and turn toothpicks to loosen; remove from bonbons. Freeze. Repeat dipping process with remaining ice cream balls and frozen cookie sheet. Freeze for 30 minutes.

Melt white chocolate with remaining 1 tablespoon shortening in heavy small saucepan over very low heat, stirring constantly. Cool to lukewarm. Rewarm bittersweet chocolate to lukewarm over very low heat, stirring constantly. Remove 1 sheet of bonbons from freezer. Dip 1 bonbon halfway into white chocolate, covering one side and hole left from toothpick. Place on same frozen sheet. Repeat with 4 more bonbons. Dip spoon into melted bittersweet chocolate and quickly move from side to side over double-dipped bonbons, allowing chocolate to fall in zigzag lines. Dip another spoon into melted white chocolate and wave from side to side over 5 solid chocolate bonbons, allowing chocolate to fall in zigzag lines. Dip finger into melted bittersweet chocolate and dab over top of one of remaining bonbons on sheet, covering hole left from toothpick. Sprinkle chocolate shavings over. Repeat with remaining 4 bonbons on sheet. Return bonbons to freezer.

Remove second sheet of bonbons from freezer. Dip half of walnut into bittersweet chocolate. Place atop 1 bonbon. Repeat with 4 more walnuts and bonbons. Roll remaining 10 bonbons in bowl of cocoa powder. Brush off excess. Place on same sheet. Freeze at least 4 hours or overnight. (*Can be prepared 1 week ahead. Store in single layer in airtight container.*)

Chocolate Chip 'Wiches

Any favorite ice cream can be used in these treats. Both the walnut cookies and the "sandwiches" themselves can be prepared several days in advance.

Makes 8

Walnut Chip Cookies
- 1 cup all purpose flour
- ⅓ cup sugar
- 2½ tablespoons cornstarch
- 1½ teaspoons grated lemon peel
- ½ teaspoon ground nutmeg
- ⅛ teaspoon salt
- ½ cup (1 stick) chilled unsalted butter, cut into ½-inch pieces
- ½ teaspoon vanilla extract
- ½ cup walnuts

- 2 ounces bittersweet (not unsweetened) or semisweet chocolate, chopped, or ⅓ cup mini chocolate chips

  Sugar

Ice Cream
- 1 pint ice cream of choice

- 3 ounces semisweet chocolate, chopped

For cookies: Preheat oven to 350°F. Combine first 6 ingredients in processor and blend. Add butter and vanilla. Process until mixture resembles fine meal and begins to stick together, using on/off turns. Add walnuts and process until finely chopped. Mix in chopped chocolate.

Transfer mixture to sheet of waxed paper. Press together. Top with another sheet of waxed paper. Roll out ¼ inch thick. Cut out cookies using 2½-inch round cookie cutter. Transfer to ungreased cookie sheet. Gather scraps, reroll and cut additional cookies. Sprinkle cookies with sugar. Bake until just beginning to color, about 22 minutes. Cool on cookie sheet on rack 5 minutes. Carefully transfer cookies to rack and cool. (*Can be prepared 3 days ahead. Store in airtight container at room temperature.*)

For ice cream: Soften ice cream slightly in refrigerator. Turn 8 cookies over and gently spread ¼ cup ice cream atop each. Top with 8 cookies, sugared side up. Freeze ice cream sandwiches until firm.

Melt 3 ounces semisweet chocolate in top of double boiler over simmering water, stirring until smooth. Dip fork in chocolate and drizzle in free-form lines over tops of sandwiches. Freeze until chocolate design is firm. (*Can be prepared up to 3 days ahead. Cover and freeze.*) Soften sandwiches slightly in refrigerator before serving if frozen very solid.

Hot Fudge Fruit Sundaes

The addition of fruit makes these irresistible sundaes a little different. The rich, creamy sauce is a do-ahead.

6 to 8 servings

Fudge Sauce
½ cup whipping cream
⅓ cup firmly packed golden brown sugar
4 ounces unsweetened chocolate (such as Baker's), chopped
½ cup orange marmalade
2 tablespoons rum

Sundaes
1 1-pint basket strawberries, thickly sliced

2 bananas, sliced
2 peaches, peeled and sliced
2 tablespoons sugar
1 tablespoon rum

2 pints vanilla Swiss almond (such as Häagen Dazs) or chocolate chip ice cream
Toasted sliced almonds

For sauce: Stir first 4 ingredients in heavy small saucepan over low heat until melted and smooth. Add rum. Strain, pressing on solids to extract as much flavor as possible. (*Can be prepared 5 days ahead. Cover and refrigerate. Rewarm over low heat, stirring constantly and thinning with more cream if necessary.*)

For sundaes: Combine first 5 ingredients in medium bowl. Stir gently. Let fruit mixture stand for 15 to 30 minutes.

Scoop ice cream into sundae or balloon glasses. Top with warm sauce, then fruits and toasted sliced almonds and serve.

Tropical Sundaes

The twist to these sundaes is a simple ginger-flavored sauce sparked with lime. It can be made ahead and rewarmed before you assemble the sundaes.

6 servings

Ginger-Lime Sauce
½ cup sugar
½ cup firmly packed golden brown sugar
6 tablespoons water
¼ cup strained fresh lime juice
3 tablespoons unsalted butter
2 pieces crystallized ginger
3 tablespoons minced crystallized ginger

Sundaes
Vanilla ice cream
3 cups diced peeled tropical fruit such as pineapple, papaya and/or mango
Toasted sweetened shredded coconut

For sauce: Combine first 6 ingredients in heavy medium saucepan. Stir over medium heat until sugars dissolve. Boil gently until reduced to 1 cup, stirring frequently, about 15 minutes. Cool to lukewarm. Discard ginger pieces and add minced ginger. (*Can be prepared 1 day ahead. Cover and store at room temperature. Reheat to lukewarm, whisking occasionally, before serving.*)

For sundaes: Scoop ice cream into balloon glasses or sundae dishes. Spoon lukewarm sauce over. Top with fruit. Sprinkle with coconut and serve.

Red Plum Sorbet

A colorful platter of assorted fresh fruit sorbets is always a popular dessert. Here's the formula for one made with plums. To use other fruits, please see the variations that follow.

Makes 3 cups

1¼ cups sugar
1 cup water

1½ pounds ripe red plums (8 or 9)
Several drops fresh lemon juice

Combine sugar and water in heavy small saucepan over low heat. Stir until sugar dissolves. Increase heat and bring to boil. Cool sugar syrup completely. (*Can be prepared 3 days ahead. Cover and refrigerate.*)

Halve and pit plums. Transfer to processor and puree. Strain puree through sieve into bowl, pushing all solids through. Stir in 1 cup sugar syrup (reserve remainder for another use). Add lemon juice to taste. Pour into ice cream maker and freeze according to manufacturer's instructions. Freeze in covered container. Soften slightly in refrigerator before serving.

Variations: For 2¾ cups mango sorbet, use 2 cups mango puree, ½ cup sugar syrup, ¼ cup water and several drops lemon juice. For 1¾ cups raspberry sorbet, use 1½ cups raspberry puree, 1 cup sugar syrup, 3 drops raspberry eau-de-vie and several drops lemon juice. For 2½ cups lemon sorbet, use 1 cup sugar syrup, ¾ cup fresh lemon juice, ¾ cup water and several drops lemon vodka. For 2¾ cups blackberry sorbet, use 1¾ cups blackberry puree, 1 cup sugar syrup, 2 tablespoons whipping cream and several drops lemon juice. For 2¼ cups kiwi sorbet, use 1½ cups kiwi puree, ¾ cup sugar syrup and several drops white rum.

Best Banana Splits

6 servings

Strawberry Sauce
1 1-pint basket strawberries, hulled
¾ cup sugar
2 tablespoons Grand Marnier or other orange liqueur

Butterscotch Sauce
½ cup whipping cream
½ cup firmly packed golden brown sugar
½ cup sugar
¼ cup (½ stick) unsalted butter, cut into pieces
1 teaspoon vanilla extract

Hot Fudge Sauce
½ cup whipping cream
4½ ounces semisweet chocolate, chopped
1 tablespoon dark rum

6 bananas, peeled and halved lengthwise
1 pint vanilla ice cream
1 pint strawberry ice cream
1 pint chocolate ice cream
Fresh strawberries, sliced
Whipped cream
Sliced toasted almonds
Crumbled cookies
Fresh mint leaves

For strawberry sauce: Puree strawberries with sugar and Grand Marnier in processor. Transfer to bowl. Cover and refrigerate until well chilled. (*Can be prepared 1 day ahead. Cover tightly.*)

For butterscotch sauce: Stir cream with both sugars in heavy medium saucepan over very low heat until sugars dissolve. Add butter and vanilla and stir until butter melts. Cool to room temperature. (*Can be prepared 1 day ahead. Cover tightly and refrigerate. Whisk sauce before using.*)

For hot fudge sauce: Bring cream to simmer in heavy small saucepan. Add chocolate and stir until melted. Mix in rum. (*Can be prepared 1 day ahead. Cover and refrigerate. Rewarm over low heat, stirring constantly, before using.*)

Arrange 2 banana halves in each of 6 oblong dishes. Place 1 scoop of each ice cream atop bananas in each dish. Spoon 1 tablespoon butterscotch sauce over vanilla ice cream, 1 tablespoon strawberry sauce over strawberry ice cream and 2 tablespoons hot fudge sauce over chocolate ice cream in each dish. Top with fresh berries, whipped cream, nuts and cookies. Garnish with mint.

Double-Decker Mocha Ice Cream Pie

10 to 12 servings

Crust
- 1 8½-ounce package chocolate wafer cookies
- 2 tablespoons sugar
- ¼ cup (½ stick) unsalted butter, melted

Filling
- ½ gallon coffee ice cream, softened
- ½ gallon chocolate ice cream, softened
- 3 ounces bittersweet (not unsweetened) or semisweet chocolate, melted

Whipped cream
Toasted sliced almonds

For crust: Preheat oven to 350°F. Butter bottom of 10-inch-diameter springform pan with 2½-inch-high sides. Finely grind cookies in processor. Transfer to bowl. Mix in sugar. Add butter and stir well. Press crumbs firmly on bottom of prepared pan. Bake 8 minutes. Transfer to rack and cool.

For filling: Spoon coffee ice cream onto crust; spread evenly. Freeze 45 minutes. Spoon chocolate ice cream over coffee ice cream; spread evenly. Freeze 30 minutes. Drizzle chocolate over ice cream. Freeze until firm. (*Can be prepared 2 days ahead. Cover tightly.*)

Release pan sides from pie. Transfer pie to plate. Spoon whipped cream into pastry bag fitted with medium star tip. Pipe cream decoratively around edge of pie. Sprinkle with almonds. Cut into wedges. Serve immediately.

🍒 *Pies, Tarts and Pastries*

Spiced Pear Pie

6 to 8 servings

- ⅔ cup plus 2 teaspoons sugar
- 2 tablespoons all purpose flour
- ¾ teaspoon ground cinnamon
- 3¼ pounds pears (about 8 medium), quartered, cored, cut into ⅛-inch-thick slices

- 1 teaspoon lemon juice
- 2 frozen unbaked 9-inch pie shells, thawed
- 1 tablespoon whipping cream

Preheat oven to 400°F. Combine ⅔ cup sugar, flour and cinnamon in large bowl. Add sliced pears and lemon juice to sugar mixture and toss to coat.

Arrange pear mixture in pie shell, mounding in center. Remove remaining pie shell from pan and place on lightly floured board. Gently roll dough flat. Place dough over filling. Trim excess. Pinch edges to seal. Crimp edges to make decorative border. Make several slashes in top to allow steam to escape. Lightly brush cream over crust. Sprinkle with remaining 2 teaspoons sugar. Bake until pastry is golden brown and fruit is tender, about 60 minutes. Cool slightly. Serve pear pie warm or at room temperature.

Armagnac Cream Pie with Fresh Fruit

Armagnac adds an elegant finish to the dessert. If fresh berries are unavailable, use any seasonal fruit.

Makes 2 pies

Crust
- 2 cups graham cracker crumbs
- ¾ cup (1½ sticks) unsalted butter, melted
- 2 tablespoons sugar
- 2 teaspoons Armagnac or other brandy

Filling
- 1 envelope unflavored gelatin
- ¼ cup Armagnac or brandy
- 2 tablespoons water
- 6 large egg yolks
- ⅔ cup sugar
- 2 cups chilled whipping cream
- 8 kiwis, peeled, cut into ½-inch pieces
- 2 1-pint baskets strawberries, hulled
- 2 ½-pint baskets fresh raspberries
- 2 tablespoons sugar

For crust: Mix all ingredients in bowl to blend. Divide mixture between two 9-inch-diameter glass pie dishes. Press crumbs on bottom and up sides of dishes. Freeze crusts while preparing filling.

For filling: Sprinkle gelatin over Armagnac and water in small bowl. Let stand 10 minutes to soften. Set in saucepan of simmering water and stir until gelatin dissolves. Remove from saucepan. Using electric mixer, beat yolks with ⅔ cup sugar in large bowl until pale yellow and slowly dissolving ribbon forms when beaters are lifted, about 3 minutes. Set egg mixture over saucepan of simmering water and whisk until heated through. Add gelatin mixture and stir. Remove from over water. Let stand until cool but not set, whisking occasionally.

Using electric mixer fitted with clean, dry beaters, whip cream in medium bowl to soft peaks. Fold into egg mixture. Divide mixture between crusts; smooth top. Freeze until firm, about 2 hours. (*Pies can be prepared up to 2 days ahead. Cover tightly and freeze.*)

Gently toss fruit with 2 tablespoons sugar in large bowl. Spoon over pies, mounding slightly. Serve immediately.

Raspberry Cheese Pie

6 to 8 servings

Crust
- 2 cups pecans, lightly toasted (about 8 ounces)
- ⅓ cup firmly packed golden brown sugar
- ¼ teaspoon ground cinnamon
- ⅛ teaspoon ground cloves
- ¼ cup (½ stick) unsalted butter, melted

Filling
- 2 8-ounce packages cream cheese, room temperature
- ½ cup whipping cream
- ½ cup sugar
- 1 teaspoon vanilla extract

Topping
- ¼ cup plus 2 teaspoons water
- 1 tablespoon cornstarch
- 4 cups fresh raspberries
- ½ cup sugar

For crust: Blend pecans, brown sugar, cinnamon and cloves to coarse crumbs in processor. Transfer to bowl. Mix in butter. Mound crumbs in bottom of 9-inch-diameter springform pan. Cover with sheet of plastic and press crumbs firmly into bottom and up sides of pan. Chill 30 minutes.

Preheat oven to 350°F. Bake crust until golden brown, about 20 minutes. Cool crust completely on rack.

For filling: Using electric mixer, beat all ingredients in large bowl until smooth, stopping occasionally to scrape down sides of bowl. Pour filling into cooled crust. Cover with plastic and refrigerate until firm, at least 4 hours. (*Can be prepared up to 1 day ahead.*)

For topping: Mix 2 teaspoons water with cornstarch in small cup. Stir 2½ cups berries with sugar and remaining ¼ cup water in heavy medium saucepan over medium heat until sugar dissolves. Increase heat and boil until berries are thoroughly crushed and have exuded their juices, stirring frequently, about 5 minutes. Add cornstarch mixture and boil until slightly thickened, stirring constantly, about 1 minute. Strain through sieve set over large bowl, pressing on solids with back of spoon. Cool sauce, then cover and refrigerate until well chilled. (*Can be prepared up to 1 day ahead.*)

Mix remaining 1½ cups berries into sauce. Cut pie into wedges. Spoon berry sauce over and serve immediately.

Fudge Pecan Pie

10 servings

Crust
1½ cups all purpose flour
Pinch of salt
3 tablespoons chilled unsalted butter, cut into small pieces
2 tablespoons chilled solid vegetable shortening
3 tablespoons (about) ice water

Filling
4 large eggs
2 egg yolks
1½ cups light corn syrup
1 cup sugar

1 cup firmly packed golden brown sugar
3 tablespoons unsalted butter, melted
1 tablespoon light unsulfured molasses
1 tablespoon vanilla extract

5 ounces bittersweet (not unsweetened) or semisweet chocolate, coarsely chopped
1 cup chopped pecans (about 4 ounces)

For crust: Combine flour and salt in processor. Add butter and shortening and cut in using on/off turns until mixture resembles coarse meal. Add enough water by tablespoons to form dough that just comes together. Gather dough into ball; flatten into disk. Wrap dough in plastic and refrigerate for at least 30 minutes. (*Can be made up to 1 day ahead.*)

Roll dough out on lightly floured surface to 12-inch round. Transfer dough to 9-inch-diameter pie dish with 2-inch-high sides. Crimp edges.

For filling: Position rack in center of oven and preheat to 350°F. Whisk eggs and yolks in large bowl until frothy. Add corn syrup, both sugars, melted butter, molasses and vanilla and mix well.

Sprinkle chocolate and pecans over pie crust. Pour filling over. Bake pie until top is dry and firm to touch but center is still soft, about 1 hour 10 minutes. Cool completely on rack. (*Can be prepared 1 day ahead. Cover and let stand at room temperature.*) Cut pecan pie into wedges and serve.

Cranberry and Apple Harvest Pie

8 servings

Pie
- ¾ cup lightly packed golden brown sugar
- 5 tablespoons cornstarch
- 1 teaspoon ground cinnamon
  Pinch of salt
- 2 pounds tart green apples, peeled, cored, cut into ¼-inch-thick wedges
- 1¾ cups cranberries
- 2 tablespoons fresh lemon juice
- 1 9-inch deep-dish frozen pie shell, thawed

Topping
- ½ cup (1 stick) unsalted butter
- ¾ cup lightly packed golden brown sugar
- 2 tablespoons evaporated milk
- 1 teaspoon vanilla extract
- 1 cup chopped walnuts (about 4 ounces)

For pie: Preheat oven to 350°F. Mix first 4 ingredients in large bowl to blend. Add apples, cranberries and lemon juice and toss well. Transfer mixture to pie shell, mounding in center. Bake until apples are almost tender, about 1½ hours. Cover with foil and bake 15 minutes more. Transfer to rack. Uncover and cool.

For topping: Melt butter with sugar and milk in heavy medium skillet over low heat, stirring frequently. Increase heat and bring to simmer, stirring constantly. Mix in vanilla, then walnuts. Pour mixture into bowl. Let stand until slightly thickened and just cool, stirring occasionally, about 10 minutes.

Spoon topping over pie, covering completely. Let stand until topping sets, about 30 minutes. (*Can be prepared 6 hours ahead. Let stand at room temperature.*) Cut pie into wedges and serve.

Peanut Butter Pie with Fudge Topping

8 servings

Crust
- 1 cup graham cracker crumbs
- ¼ cup sugar
- ¼ cup (½ stick) unsalted butter, cut into pieces, room temperature

Filling
- 8 ounces cream cheese, room temperature
- 1 cup creamy peanut butter (do not use old-fashioned style or freshly ground)
- 1 cup plus 2 tablespoons powdered sugar
- 2 tablespoons (¼ stick) unsalted butter, room temperature
- ½ cup chilled whipping cream
- 1 tablespoon vanilla extract

Topping
- ½ cup whipping cream
- 6 ounces semisweet chocolate, chopped

For crust: Generously butter 9-inch-diameter pie plate. Mix all ingredients in medium bowl. Press mixture evenly in prepared pan. Refrigerate 1 hour.

For filling: Using electric mixer, beat cream cheese and peanut butter in large bowl until well blended. Add 1 cup powdered sugar and butter and beat until fluffy. Beat cream in medium bowl until soft peaks form. Gradually add remaining 2 tablespoons sugar and vanilla and beat to stiff peaks. Fold ⅓ of cream into peanut butter mixture to lighten. Gently fold in remaining cream. Spoon into crust. Refrigerate until firm, about 3 hours.

For topping: Bring cream to simmer in heavy small saucepan over low heat. Add chocolate and stir until smooth. Cool to lukewarm. Spread topping over pie. Refrigerate until firm, about 3 hours. (*Can be prepared 1 day ahead. Cover.*) Cut into wedges and serve immediately.

Apple Strudel Tartlets

You won't need tartlet molds for these crisp, free-form sweets.

6 servings

4 large Granny Smith apples, peeled, cored, cut into ½-inch-thick slices
2 teaspoons fresh lemon juice
⅓ cup sugar
12 tablespoons (1½ sticks) unsalted butter

2 tablespoons Armagnac or brandy
7 fresh or frozen phyllo pastry sheets, thawed
1 tablespoon honey
Additional Armagnac or brandy
Powdered sugar

Place apple slices in large bowl. Sprinkle lemon juice and ⅓ cup sugar over apples and toss. Melt 3 tablespoons butter in heavy large skillet over high heat. Add apple mixture to skillet and sauté until apples are tender and light brown, about 6 minutes. Add 2 tablespoons Armagnac to skillet and heat briefly. Remove from heat and ignite with match. When flames subside, strain apples, reserving cooking juices. Set aside.

Preheat oven to 350°F. Melt remaining 9 tablespoons butter in small saucepan. Brush large cookie sheet lightly with melted butter. Stack 6 phyllo sheets. Cut in half lengthwise, then crosswise, forming 4 rectangles from each phyllo sheet. Place 1 phyllo rectangle atop sheet of waxed paper. Brush with melted butter. (Cover remaining pieces with plastic wrap, then with clean, damp towel.) Arrange second phyllo rectangle crosswise over first. Brush with butter. Arrange third phyllo rectangle at 45° angle over second phyllo rectangle. Brush with butter. Place fourth phyllo rectangle crosswise over third phyllo rectangle. Brush with butter. Arrange ⅙ of apples in center. Fold ends of phyllo pieces over apples 1 at a time, enclosing apples completely and forming round tartlet. Brush top with butter. Transfer to prepared cookie sheet, using spatula as aid. Repeat layering, filling and folding to make 5 more tartlets.

Butter remaining whole phyllo sheet. Cut sheet into 6 strips of approximately 12 × 2 inches. Fold each strip in half lengthwise. Coil 1 strip, folded side down, around pencil. Phyllo strip should be rolled tightly at bottom and loosely at top, creating rose-shaped coil. Repeat with remaining strips. Place 1 phyllo rose atop each tartlet. Combine honey with 1 tablespoon remaining melted butter in small bowl. Brush honey mixture over tartlets. Bake until pastry is golden brown and apples are tender, about 40 minutes. Cool slightly. If desired, pierce top of tartlets with toothpick or skewer. Sprinkle lightly with Armagnac. Sift powdered sugar over tartlets. Transfer to plates and serve immediately, passing reserved cooking juices from apples separately.

Strawberries and Cream Tart

This beautiful tart is also low in calories—only about 200 per serving.

8 servings

Crust
¾ cup all purpose flour
Pinch of salt
¼ cup (½ stick) chilled unsalted butter, cut into pieces
¼ cup farmer cheese*
2 tablespoons (about) cold water

Sauce
2 cups hulled strawberries
¼ cup fresh orange juice

2 tablespoons Grand Marnier or other orange liqueur
1 tablespoon sugar

Filling
1 cup lowfat cottage cheese
2 tablespoons sugar
½ teaspoon grated orange peel
2 1-pint baskets strawberries, hulled, thinly sliced

3 tablespoons apricot jam

For crust: Combine flour, salt, butter and farmer cheese in processor. Mix using on/off turns until mixture resembles coarse meal. With machine running, add just enough water through feed tube to bind dough, mixing just until dough begins to come together. Gather into ball. Flatten into disk. Wrap disk in plastic and refrigerate 30 minutes. (*Crust can be prepared 1 day ahead. Let stand at room temperature to soften slightly before continuing.*)

Preheat oven to 375°F. Roll dough out on lightly floured surface to 11-inch round. Transfer dough to 9-inch-diameter tart pan with removable bottom. Trim edges. Line pastry with parchment or foil. Fill with dried beans or pie weights. Bake 15 minutes. Remove parchment and beans. Bake until crust is golden, about 8 minutes. Cool completely on wire rack.

For sauce: Puree 2 cups strawberries, orange juice, Grand Marnier and sugar in processor until smooth. Refrigerate. (*Can be prepared 1 day ahead.*)

For filling: Blend cottage cheese, sugar and orange peel in processor until smooth. Spread filling in crust. Place strawberry slices over filling in concentric circles, tips pointing toward outer edge of tart and overlapping slightly.

Melt jam in heavy small saucepan over medium heat, stirring until smooth. Cool slightly. Carefully brush jam over tart. Refrigerate until glaze is set, about 20 minutes. (*Can be prepared 2 hours ahead.*) Serve with sauce.

*Farmer cheese is available at specialty foods stores and some supermarkets.

Espresso Cream and Chocolate Tartlets

A creamy coffee mousse spiked with rum is mounded in chocolate-lined tartlet shells.

Makes 24

Crust
- 2 cups all purpose flour
- 1 cup cake flour
- ²/₃ cup sugar
- ¹/₈ teaspoon salt
- 1 cup (2 sticks) chilled unsalted butter, cut into pieces
- 2 egg yolks
- 2 teaspoons vanilla extract
- 4 tablespoons (about) cold water

- 8 ounces bittersweet (not unsweetened) or semisweet chocolate, melted

Filling
- 6 tablespoons instant espresso powder
- ¹/₂ cup boiling water
- 5 large egg yolks
- ¹/₂ cup sugar
- 2 tablespoons dark rum

- 1 pound cream cheese, room temperature
- 1 cup sour cream
- ¹/₃ cup sugar
- ¹/₂ cup chilled whipping cream

Chocolate coffee bean candies* (optional)

For crust: Mix flours, sugar and salt in large bowl. Add butter and cut in until mixture resembles coarse meal. Beat yolks with vanilla to blend. Pour over flour mixture and stir until dough comes together, adding just enough water to bind dough. Gather dough into 2 balls. Flatten into disks. Wrap separately in plastic and refrigerate 30 minutes. (*Can be prepared one day ahead. Let dough soften slightly at room temperature before continuing.*)

Grease twenty-four 3-inch-diameter brioche pans with 1½-inch-high sides or 3½-inch-diameter tartlet pans with ¾-inch-high sides. Roll 1 piece of dough out on lightly floured surface to thickness of ⅛ inch. Cut out twelve 4-inch-diameter rounds using cookie cutter or small bowl. Press pastry rounds into prepared pans. Repeat with remaining dough. Transfer pans to cookie sheet and refrigerate pastry until well chilled, about 30 minutes.

Preheat oven to 400°F. Line tartlets with foil or parchment and fill with dried beans or pie weights. Bake 10 minutes. Remove beans and foil and continue baking until golden brown, about 8 minutes. Cool on rack.

Using back of spoon, spread insides of crusts with melted chocolate, coating insides completely. Refrigerate until chocolate is set, about 10 minutes.

For filling: Place espresso powder in small bowl. Pour boiling water over and stir until dissolved. Cool. Using portable mixer, beat egg yolks and ½ cup sugar in top of double boiler to blend. Beat in espresso mixture and rum. Set over simmering water and continue beating until mixture is thick and foamy and tripled in volume, about 7 minutes; do not boil. Remove from over water. Pour sabayon into medium bowl and cool completely.

Using electric mixer, beat cream cheese in large bowl until fluffy. Beat in sour cream and sugar. Whip cream in another medium bowl until soft peaks form. Gently fold into cream cheese mixture. Fold in coffee sabayon.

Remove crusts from pans. Spoon ¼ cup filling into each tartlet crust. Refrigerate in airtight container until filling is set, approximately 2 hours. (*Tartlets can be prepared up to 1 day ahead.*)

Garnish each tartlet with chocolate coffee bean if desired and serve.

*Candies are available at candy shops and some specialty foods stores.

Sweet Ravioli with Cherry Custard Sauce

These puff-pastry ravioli look-alikes are filled with dates, toasted hazelnuts and white chocolate.

6 servings

Ravioli
½ cup pitted dates
2 tablespoons amaretto liqueur

2 ounces white chocolate, chopped
3 tablespoons cream cheese, room temperature
2 tablespoons chopped toasted and husked hazelnuts

½ teaspoon ground cinnamon

½ 17¼-ounce package frozen puff pastry (1 sheet)
3 egg whites, beaten to blend

Cherry Custard Sauce (see recipe)
Powdered sugar

For ravioli: Soak dates in amaretto in small bowl until softened, about 30 minutes. Transfer dates and soaking liquid to processor and puree until smooth. Transfer date mixture to bowl.

Meanwhile, melt white chocolate in top of double boiler over gently simmering water. Stir until smooth. Add to date mixture. Stir in cream cheese, chopped toasted hazelnuts and cinnamon.

Preheat oven to 375°F. Roll pastry out on lightly floured surface to 20 × 12-inch rectangle. Fold pastry in half to make seam, then open again. Brush pastry with egg whites. Using ravioli cutter, mark off 2-inch squares in half of dough; do not cut through dough with cutter. Using pastry bag or 2 spoons, pipe or spoon 1 rounded teaspoon date mixture into center of each marked-off square. Fold uncovered half of pastry over covered half. Press pastry down and around each mound of date mixture to eliminate air and seal raviolis. Using ravioli cutter, cut between squares. (*Ravioli can be prepared ahead. Cover tightly and refrigerate 1 day or freeze up to 1 week.*)

Brush top of pastries with egg whites. Arrange ravioli on nonstick cookie sheet. Bake 10 minutes. Brush with egg whites. Bake 5 minutes. Brush with egg whites. Continue baking until golden brown, about 5 minutes.

Spoon sauce onto plates. Top with ravioli. Dust with powdered sugar.

Cherry Custard Sauce

Makes 2²/₃ cups

2¼ cups whipping cream
6 egg yolks
½ cup sugar
1 teaspoon vanilla extract

½ cup cherry preserves
2 tablespoons kirsch (clear cherry brandy)

Scald cream in heavy medium saucepan. Whisk yolks, sugar and vanilla in bowl. Whisk cream into yolk mixture. Return to saucepan and stir until mixture is thick enough to coat back of spoon, about 3 minutes; do not boil. Stir in preserves and kirsch. Chill. (*Can be prepared 1 day ahead.*)

 # Cakes

Double Chocolate Cheesecake

This decadent dessert combines white and dark chocolates with an elegant touch of orange. Begin preparations at least one and up to two days ahead.

12 servings

Crust
18 chocolate wafer cookies (about 4 ounces), broken up
1 cup pecans (about 4 ounces)
¼ cup sugar
2 ounces semisweet chocolate, coarsely chopped
¼ cup (½ stick) chilled unsalted butter, cut into pieces

Filling
4½ ounces unsweetened chocolate (such as Baker's), chopped

28 ounces cream cheese, very soft room temperature
½ cup sugar
5 large eggs, room temperature
1 cup plus 2 tablespoons firmly packed golden brown sugar
1 tablespoon light corn syrup

¼ cup whipping cream
1 tablespoon plus 1 teaspoon grated orange peel

1 teaspoon grated lemon peel
6 ounces imported white chocolate (such as Lindt), finely chopped
¼ cup Grand Marnier or other orange liqueur

Dark and White Chocolate Leaves
3 ounces semisweet chocolate, chopped
1 teaspoon solid vegetable shortening
12 medium camellia or lemon leaves, wiped clean

3 ounces imported white chocolate (such as Lindt), chopped

Orange Threads
1 orange

Whipped Cream Topping
⅔ cup chilled whipping cream
1 tablespoon powdered sugar
2½ teaspoons Grand Marnier or other orange liqueur

For crust: Position rack in center of oven and preheat to 350°F. Place cookies, pecans, sugar and chocolate in processor. Process until finely chopped. Add butter and process until moist crumbs form. Transfer crumb mixture to 10-inch-diameter springform pan with 2¾-inch-high sides. Press crumb mixture 2 inches up sides and onto bottom of pan. Set on cookie sheet and bake 10 minutes. Transfer crust to rack and cool.

For filling: Preheat oven to 350°F. Place unsweetened chocolate in top of small double boiler over barely simmering water. Cook until chocolate is melted and smooth, stirring occasionally. Remove from over water. Cool slightly.

Using electric mixer, beat cream cheese with ½ cup sugar in large bowl until fluffy. Add eggs 1 at a time, beating until just incorporated and stopping occasionally to scrape down bottom and sides of bowl. Transfer 2½ cups plain batter to medium bowl and set aside for white chocolate batter. Add brown sugar to remaining plain batter in large bowl and beat until combined. Mix corn syrup, then melted chocolate into plain batter in large bowl. Pour ⅔ cup chocolate batter into small bowl and set aside. Pour remaining chocolate batter into prepared crust. Set on cookie sheet and bake until filling is barely set, about 15 minutes. Transfer to rack and cool 5 minutes. Maintain oven temperature.

Meanwhile, scald cream with orange and lemon peels in heavy saucepan. Remove from heat. Add white chocolate and stir until melted and smooth. Cool mixture slightly. Add white chocolate mixture to reserved 2½ cups plain batter and stir to combine. Mix in Grand Marnier.

Starting at outside edge, carefully spoon white chocolate batter over chocolate layer in pan. Set on cookie sheet and bake until cake sides are puffed and center moves only slightly when pan is shaken, 35 to 40 minutes. Transfer to rack and cool 5 minutes. Maintain oven temperature.

Spoon reserved ⅔ cup chocolate batter by tablespoons onto center of white chocolate layer. Using back of spoon, spread chocolate in smooth even circle to within ½ inch of cake edge. Set on cookie sheet and bake 10 minutes. Transfer to rack. Using small sharp knife, cut around cake pan sides to loosen. Cool completely in pan. Refrigerate overnight. (*Can be prepared 2 days ahead.*)

For chocolate leaves: Line 2 cookie sheets with foil. Place semisweet chocolate and ½ teaspoon shortening in small bowl. Set bowl over saucepan of barely simmering water. Cook until melted and smooth, stirring occasionally. Remove from over water. Using small metal spatula or spoon, spread thin layer of chocolate over veined underside of 6 leaves, being careful not to drip over edges. Place on 1 prepared cookie sheet. Chill until set, about 5 minutes. Spread second thin layer of chocolate on each leaf, remelting chocolate over barely simmering water if necessary. Refrigerate leaves until chocolate sets, about 30 minutes.

Place white chocolate and ½ teaspoon shortening in small bowl. Set bowl over saucepan of barely simmering water. Cook until melted and smooth, stirring occasionally. Remove from over water. Spread thin layer of white chocolate on veined underside of 6 leaves, being careful not to drip over edges. Place on second prepared cookie sheet. Chill until set, about 5 minutes. Spread second thin layer of white chocolate on each leaf, remelting chocolate over barely simmering water if necessary. Refrigerate white chocolate leaves until chocolate is completely set, about 30 minutes.

Starting at stem end, gently peel leaves off dark and white chocolate. (*Can be prepared up to 1 day ahead. Refrigerate dark and white chocolate leaves in single layers in airtight containers.*)

For orange threads: Using vegetable peeler, remove orange peel in large strips. Cut into matchstick-size strips. Blanch orange strips in saucepan of boiling water 30 seconds. Drain well. Dry thoroughly on paper towels. (*Orange threads can be prepared 1 day ahead. Cover and refrigerate.*)

For topping: Beat cream and sugar in medium bowl to soft peaks. Add Grand Marnier and beat until stiff peaks form.

Release pan sides from cheesecake. Spoon whipped cream into pastry bag fitted with large star tip. Pipe decorative border of whipped cream around edge of cake. Set alternating white and dark chocolate leaves at a slight angle atop whipped cream border. Arrange orange threads on cake. Cut into wedges.

Chocolate-Orange Decadence Cake

12 servings

Cake
- 2 medium oranges
- 1⅓ cups sugar
- ¼ cup orange marmalade
- ¾ cup (1½ sticks) unsalted butter, room temperature
- 1 teaspoon vanilla extract
- 4 large eggs, room temperature
- 2½ cups cake flour
- ½ teaspoon baking powder
- ¼ teaspoon baking soda
- ¾ cup orange juice

Chocolate Ganache
- 2½ cups whipping cream
- 9 tablespoons unsalted butter
- 30 ounces bittersweet (not unsweetened) or semisweet chocolate, chopped
- 7 tablespoons Grand Marnier or orange juice
- 3 tablespoons thawed frozen orange juice concentrate
- 2 tablespoons minced orange peel

Orange Glaze
- 6 tablespoons orange marmalade
- 6 tablespoons Grand Marnier or orange juice

3½ ½-pint baskets (about) raspberries or 5¼ cups frozen unsweetened raspberries, thawed and drained

Mint sprigs

For cake: Preheat oven to 350°F. Butter two 9-inch-diameter cake pans with 1½-inch-high sides. Line pan bottoms with waxed paper. Using vegetable peeler, remove peel from oranges in strips. Coarsely chop peel in processor, stopping occasionally to scrape down sides of bowl. Add ⅓ cup sugar and blend until peel is minced. Add marmalade and puree. Using electric mixer, cream butter with pureed mixture and vanilla in large bowl until light and fluffy. Beat in remaining 1 cup sugar. Add eggs 1 at a time, beating well after each addition. Sift dry ingredients into small bowl. Mix dry ingredients into batter alternately with orange juice.

Divide batter between prepared pans. Bake cakes until tops are golden brown and tester inserted in centers comes out clean, about 38 minutes. Cool cakes in pans on racks 10 minutes. Run sharp knife around pan sides to loosen cakes. Turn cakes out onto racks; cool. Peel off paper.

For chocolate ganache: Bring cream and butter to simmer in heavy large saucepan. Reduce heat to low. Add chopped chocolate and stir until melted. Mix in remaining ingredients. Pour ganache into large bowl. Freeze until very thick but still spreadable, stirring frequently, about 1 hour 15 minutes.

For glaze: Melt marmalade in heavy small saucepan over low heat. Remove from heat. Mix in Grand Marnier.

Cut each cake into 2 layers. Place 1 layer on plate. Brush with ¼ of glaze. Spread 1 cup ganache over. Top with second cake layer. Brush with ¼ of glaze. Spread ¾ cup ganache over. Top with 1½ baskets berries (about 2½ cups). Spread ½ cup ganache over third cake layer. Invert, chocolate side down, over berries. Brush with ¼ of glaze. Spread 1 cup ganache over. Top with fourth cake layer. Brush with remaining glaze. Spread ¾ cup ganache over top of cake. Freeze cake 20 minutes. (*Can be prepared 1 day ahead. Cover cake and remaining ganache separately and chill both. If necessary, let ganache stand at room temperature to soften to spreading consistency before using.*)

Spoon 1 cup ganache into pastry bag fitted with medium star tip. Spread remaining ganache over sides of cake, drawing icing spatula up to create vertical lines. Pipe decorative border of ganache around top and bottom edges of cake. Arrange remaining berries atop cake, covering completely. Garnish cake with mint sprigs. Serve at room temperature.

Bitter Chocolate Cake

This recipe is simplicity itself, but the results are unbelievably delicious. The French would use a bitter chocolate called chocolat noir, *but the same flavor can be achieved by using a blend of semisweet and unsweetened chocolate.*

10 servings

Sugar
1 cup (2 sticks) unsalted butter
6 ounces semisweet chocolate, chopped
3 ounces unsweetened chocolate, chopped

1¼ cups sugar
4 extra-large eggs
1 tablespoon all purpose flour

Lightly sweetened whipped cream

Preheat oven to 325°F. Butter 9-inch-diameter springform pan. Sprinkle bottom and sides with sugar. Tap out excess. Wrap foil around bottom and 2 inches up outside of pan. Combine 1 cup butter and both chocolates in top of double boiler. Melt over simmering water, stirring until smooth. Remove from over water. Whisk sugar and eggs in large bowl to blend. Mix in flour. Stir in warm chocolate mixture. Pour batter into prepared pan. Place cake in large baking pan. Pour enough boiling water into baking pan to come ½ inch up sides of cake. Bake cake until top is firm and toothpick inserted into center comes out with some moist crumbs attached, about 1 hour.

Remove cake from water and cool completely on rack. Transfer cake to platter; release pan sides. Cut into wedges and serve with whipped cream.

Three-Layer Chocolate Cake

10 servings

Cake
1 cup milk
4 ounces unsweetened chocolate, chopped

3 cups all purpose flour
1½ teaspoons baking powder
½ teaspoon salt
¼ cup (½ stick) unsalted butter, room temperature
6 tablespoons vegetable oil
2 cups sugar
2 teaspoons vanilla extract

5 large eggs, room temperature
¼ cup grenadine syrup

Frosting
12 ounces semisweet chocolate, chopped
1 tablespoon instant coffee granules
2 teaspoons vanilla extract
2 cups (4 sticks) unsalted butter, room temperature
2 large egg yolks
2½ cups powdered sugar

For cake: Preheat oven to 350°F. Butter three 8-inch-diameter cake pans with 2-inch-high sides. Bring milk to simmer in heavy medium saucepan. Reduce heat to low. Add chocolate and stir until melted. Cool.

Sift flour, baking powder and salt into small bowl. Using electric mixer, beat butter and oil in large bowl until well blended. Gradually beat in sugar and vanilla. Add eggs 1 at a time, beating well after each addition. Mix in dry ingredients alternately with chocolate mixture. Mix in grenadine.

Divide batter evenly among prepared pans. Bake until toothpick inserted in centers comes out clean, about 25 minutes. Cool cakes in pans on racks 10 minutes. Run small sharp knife around pan sides to loosen cake, if necessary. Turn cakes out onto racks and cool completely. (*Can be prepared 1 day ahead. Wrap cakes separately in plastic and store at room temperature.*)

For frosting: Melt chocolate in top of double boiler over simmering water, stirring until smooth. Remove from over water. Cool just to room temperature. Combine coffee granules and vanilla extract in small cup; stir to dissolve. Using electric mixer, cream butter in medium bowl until light. Add yolks 1 at a time, beating well after each addition. Add chocolate and beat well. Beat in coffee mixture. Gradually add sugar and beat until smooth.

Place 1 cake layer on plate. Spread 1 cup frosting over. Top with second cake layer. Spread 1 cup frosting over. Top with third cake layer. Spread top and sides of cake with as much remaining frosting as desired (reserve any remainder for another use). (*Can be prepared 1 day ahead. Cover with cake dome and refrigerate. Bring cake to room temperature before serving.*)

Bridal Shower Cake

This pretty cake is flavored with almond, filled with assorted berries and frosted with a rich mixture of white chocolate and cream cheese. It's perfect for a bridal shower or any special occasion and can be prepared up to two days ahead. To make sure the frosting sets properly, use a high-quality imported white chocolate, such as Lindt.

25 servings

Cake
2¼ cups blanched slivered almonds
2 cups cake flour
1 tablespoon baking powder

1 cup plus 2 tablespoons (2¼ sticks) unsalted butter, room temperature
1½ cups sugar
21 ounces almond paste, cut into small pieces
12 large eggs, room temperature
1 tablespoon vanilla extract

Berry Filling
2 cups frozen blueberries, thawed
2 cups frozen unsweetened boysenberries or blackberries, thawed
2 cups fresh raspberries
⅔ cup sugar

Frosting
15 ounces imported white chocolate (such as Lindt), chopped

2¼ cups (4½ sticks) unsalted butter, room temperature
2½ pounds cream cheese, room temperature
3 tablespoons vanilla extract
1¼ teaspoons almond extract
6½ cups powdered sugar
1 cup sour cream

Assembly
1 11-inch-diameter cardboard round

1 7-inch-diameter cardboard round

2 yards lavender or pink ribbon (about 1 inch wide)

4 6-inch-long ¼-inch-wide wood dowels*

Assorted fresh flowers

For cake: Preheat oven to 325°F. Butter and flour one 8-inch-diameter cake pan with 2-inch-high sides and one 12-inch-diameter cake pan with 2-inch-high sides. Finely grind blanched slivered almonds in processor. Sift flour and baking powder into small bowl. Set aside.

Using heavy-duty mixer, cream butter with sugar in large bowl until blended. Beat in almond paste a few pieces at a time. Beat until mixture resembles smooth paste. Add eggs 1 at a time, beating well after each addition. Add vanilla and beat until batter increases slightly in volume, about 5 minutes. Mix in almonds, then dry ingredients.

Divide batter between prepared pans. Bake until tester inserted in center of cakes comes out clean, about 55 minutes for 8-inch cake and 65 minutes for 12-inch cake. Cool cakes in pans on racks 10 minutes. Run small sharp knife around cake pan sides to loosen. Turn cakes out onto racks; cool completely. (*Can be prepared 1 day ahead. Wrap in plastic; store at room temperature.*)

For berry filling: Combine berries in heavy large saucepan. Sprinkle with sugar. Let stand 45 minutes, stirring occasionally. Bring berries to boil. Reduce heat and simmer until mixture is reduced to 2 cups, stirring occasionally, about 20 minutes. Transfer to bowl. Cover and refrigerate until well chilled. (*Berry filling can be prepared up to 1 day ahead.*)

For frosting: Melt chocolate in top of double boiler over barely simmering water, stirring until smooth. Cool chocolate until just slightly warm.

Using electric mixer, beat butter in large bowl until light. Gradually add cream cheese, beating until just combined. Beat in both extracts. Add sugar and beat just until smooth. Add melted chocolate and beat until just combined. Stir in sour cream. If necessary, chill frosting until spreadable.

To assemble: Using serrated knife, cut each cake horizontally into 3 layers. Place bottom 12-inch cake layer on 11-inch cardboard round. Spread with ⅔ cup berry filling, leaving ½-inch border uncovered. Carefully spread 2 cups frosting over entire layer. Top with middle 12-inch cake layer. Spread with ⅔ cup berry filling, leaving ½-inch border uncovered. Carefully spread 2 cups frosting over entire layer. Top with top 12-inch cake layer. Spread 3 cups frosting over top and sides of cake. Set 12-inch cake aside.

Place bottom 8-inch cake layer on 7-inch cardboard round. Spread with ¼ cup berry filling, leaving ¼-inch border uncovered. Carefully spread ¾ cup frosting over entire layer. Top with middle 8-inch cake layer. Spread with ¼ cup berry filling, leaving ¼-inch border uncovered. Carefully spread ¾ cup frosting over entire layer. Top with top 8-inch cake layer. Spread 2 cups frosting over top and sides of cake. Set aside.

Cut one 3-foot, 4-inch-long piece of ribbon and wrap around base of 12-inch cake. Press gently onto sides to adhere. Cut one 2-foot, 3-inch-long piece of ribbon and wrap around base of 8-inch cake. Press gently onto sides to adhere. Refrigerate both cakes until frosting sets, about 3 hours.

Place 12-inch cake on platter. Press dowel into center of cake. Mark dowel ⅛ inch above top of cake. Remove and cut with serrated knife at marked point. Cut remaining dowels to same length. Carefully press dowels into bottom cake tier 3½ to 4 inches in from cake edges, spacing evenly. Gently place 8-inch cake on cardboard atop bottom cake tier, centering carefully, with cake resting on dowels.

Spoon remaining frosting into pastry bag fitted with small round tip. Pipe dots of frosting on top edge of both cakes. Refrigerate until frosting sets, about 1 hour. (*Can be prepared 2 days ahead. Cover loosely with plastic.*)

Arrange flowers decoratively atop cake. (*Can be prepared 4 hours ahead.*) Serve cake cold or at room temperature.

*Dowels are available at cake supply stores and most hardware stores.

Mixed Berry and Pecan Shortcakes

It's easy to make these processor-quick biscuits ahead, if you like. Then reheat, split and fill them with the ice cream and berries just before serving.

6 servings

Biscuits

1½ cups all purpose flour
⅓ cup sugar
2¼ teaspoons baking powder
½ teaspoon baking soda
¼ teaspoon salt
6 tablespoons (¾ stick) chilled unsalted butter, cut into ½-inch pieces
¾ cup pecans
¾ cup plus 3 tablespoons (about) buttermilk
¾ teaspoon vanilla extract

Sugar

Filling

2 1-pint baskets strawberries, sliced
2 ½-pint baskets raspberries
6 tablespoons sugar

1 pint butter pecan or pralines-and-cream ice cream

For biscuits: Preheat oven to 450°F. Line cookie sheet with parchment. Mix first 5 ingredients in processor. Add butter and cut in until coarse meal forms. Add pecans and chop. Transfer mixture to large bowl. Combine ¾ cup buttermilk and vanilla in large cup. Mix into dry ingredients, tossing gently with fork and adding enough buttermilk to form fluffy, moist dough.

Drop dough by slightly rounded ⅓ cupfuls onto prepared sheet, spacing 3 inches apart. Sprinkle top of each biscuit with sugar. Bake until golden and just firm to touch, about 15 minutes. Transfer biscuits to rack. (*Can be prepared up to 1 day ahead. Let cool. Wrap biscuits in foil and store at room temperature. Rewarm biscuits in foil in 350°F oven.*)

For filling: Combine berries and sugar in large bowl. Mix gently. Let stand at least 15 minutes. (*Can be prepared 3 hours ahead. Cover and refrigerate.*)

Split warm biscuits. Place bottoms in shallow bowls. Spoon some fruit over each. Top each with ⅓ cup ice cream and biscuit tops. Spoon remaining fruit over tops of biscuits. Serve immediately.

Chocolate-Hazelnut Panforte

This Italian version of fruitcake is dense, chewy and candylike.

Makes 2

¼ cup (½ stick) unsalted butter, melted

1½ cups hazelnuts (about 7½ ounces)
1 cup whole unblanched almonds (about 5 ounces)

1½ cups lightly packed chopped dried Calimyrna figs (about 9 ounces)
1½ cups lightly packed chopped dried apricots (about 9 ounces)
1 cup diced candied citron (about 5 ounces)
2 tablespoons grated orange peel
1 tablespoon grated lemon peel

¾ cup unbleached all purpose flour
¾ cup cocoa powder (preferably Dutch-process)
1½ teaspoons ground cinnamon
1 scant teaspoon ground nutmeg
1 scant teaspoon ground coriander
¼ teaspoon pepper
¼ teaspoon ground cloves

1 cup plus 2 tablespoons sugar
1 cup plus 2 tablespoons honey

6 ounces bittersweet or semisweet chocolate, melted

Additional cocoa powder

Position rack in center of oven and preheat to 400°F. Brush two 8-inch-diameter cake pans with melted butter. Line bottoms with parchment paper. Brush parchment generously with butter. Reserve remaining butter.

Place hazelnuts on small cookie sheet; place almonds on another small cookie sheet. Toast in oven until nuts are brown and fragrant, stirring occasionally, about 10 minutes for almonds and 14 minutes for hazelnuts. Cool slightly. Gather hazelnuts in dish towel. Rub hazelnuts in towel to remove husks. Transfer hazelnuts and almonds to large bowl. Reduce oven temperature to 300°F.

Add figs, apricots, citron, orange and lemon peels to nuts. Combine flour, ³⁄₄ cup cocoa powder and spices in small bowl. Add to nut mixture and mix well.

Combine sugar, honey and remaining melted butter in heavy medium saucepan. Stir over medium heat until mixture is smooth and sugar is mostly dissolved, about 5 minutes. Bring to boil. Continue cooking until candy thermometer registers 248°F (firm-ball stage). Immediately pour over nut mixture. Stir batter to combine thoroughly.

Divide batter between prepared pans, using back of buttered spoon to spread evenly. Bake until tops and edges begin to brown and tops feel dry, about 1¼ hours. Cool slightly on rack. Run small sharp knife around edges of pans to loosen cakes. Turn cakes out onto work surface; peel off parchment. Cool.

Arrange cakes top sides up on 8-inch-diameter cardboard rounds. Spread half of chocolate over each. Refrigerate until chocolate is set, about 1 hour.

Brush tops of cakes with cocoa powder. Wrap tightly in plastic wrap. (*Can be prepared 1 month ahead. Store at cool room temperature.*)

 Cookies

Raspberry Brownies

Delicate cocoa brownies, spangled with juicy fresh berries and drizzled with dark chocolate, are an informal yet sophisticated conclusion to a meal.

Makes about 16

Brownies
- 1 cup (2 sticks) unsalted butter, room temperature
- 1¼ cups sugar
- ½ cup firmly packed golden brown sugar
- 4 large eggs
- ½ cup unsweetened cocoa powder
- 1 tablespoon framboise eau-de-vie (clear raspberry brandy) or brandy
- 1 teaspoon vanilla extract
- ¼ teaspoon salt
- 1¼ cups unbleached all purpose flour
- 1 ½-pint basket fresh raspberries

Glaze
- 4 ounces semisweet chocolate, chopped
- 2 tablespoons framboise eau-de-vie (clear raspberry brandy) or brandy
- 2 teaspoons hot water

Powdered sugar

For brownies: Preheat oven to 325°F. Grease 9 × 13-inch pan. Beat 1 cup butter, sugar and brown sugar in large bowl until fluffy. Add eggs 1 at a time, beating well after each addition. Stir in cocoa, framboise, vanilla and salt. Gently mix in flour. Pour batter into prepared pan. Sprinkle raspberries evenly over batter. Bake until tester inserted into center of brownies comes out clean, about 30 minutes. Cool completely in pan on rack.

For glaze: Combine chocolate, framboise and water in top of double boiler. Set over barely simmering water and stir until smooth. Cool slightly.

Cut brownies into 3 × 2-inch bars. Sift powdered sugar lightly over brownies. Dip fork into glaze and drizzle glaze decoratively over brownies. Let stand until glaze sets, about 30 minutes. (*Can be prepared 8 hours ahead. Cover and store at room temperature.*) Transfer brownies to plate and serve.

Toffee Brownies

Crunchy, chewy, chocolaty. Begin this recipe on the morning of the day you plan to serve them.

Makes 24

Brownies

6 ounces unsweetened chocolate, chopped
¾ cup (1½ sticks) unsalted butter
4 teaspoons instant espresso powder

4 eggs
2 cups sugar
1½ teaspoons vanilla extract
¼ teaspoon salt
1 cup all purpose flour

Topping

6 ounces cream cheese, room temperature
1 tablespoon whipping cream
1½ teaspoons vanilla extract
6 tablespoons sifted powdered sugar

1⅓ cups chopped Almond Roca or Heath Bars (about 7 ounces)

For brownies: Preheat oven to 350°F. Butter and flour 13½ × 8½-inch baking dish. Melt chocolate and butter with espresso powder in top of double boiler over simmering water; stir until smooth. Cool slightly.

Whisk eggs in large bowl to blend. Gradually whisk in sugar. Add vanilla and salt. Whisk in melted chocolate. Add flour and stir until just blended. Spread batter in prepared dish. Bake until tester inserted in center comes out with a few moist crumbs, about 30 minutes. Cool brownies completely in pan on rack. (*Can be prepared 8 hours ahead. Cover tightly.*)

For topping: Blend cream cheese, cream and vanilla extract in processor until smooth. Mix in powdered sugar.

Spread topping over brownies. Sprinkle with Almond Roca. (*Can be prepared 2 hours ahead. Store at room temperature.*)

S'More Brownies

All the components of those famous childhood delights—marshmallows, graham crackers and creamy milk chocolate—in a delectable brownie.

Makes about 2 dozen

Crust

6 whole graham crackers, broken into small pieces
3 tablespoons sugar
3 tablespoons unsalted butter, cut into pieces, room temperature

Brownies

8 ounces milk chocolate, chopped
6 tablespoons (¾ stick) unsalted butter, cut into pieces

¼ cup sifted all purpose flour
⅛ teaspoon salt
2 extra-large eggs, room temperature
¼ cup plus 1½ teaspoons sugar
4 ounces milk chocolate, cut into ¼-inch pieces

25 large marshmallows, cut crosswise in half

1 ounce milk chocolate, grated

For crust: Position rack in center of oven and preheat to 325°F. Butter sides of 9-inch square cake pan with 2-inch-high sides. Fold 18 × 12-inch piece of foil in half crosswise. Line pan with foil, allowing foil to extend over two sides. Butter foil. Blend graham crackers, sugar and butter in processor until moist crumbs form. Press crumbs evenly into bottom of prepared pan. Bake until light golden brown, about 7 minutes. Cool crust on rack.

For brownies: Melt 8 ounces milk chocolate and 6 tablespoons butter in heavy medium saucepan over very low heat, stirring until smooth. Cool chocolate-butter mixture to room temperature.

Sift flour and salt into small bowl. Whisk eggs and sugar in medium bowl until well blended. Whisk in melted chocolate-butter mixture. Gently fold in dry ingredients. Mix in 4 ounces chopped chocolate. Spread batter over crust. Bake until toothpick inserted in center comes out clean, about 23 minutes (surface of brownies may crack).

Place marshmallows over hot brownies, spacing evenly. Cover tightly with foil and let brownies stand for 15 minutes.

Remove foil cover from pan. Using wet fingertips, press marshmallows together to fill in any uncovered spaces. Sprinkle grated chocolate over. Cool completely on rack. Lift brownies from pan using foil sides as aid. Fold down foil sides. Cut into squares. (*Brownies can be prepared 1 day ahead. Store in airtight container at room temperature.*)

Grand Slam Brownies

Fudgy, creamy and nutty— these incredible brownies cover all the bases.

Makes about 2 dozen

Brownies
- 4 ounces unsweetened chocolate, chopped
- 6 tablespoons (¾ stick) unsalted butter, cut into pieces
- ½ cup sifted all purpose flour
- ⅛ teaspoon baking powder
- ¼ teaspoon salt
- ½ teaspoon instant coffee powder
- 2 teaspoons water
- 2 extra-large eggs, room temperature
- 1½ cups sugar
- ½ cup walnut pieces, toasted
- ⅓ cup milk-chocolate-covered raisins

Topping
- 4½ ounces semisweet chocolate, chopped
- 8 ounces cream cheese, room temperature
- ¼ cup sugar
- 1 extra-large egg, room temperature

For brownies: Position rack in center of oven and preheat to 325°F. Butter sides of 9-inch square baking pan with 2-inch-high sides. Fold 18 × 12-inch piece of foil in half crosswise. Line pan with foil, allowing foil to extend over two sides. Butter foil. Dust pan and foil with flour; tap out excess.

Melt unsweetened chocolate and butter in heavy small saucepan over very low heat, stirring until smooth. Cool to room temperature.

Sift flour, baking powder and salt into small bowl. Place coffee powder in large bowl. Add water and stir to dissolve. Add eggs and sugar. Using electric mixer, beat mixture until pale yellow and slowly dissolving ribbon forms when beaters are lifted. Fold in melted chocolate, then dry ingredients. Mix in walnuts and raisins. Spread batter in prepared pan. Bake until top is dry and cracked and toothpick inserted in center comes out with some wet batter still attached, about 38 minutes (surface may crack). Transfer to rack. Gently press down any raised edges to flatten slightly. Maintain oven temperature.

For topping: Melt semisweet chocolate in top of double boiler over simmering water, stirring until smooth. Remove from over water. Blend cream cheese and sugar in processor until smooth, stopping occasionally to scrape down sides of bowl. Add warm melted chocolate and blend well. Add egg and blend just until combined. Pour topping over hot brownie. Bake until topping moves just slightly in center when shaken, about 10 minutes. Transfer to rack and cool completely. Cover with foil. Refrigerate overnight.

Lift brownies from pan using foil sides as aid. Fold down foil sides. Cut brownies into squares and serve immediately.

U.S. Mints

Rich chocolate brownies accented with mint.

Makes about 2 dozen

Brownies

1¼ **cups mint chocolate chips**
1½ **ounces unsweetened chocolate, finely chopped**
½ **cup (1 stick) unsalted butter, cut into pieces**

½ **cup sifted all purpose flour**
Pinch of salt
1½ **teaspoons whipping cream**
1½ **teaspoons instant espresso powder**
½ **teaspoon white crème de menthe liqueur**

3 **extra-large eggs, room temperature**
¾ **cup plus 2 tablespoons sugar**

Glaze

6 **tablespoons mint chocolate chips**
½ **ounce unsweetened chocolate, finely chopped**
5 **tablespoons unsalted butter, cut into pieces**

For brownies: Position rack in lowest third of oven and preheat to 350°F. Butter sides of 9-inch square baking pan with 2-inch-high sides. Fold 18 × 12-inch piece of foil in half crosswise. Line pan with foil, allowing foil to extend over two sides. Butter foil. Melt both chocolates and butter in heavy medium saucepan over very low heat, stirring until smooth. Cool.

Sift flour and salt into small bowl. Mix cream, espresso powder and crème de menthe in small cup. Using electric mixer, beat eggs and sugar in large bowl until frothy. Fold in coffee mixture and then melted chocolate. Fold in dry ingredients. Spread batter evenly in prepared pan. Bake until toothpick inserted in center comes out with some moist crumbs still attached, about 25 minutes (surface may crack). Gently press down on any raised surfaces to flatten slightly. Cool brownies for 30 minutes on rack.

For glaze: Melt both chocolates and butter in heavy small saucepan over low heat, stirring until smooth. Let stand until cool enough to spread. Spread glaze over brownies. Let stand 4 hours at room temperature.

Lift brownies from pan using foil sides as aid. Fold down foil sides. Cut into squares. (*Can be prepared 1 day ahead. Store in airtight container.*)

Mocha-Hazelnut Macaroon Domes

If you're running short on time, you can skip the melted white chocolate decoration called for here.

Makes about 30

Macaroons

½ **cup hazelnuts, lightly toasted (about 2½ ounces)**
½ **cup sugar**
1 **tablespoon all purpose flour**
1 **large egg white**
1 **teaspoon vanilla extract**

Mocha Ganache

½ **cup plus 2 tablespoons whipping cream**
3 **tablespoons unsalted butter**
1 **teaspoon instant coffee granules**
9 **ounces imported milk chocolate (such as Lindt), chopped**
1 **teaspoon vanilla extract**

Coating

9 **ounces bittersweet (not unsweetened) or semisweet chocolate, chopped**
1 **tablespoon solid vegetable shortening**
30 **(about) small raspberries or hazelnuts**

3 **ounces imported white chocolate (such as Lindt), chopped**

For macaroons: Preheat oven to 350°F. Line 1 large cookie sheet with parchment. Brush lightly with vegetable oil. Finely grind hazelnuts in processor. Add sugar and flour and blend to powder. With machine running, add egg white and vanilla extract and blend to paste.

Spoon mixture into pastry bag fitted with no. 4 (³⁄₈-inch-diameter) round tip. Pipe ¾- to 1-inch-wide mounds on parchment about ½ inch high and spacing 1 inch apart. Dip finger into water and gently press on top of cookie to flatten center slightly. Bake until golden brown, about 12 minutes (cookies will spread to about 1½ inches). Turn parchment over onto work surface. Brush parchment with water to moisten. Let stand until parchment can easily be pulled off cookies, about 2 minutes. Remove parchment.

For ganache: Bring cream and butter to simmer in heavy medium saucepan over medium heat. Add espresso powder and stir to dissolve. Reduce heat to low. Add chocolate and stir until melted. Mix in vanilla. Pour into shallow bowl. Refrigerate chocolate ganache just until firm enough to spread, stirring occasionally, approximately 45 minutes.

Line cookie sheet with foil. Using icing spatula, spread 1 heaping teaspoon ganache onto flat side of each cookie, mounding to dome in center. Place rounded side up on prepared sheet. Repeat with remaining cookies. Refrigerate until ganache is firm, about 20 minutes.

For coating: Line cookie sheet with foil. Melt bittersweet chocolate with vegetable shortening in top of double boiler over simmering water, stirring until smooth. Remove from over water. Grasp 1 cookie between thumb and index finger. Dip ganache portion into melted chocolate. Shake off excess. Turn chocolate side up and place on foil-lined cookie sheet. Top with berry or nut. Repeat with remaining cookies. Refrigerate until chocolate sets, about 30 minutes.

Melt white chocolate in top of double boiler over simmering water, stirring until smooth. Dip spoon into chocolate. Wave from side to side over cookies, forming zigzag lines. Refrigerate until chocolate sets, about 15 minutes. Place cookies in single layer in airtight containers and refrigerate overnight. (*Can be made 3 days ahead.*) Let stand 10 minutes at room temperature before serving.

Chocolate-dipped Orange-Ginger Florentines

Chewy, candylike caramel cookies enhanced with orange and crystallized ginger. The leftover orange sugar syrup is delicious as a sweetener for hot tea or coffee.

Makes 24

Sugared Orange Peel
  3 oranges
  ½ cup plus 4 tablespoons sugar
  ½ cup water

Cookies
  ½ cup plus 2 tablespoons whipping cream
  ½ cup sugar
  ¼ cup firmly packed golden brown sugar

  2 tablespoons (¼ stick) unsalted butter
  ⅔ cup lightly toasted sliced almonds
  ¼ cup all purpose flour
  2 tablespoons finely chopped crystallized ginger

  6 ounces bittersweet (not unsweetened) or semisweet chocolate, chopped

For peel: Remove peel from oranges (orange part only) in strips using vegetable peeler. Finely chop enough peel to measure 2 teaspoons and set aside for cookie batter. Blanch remaining peel in small saucepan of boiling water 2 minutes. Drain. Return blanched orange peel strips to saucepan. Add ½ cup sugar and water and bring to boil, stirring frequently. Boil mixture for 5 minutes. Drain; reserve orange syrup for another use.

Sprinkle 2 tablespoons sugar on plate. Arrange peel atop sugar. Sprinkle with remaining 2 tablespoons sugar. Let stand 15 minutes. Remove peel from sugar. Finely chop enough orange peel to measure 2 tablespoons; set aside. Reserve remainder for another use.

For cookies: Preheat oven to 350°F. Line 2 heavy large cookie sheets with foil. Lightly butter foil. Combine first four ingredients in heavy small saucepan. Cook over medium heat just until sugar dissolves, stirring constantly. Add 2 teaspoons minced unsugared peel, 2 tablespoons chopped sugared orange peel, almonds, flour and ginger. Bring to boil over medium heat, stirring frequently.

Drop 1 level tablespoon mixture (mixture will be runny) onto prepared sheet. Repeat 5 more times, spacing cookies about 3 inches apart. Repeat procedure with second cookie sheet. Bake cookies until edges are pale golden brown, about 8 minutes (cookies will spread). Remove cookie sheets from oven. Using 3-inch round cookie cutter, push cookie sides in to reshape cookies into 3-inch rounds. Slide foil off sheets. Cool cookies on foil. Turn foil over. Carefully peel off cookies. Line same cookie sheets with new foil. Repeat procedure with remaining cookie batter.

Line 2 cookie sheets with foil. Melt chocolate in top of double boiler over simmering water, stirring occasionally until smooth. Remove from over water. Dip 1 cookie halfway into chocolate; shake off excess chocolate. Place cookie on prepared sheet. Repeat with remaining cookies. Refrigerate until chocolate sets, about 30 minutes. Remove cookies from foil. (*Can be prepared 2 weeks ahead. Refrigerate in airtight container between sheets of waxed paper. Let stand 20 minutes at room temperature before serving.*)

Cran-Raspberry Star Cookies

Cranberries add tang to the filling of these colorful sandwich cookies. You will have some small unsandwiched cookies, too.

Makes about 36

Cookies
¾ cup (1½ sticks) unsalted butter, room temperature
1 teaspoon vanilla extract
¼ teaspoon grated lemon peel
1 cup sugar
1 large egg
1 egg yolk
2¼ cups all purpose flour
¼ cup cornstarch
¼ teaspoon (generous) ground cloves

Filling
1 cup fresh cranberries
¼ cup sugar
¾ cup raspberry preserves

Powdered sugar

For cookies: Using electric mixer, cream butter, vanilla and lemon in medium bowl until light. Gradually add sugar and beat until blended. Beat in egg and yolk. Combine flour, cornstarch and cloves. Beat half of dry ingredients into butter mixture. Stir in remaining dry ingredients. Gather dough into ball (dough will be soft). Divide dough into 4 pieces; flatten each into disk. Wrap each in plastic and refrigerate 1 hour.

Preheat oven to 350°F. Butter heavy large nonstick cookie sheets. Roll 1 dough piece out (keep remainder refrigerated) on floured surface to thickness of ⅛ inch. Cut out star-shaped cookies using floured 3-inch star cutter. Transfer to prepared cookie sheets spacing ½ inch apart. Repeat rolling and cutting with second dough piece. Gather scraps and reroll, chilling dough briefly if soft. Cut out more star cookies. Transfer to prepared cookie sheets. Chill cookies 10 minutes. Bake cookies until edges are golden brown, about 10 minutes. Transfer cookies to rack and cool completely.

Roll third dough piece out on lightly floured surface to thickness of ⅛ inch. Cut out star-shaped cookies using floured 3-inch star cutter. Cut smaller star out of center of each 3-inch star using 1¾- to 2-inch star cutter. Transfer star outlines to prepared sheets using floured metal spatula as aid. Repeat rolling and cutting star outlines with fourth dough piece. Gather scraps and star centers and reroll, chilling dough briefly if soft. Cut out 3-inch stars. Cut smaller stars out of each 3-inch star. Transfer star outlines and centers to prepared cookie sheets. Chill cookies 10 minutes. Bake until edges are golden brown, about 9 minutes. Transfer cookies to rack; cool.

For filling: Finely chop cranberries and sugar in processor. Transfer mixture to heavy medium saucepan. Mix in preserves. Cook over medium-high heat until mixture is reduced to scant 1 cup, stirring occasionally, about 8 minutes. Pour filling into bowl and cool completely.

Using metal icing spatula, spread 1 teaspoon jam filling in center of each 3-inch cookie, spreading slightly toward points of star. Lightly sift powdered sugar over star outlines. Place sugared cookies sugar side up over jam-topped cookies. (*Can be prepared ahead. Place in single layers in airtight containers. Refrigerate up to 4 days or freeze up to 2 weeks. Let cookies stand for 10 minutes at room temperature before serving.*)

Molasses Spice Leaves

These cookies are topped with white icing and silver dragées for added elegance. Look for the dragées in the cake decorating section of your supermarket.

Makes about 48

Cookies
- ½ cup walnuts (about 2 ounces)
- 2 cups all purpose flour
- ¼ cup sugar
- ½ cup (1 stick) unsalted butter, room temperature
- ½ cup firmly packed golden brown sugar
- 2 teaspoons vanilla extract
- ¼ cup unsulfured molasses
- 1 egg
- ½ teaspoon ground cardamom
- ½ teaspoon ground ginger
- ½ teaspoon ground allspice
- ½ teaspoon ground cinnamon
- ½ teaspoon baking soda

Icing
- 3 cups powdered sugar
- 2 large egg whites

Silver dragées

For cookies: Finely grind walnuts in processor. Add ¼ cup flour and ¼ cup sugar and blend to powder. Using electric mixer, cream butter with brown sugar and vanilla in large bowl until fluffy. Beat in molasses and egg. Mix remaining 1¾ cups flour with nut mixture, spices and baking soda. Stir into butter mixture (dough will be soft). Divide dough into 2 pieces. Flatten each into disk. Wrap each in plastic and refrigerate 1 hour.

Preheat oven to 350°F. Butter heavy large cookie sheets. On heavily floured surface, roll 1 dough piece out (keep remainder refrigerated) to thickness of ⅛ to ¼ inch. Cut out cookies using 3-inch leaf cookie cutter. Transfer to prepared cookie sheets, spacing ½ inch apart. Repeat rolling and cutting with second dough piece. Gather scraps and refrigerate 15 minutes. Reroll scraps and cut out more cookies. Bake until light golden brown, about 10 minutes. Cool on racks.

For icing: Using electric mixer, beat sugar and egg whites until smooth.

Spoon icing into pastry bag fitted with 1/16-inch round tip. Pipe icing decoratively atop cookies. Decorate with dragées. Let stand until icing sets. (*Can be prepared 2 weeks ahead. Store refrigerated between layers of waxed paper in airtight container. Let stand 5 minutes at room temperature before serving.*)

 *Index*

News '90

The Year of Food and Entertaining in Review

Trends & New Products

Foods & Info by Mail

Books

Restaurants & People

Getaways

For the Kitchen & Table

Diet News

Trends & New Products

Environmental groups have warned that bleached paper contains dioxin, a toxic chemical. So Melitta has introduced a coffee filter made of brown, unbleached paper. Not only is it ecologically safe, but the filter may also produce a milder-tasting coffee. Available at supermarkets.

Riz Cous, a wheat-free version of couscous made from brown rice, is a smart product now in natural foods sections of supermarkets. Flavors include Original, Cajun spice and French country herb. Find out where you can get it by contacting Lundberg Family Farms, 5370 Church Street, P.O. Box 369, Richvale, CA 95974; 916-882-4551.

Lavazza and Illycaffè, Italy's most famous coffee producers, are beginning to move into the U.S. market. Lavazza is presently sold at fine supermarkets in New York, Philadelphia, Boston and Seattle. To find out where Illycaffè is sold, call 800-USA-ILLY.

Enrico Serafino Winery in Canale, Italy, one of the first producers of Asti Spumante, has introduced a new premium sparkling Asti wine called Mondoro. Zesty, fruity, refreshing and packaged in a handsome green fluted bottle with gold foil, it's ideal for any occasion. The wine is available in liquor stores for $18.

Long a favorite all over Europe, Ferrero's Mon Cheri candy, a whole hazelnut or almond encased in smooth milk chocolate, is now joined in popularity by a brand-new praline confection, Ferrero Rocher. A glamorously wrapped treat made of the finest hazelnuts, it has a smooth chocolate cream and whole nut center and a crisp wafer shell that is dipped in chocolate. These luxe sweets are 99 cents for a pack of four Mon Cheri and about $2.49 for eight of the Rocher. Find them in department and specialty foods stores, or phone 212-683-8282.

The fashionable new cracker is basic black—a rice cracker from San-J made with whole black unhulled sesame seeds, whole brown rice and soy sauce. Crisp and flavorful, they are the perfect foil for chèvre and other white cheeses, making a very sophisticated appetizer. A 3½-ounce package costs about $2 at natural and specialty foods stores. For a shop in your area, call 800-222-3390 or, in the state of California, call 415-821-4041.

Huston's Yukon Gold—a yellow potato that is creamy in texture and buttery in flavor—is finally in your supermarket. It took the people at Michigan State University ten years to develop this delicious discovery. It was worth the wait. Try it without butter for a tasty, low-calorie treat.

New and noteworthy at the greengrocers are green-topped baby Vidalia onions, young versions of the giant, sweet and crunchy vegetables from Georgia. For details, call 800-843-2542.

Last April 20 climbers from the United States, the Soviet Union and the People's Republic of China ascended Mount Everest. The purpose of their effort was to demonstrate that "through international cooperation, commitment and teamwork, the highest goals on earth can be reached: the summit of Everest, solutions to global environmental problems and world peace." Barbara A. Fromm, director of food for the project, came up with a powder to spice up the climbers' meals. Because, while little else is appealing at high altitudes, spicy food is most welcome. Called The Spice House Peace Climb Chili Powder, a four-ounce jar is $4.98. Orders will include a sample of the wine-mulling mixture also specially formulated for the climb. Contact Kavanaugh Hill Spice Shop, 1244 North Glenview Avenue, Wauwatosa, WI 53213; 414-258-7727.

There's something new on the market for your salads. Developed in France and called Sangria, it's a butter, or Boston, lettuce that's rosy red and dark green all year long except for summer, when it turns a brilliant red-brown. Seeds for your home garden are distributed by Johnny's Selected Seeds, Foss Hill Road, Albion, ME 04910; 207-437-9294.

Last March's *Bon Appétit's* Taste of the Nation benefit for hunger relief in America and overseas raised more than $1.2 million for the cause. And those were not the only impressive numbers: More than 30,000 people attended events in 65 cities across the country, with 2,000 chefs providing superb food for sampling. Seventy percent of the proceeds from each event will be awarded to food banks and shelters within that community; 10 percent is earmarked for a high-need rural area of the state; and 20 percent is pooled nationally for grants to international relief agencies.

The Chukar Cherry Company offers a neat alternative to raisins—dried Bing cherries; they are available plain and chocolate covered in snack and gift-package sizes. The company also produces a line of products using the Washington State sweet cherries, including chutney, a dessert sauce and preserves. For information, call 800-624-9544 or, in the state of Washington, call 509-786-2055.

New herb blends (for the barbecue coals, not for the food) make grilled fare taste great. The hot herbs create a fragrant smoke that permeates the food. A two-ounce bag (enough for several meals) from The The Spice Hunter costs about three dollars at specialty foods stores nationwide, or call 800-541-0225 for information.

While you're busy tying up newspapers for the recycling center, consider investing in a reusable canvas bag for carrying groceries from the supermarket. Treekeepers offers a big and sturdy 100 percent cotton bag for groceries. Their green logo is a reminder of the three Rs: reduce, recycle and reuse. To order, send $9.95 for one bag, $21 for three or $30 for five, plus $3.50 shipping to Treekeepers, 249 South Highway 101, Suite 518, Solana Beach, CA 92075, or call 619-481-6403.

Rich, soft, spoonable Italian-style *mascarpone* cheese is now being made in the United States. It's perfect for making *tiramisù*, or simply serve it drizzled with honey accompanied by fresh fruit and *biscotti*. Seven ounces cost about $4, 16 ounces about $5; at specialty stores and selected supermarkets. For more information, contact Auricchio Cheese at 414-863-2123.

❦ Foods & Info by Mail

Delicious bread can turn a simple bowl of soup (or an omelet or a salad) into a special meal. Gayle's Bakery bread—chewy, crusty and oh, so satisfying—is some of the best we've tasted. Order by mail for a special party or to send along to a carb-loving friend. Choose from richly textured combinations, like walnut-raisin or pumpkin-seed rye, plus simple whole wheat country loaves. For more information, write or call Gayle's Bakery, 504 Bay Avenue, Capitola, CA 95010; telephone number 408-462-1127.

American Spoon Foods's cherry-chocolate cake takes fruitcake to another realm. It's dense and chocolaty, with the tang of dried cherries. The 14½-ounce fruitcake is $18.50 plus shipping. To order, call American Spoon Foods at 800-222-5886.

Dried fruits and nuts are always a welcome gift, but a can of From the Rain Forest Tropical Mix does more than just make a great snack. A portion of the profits from this all-natural, no-preservative blend of cashews and Brazil nuts goes to Cultural Survival, a nonprofit human rights group that assists the rain forest and its people. You can purchase the 30-ounce can of tropical mix for $9.95 plus shipping; or, for the same price, get a 12-ounce can of the mix and a 12-ounce can of roasted unsalted cashews. To order, call 800-327-8496 or, in New York, the number is 212-627-2508.

Doll up your favorite ice cream desserts with fruity toppings from the Northwest. Berry Fudge Toppings combine rich, dark cocoa and sweet butter with fresh strawberries, blueberries or raspberries. The Berry Syrups have deep fruit flavors with just a whisper of liqueur. The toppings cost $8 per 11-ounce jar; the syrups, $8.50 per 16-ounce bottle. Berry jams are also available in a gift pack of three 11-ounce jars for $20.50. All prices include shipping. To order, contact From Oregon, 2787 Olympic Street, Springfield, OR 97477; toll free number 800-447-5365 or 503-747-4222.

Andrea Safran and Joyce Weiner, co-owners of Wild About Chocolate!, have succeeded in putting homemade brownies to shame. One taste of theirs and you'll never want to melt chocolate again. The selection includes chocolate chip blondies, peanut butter fudge, butterscotch fudge, Heathchip, double fudge, fudge mint, walnut fudge, amaretto almond, cream cheese, raspberry and Kahlúa almond. A dozen costs $25, including shipping. Contact Wild About Chocolate!, 166A Great Road, Acton, MA 01720; telephone 508-263-1153.

Favorite Pumpkin Recipes, a new booklet from Libby's, offers mouth-watering recipes for muffins, waffles, sauces and soups, plus a low-calorie crustless version of pumpkin pie. To order, send $1.98 and two labels from any Libby's pumpkin product to Libby's *Favorite Pumpkin Recipes,* P.O. Box 360-FE Pico Rivera, CA 90665.

If you still enjoy peanut butter and jelly sandwiches when you brown-bag it to work, imagine your lunchtime treat made with cinnamon-raisin or chocolate-chip peanut butter. Both flavors are available from Peanut Butter Classics, and they're delightful when spread on English muffins or whole wheat toast for breakfast. (They're also good right off the spoon.) Your kids will love them too. Available in chunky or creamy, 12-ounce jars are $5 each plus shipping from Peanut Butter Classics, P.O. Box 355, 5 Broad Street, Pawling, NY 12564; telephone 914-855-1145.

Along with Martinis and fondue, beef Wellington is making a comeback. But now, with almost no effort at all, it can be the star of your fancy dinner party. Omaha Steaks is selling a ready-for-the-oven beef Wellington, delivered to your home in just two days. The closely trimmed filet mignon is topped with a rich liver pâté and wrapped with a light puff pastry. It comes in 4-, 6-, 8- and 12-portion sizes at about $60, $82, $107 and $147 respectively, plus shipping. A recipe book and cooking instructions come with each. To order, call 800-228-9055.

If you're having problems finding a special herb, spice or tea, Herbal Effect in Monterey, California, will probably be able to help you. They carry a wide variety of rare and common culinary spices and popular and exotic teas. Call 408-375-6313 for a catalog.

Convito Italiano, the charming market and cafe located in Chicago and Wilmette, Illinois, now makes its delicious homemade breads available by mail. A trio of freshly baked pepper-cheese, walnut whole wheat and raisin-and-rosemary breads is $27.50, including next-day air delivery. Other breads can be substituted for the above. Order from Convito Italiano, 11 East Chestnut Street, Chestnut Galleria, Chicago, IL 60611; 312-943-2983.

Add chocolate and pecans to short-bread and what have you got? A sweet sensation from Bittersweet Pastries. This one-pound temptation serves six to eight and costs $22, including shipping. To order, contact Bittersweet Pastries, 460 Piermont Avenue, Piermont, NY 10968; 800-537-7791 or, in New York, 914-359-7103.

Homemade and outrageously habit forming, My Sister's Caramels are meltingly chewy and the perfect gift for a hostess with a sweet tooth. Available in six tempting flavors—vanilla, chocolate, praline, coffee, peanut butter caramel and new chocolate-covered caramel-pecan myrtles. For more information, contact My Sister's Caramels, 1884 Bret Harte Street, Palo Alto, CA 94303; 415-321-2582.

Varney's Chemist Laden, located in the Texas Hill Country, offers one of the largest selections of herbal products you might ever hope to find. Bill and Sylvia Varney, who opened their charming shop about five years ago, also have a tearoom plus bed and breakfast on the premises and run the Fredericksburg Herb Farm on the property. All products in the chemist shop—teas, seasonings, vinegars, herb wreaths and more—are made with items that come directly from the Varneys' farm. For a copy of their mail-order catalog ($1.50), contact Fredericksburg Herb Farm, P.O. Drawer 927, Fredericksburg, TX 78624; 512-997-8615.

The Mocodamia Torte gets its name from an inspired mixture of espresso, chocolate and macadamia nuts. All dense and fudgy, it's dotted throughout with white chocolate chips and buried in a topping of toasted macadamias—and is rich beyond the wildest dreams of any chocoholic. Offer it as a finale to a dinner party. Serves eight. Order for $23.95 outside California, and $20.95 inside California, including shipping from Gwetzli Foods, P.O. Box 20298, Oakland, CA 94620; telephone number 415-655-5621.

What could be next, after smoked trout? Trout Nouveau, all done up in fancy clothes, that's what. Packed like *haute* sardines, they come in lemon pepper, white wine, smoked and plain flavors. These fancy fish make wonderful gifts to *bec fin* friends. Pretty wooden gift boxes with two 3¾-ounce cans are $19.95, or $29.95 for four cans. Single cans are $4.50. Available from Red-Wing Meadow Farm, P.O. Box 484, Sunderland, MA 01375; telephone number 413-549-4118.

Looking for a new and interesting sauce or an old favorite that's been eluding you in the stores? Le Saucier offers a handy catalog of more than five hundred wonderful sauces—including vinaigrettes, marinades, chutneys and salsas—that can be mail-ordered. Just call 617-522-5446 for a free copy.

Mexican foods are quickly becoming a favorite in American kitchens—they have even made their way into Yankee hearts. San Angel Salsa in Vermont is a delicious example. Using a variety of chilies grown in Mexico and New Mexico, the company produces four terrific salsas available in specialty foods stores and by mail. Spice intensity ranges from mild to hot. A sample pack of three nine-ounce jars costs $13.50. Contact San Angel, 668 Worcester Road, Stowe, VT 05672; telephone 802-253-8117.

Serve it hot, cold or at room temperature and dinner is a snap. The Princess Anne Brand spiral-sliced honey-glazed ham even relieves you of most carving chores. It comes from Smithfield, Virginia, the town renowned for its authentic country hams. A whole fully cooked 13- to 14-pound ham costs $64.95 plus $6.50 shipping. Contact The Smithfield Collection, P.O. Box 487, Smithfield, VA 23430; toll free 800-628-2242.

Beyond truffles, cookies and brownies, Boomer's Oogies are chocolate morsels that defy analysis or description, but we'll try. Rich, dense and nutty, they are moist on the inside and crumbly on the outside. A package of three dozen costs $21.99 plus $3.50 shipping from Boomer's Oogies, P.O. Box 2669, Pittsfield, MA 01202; toll free 800-332-6649.

Headed by New York restaurateur Tony May, the Gruppo Ristoratori Italiani is one organization that has furthered the quality and appreciation of Italian food here. They publish a newsletter, sponsor events, promote education and work with the Italian government to promote the country's fine cuisine. For additional information, call 203-857-0253.

🍎 *Books*

For those with a penchant for pork and pone, there are two new books to celebrate. Joni Miller's *True Grits* (Workman Publishing, 1990) is a mail-order source for everything southern, from Tennessee Goo Goo Clusters to soft white flour for making the perfect biscuits. *Biscuits, Spoonbread and Sweet Potato Pie* (Alfred A. Knopf, 1990) by Bill Neal is one of the best books around on southern baking. Easy-to-follow recipes plus quotes, anecdotes and historical references should make this a favorite of arm-chair cooks everywhere.

The New American Kitchen (Simon & Schuster, 1990) by Michael McLaughlin is chock-full of mouth-watering recipes that will make you want to get out the whisk and spatula—fast. Try his fennel and watercress salad, molasses-glazed duck with turnips, pumpkin spoon bread and bourbon-baked apples.

Recipes from the Night Kitchen (Fireside Books, 1990) by Sally Nirenberg is a delicious collection of recipes for soups, stews and chilies. The author, formerly the chef-owner of a take-out soup shop, offers recipes for any time of year. A cool ginger and melon soup is ideal for summer, while a hearty butternut squash one with apples will hit the spot on a cold night.

If ever there were a book for chocolate lovers, this one is it. Alice Medrich's *Cocolat: Extraordinary Chocolate Desserts* (Warner Books, 1990) offers more than 50 recipes for wickedly tempting delights. Medrich, who owns a number of confectionery shops called Cocolat in the San Francisco Bay Area, shares her vast knowledge of and passion for this dessert favorite in recipes like chocolate ladyfingers and a light chocolate torte lavishly decorated with chocolate ruffles.

Abbie Zabar's *Alphabet Soup* (Stewart, Tabori & Chang, 1990) is a delightful learning book for eaters of all ages. Little ones learn the whys and hows of food. Older readers will love Zabar's whimsical drawings, reminiscent of those by Miró and Klee.

One of the loveliest cookbooks of the year is *Monet's Table: The Cooking Journals of Claude Monet* (Simon & Schuster, 1990), with text by Claire Joyes and photographs taken at Giverny by Jean-Bernard Naudin. A favorite recipe here: baked peaches.

Britain's celebrated seafood authority, Alan Davidson, has written a truly magnificent opus, *Seafood, A Culinary Work of Art* (Simon & Schuster, 1989). It is thoroughly researched and an enchantment to read. Davidson, a former British ambassador to Laos, is both erudite and entertaining, and his recipes honor the bounty of the sea in the most mouth-watering ways.

Patricia Quintana's *Mexico's Feasts of Life* (Council Oak Books, 1989) is a handsome, lovingly assembled collection of recipes from four generations of family. The charm of the book is in its blending of Mexican culture and food, with feasts celebrating life's passages through family tradition.

🍃 Restaurants & People

After decades of decay, the Art Deco District of Miami Beach is again becoming a mecca for fine dining. The hottest new restaurant in SoBe (short for South Beach) is Johnny's. Three-piece-suiters rub elbows with pony-tailed trendies in a stylish dining room with peach-colored walls, mint green banquettes and black floral carpeting. The young, brash, self-trained chef and owner, Johnny Circharo, works wonders with all kinds of seafood. Johnny's is located on Lincoln Road, the epicenter of the Miami art scene. (Johnny's, 915 Lincoln Road, Miami Beach, FL 33139; 305-534-3200.)

Noted chef Jimmy Schmidt (whose résumé includes Denver's The Rattlesnake Club and Adirondacks located in Washington, D.C.) has opened Tres Vite, a modern cafe-style restaurant in Detroit's Fox Centre Building. The fresh, contemporary interior (including chairs from the Memphis Collection and Stelton flatware) reflects the urban renewal of Motor City. The moderately priced menus feature grilled entrées, pastas and homemade breads. (Tres Vite, Fox Centre Building, 2203 Woodward Avenue, Detroit, MI 48201; 313-964-4144.)

When we last caught up with him, chef Bradley Ogden was busy at the Campton Place Hotel restaurant in San Francisco, refining the superb American-style cooking that first brought him national attention at the American Restaurant in Kansas City. Now Ogden has moved on to nearby Larkspur, where he and Michael Dellar have opened the intimate Lark Creek Inn restaurant. With this new venture, Ogden says his philosophy continues to be to "keep it simple, use the freshest ingredients available and put them together in such a way that the flavors, colors and textures combine to bring out the best in each other." His menu will not disappoint. (The Lark Creek Inn, 234 Magnolia Ave., Larkspur, CA 94939; 415-924-7766.)

Los Angeles restaurateurs Yuji Tsunoda and Riku Suzuki have teamed up with cutting-edge architects Elyse Grinstein and Jeffrey Daniels to add yet another eatery to the Chaya dynasty: Chaya Venice. In almost no time, it has become as popular as its two West Hollywood siblings, Chaya Brasserie and Chaya Diner. The restaurant is located in an elegant Italian-style complex on Main Street, the lively thoroughfare that cuts right through Venice and Santa Monica. Given its proximity to the Pacific, it's no surprise that the emphasis here is on fresh fish. There's an oyster and sashimi bar, as well as wonderful specialties from the kitchen of chef Kondo Yoshikazu—meat and chicken included. (Chaya Venice, 110 Navy Street, Venice, CA 90291; 213-396-1179.)

At lunchtime, City Seen, a sleek, casual spot in downtown Kansas City, Missouri, hops with an urbane, smartly dressed crowd. You'll see diehard deal makers in the polished hardwood-framed leather booths—each equipped with a telephone. The service is quite knowledgeable and upbeat, and the menu is imaginative without excess. Lunch dishes include a Mandarin steak salad with wild mushrooms and the Inner City Caesar, tossed with creamy Parmesan and anchovy dressing and red chili croutons. Sandwich lovers will enjoy the smoked chicken and mozzarella club with *ancho* mayonnaise or the turkey and Monterey Jack cheese combo with cilantro mayonnaise. For dinner, try their hefty 24-ounce T-bone steak with *chipotle* chili butter. (City Seen, 1111 Main, AT&T Town Pavilion, Kansas City, MO 64106; 816-472-8833.)

Outside of Italy, New York may have more Italian restaurants than any other city in the world. All aficionados have their favorites, from casual trattorias to sumptuous high tech affairs. And the relatively little-known tucked-away spots are usually the best (and usually kept secret by their discoverers). One such, Stella del Mare, is located on the first two floors of a former Murray Hill town house. Chef Mario Medich serves up the full flavors of northern Italy, with an emphasis on seafood, and the ambience is pure romance. (Stella del Mare, 346 Lexington Avenue, New York, NY 10016; 212-687-4425.)

Carolyn's restaurant in the city of Columbus was formerly a private home and, just like home, it's a place where you can spend an entire evening in low-key comfort. After a drink at the stately wood bar (in what used to be the living room), a relaxed evening unfolds in the intimate dining room. Executive chef-owner Carolyn Claycomb prints a new menu daily, based on what's in season. Dinner might begin with smoked salmon with avocado blini and *crème fraîche* or an escargot and truffle tartlet, followed by spiced grilled tuna or saffron-flavored seafood pasta. And save room for dessert: Try the elegant hazelnut coronet filled with Grand Marnier mousse, or a down-home upside-down pear pie with caramel-pecan glaze. (Carolyn's, 489 City Park Avenue, Columbus, OH 43215; 614-221-8100.)

Gérard, the flagship restaurant at Vancouver's Le Meridien hotel, is a splendid place to spend an evening. Chef Olivier Chaleil, who earned his stripes in France at a series of two- and three-star restaurants, took over Gérard with a plan to keep the food as simply tasteful as the decor. Devotees of the cuisine here favor the chef's "Le menu surprise." It's a degustation of Chaleil's favorites, always the freshest of local meats, fish and produce. And be sure to try one of the surprising wines of British Columbia with your meal. (Restaurant Gérard, 845 Burrard Street, Vancouver, British Columbia, Canada; 604-682-5511.)

Planning on visiting the Metropolitan when you're next in Manhattan? Then plan to finish off the afternoon with tea across Fifth Avenue at a beautifully refurbished hotel, The Stanhope. Executive chef Bruno Mella supervises the lovely tea here, as well as the fabulous lunches and dinners. It's the per-

fect way to refresh yourself in the late afternoon. The hotel is a nice place to stay, too. (The Stanhope, 995 Fifth Avenue, New York, NY 10028; telephone 212-288-5800.)

If you think midwestern fare is old-fashioned, think again. At Kansas City's Venue, diners can sample dishes like veal chop with Madeira and thyme and fish on eggplant *confit*. The spare, elegant interior was conceived by Josh Schweitzer, designer of Los Angeles's City and Campanile restaurants. It's the perfect setting for chef-owner Dennis Kaniger's menu. (Venue, 4532 Main Street, Kansas City, MO 64111; telephone 816-561-3311.)

Monsoon, the restaurant opened earlier in the year by cookbook author Bruce Cost and chef Tony Gulisano, is one of San Francisco's best. Gulisano magically transforms standard Asian recipes into deliciously innovative dishes. Some favorites are spicy Thai seafood salad; rich, tangy "roast" eggplant; salt and pepper shrimp; and the full-flavored braised oxtail clay pot. And don't miss dessert: Pastry chef David Lebovitz (formerly of Chez Panisse) offers such delectables as warm pears in passion fruit tea, and plum wine-raspberry ice. Cost and Gulisano may not be Chinese surnames, but from the first bite, you'll know you've found true Asian inspiration. (Monsoon, 601 Van Ness Avenue, San Francisco, CA 94102; 415-441-3232.)

Now is the perfect time to rediscover the pleasures of dining at one of Los Angeles's most beautiful restaurants, L'Orangerie. After more than 12 years at its landmark La Cienega Boulevard location, it's still rated among the city's best, thanks to the combined creative talents of owners Gerard and Virginie Ferry and chef Jean-François Meteigner. Warm L.A. evenings present a delightful excuse to reserve a table on the romatic patio. Candlelight glows, illuminating the restaurant's exquisite flower arrangements and enhancing its quietly striking architecture. Chef Meteigner's superb cuisine matches the lovely surroundings. Favorites and brand-new dishes are all complemented by an extensive wine list, and desserts are memorable. Gilles Lagourgue is the personable maître d' who makes sure the service is as top-notch as the food. (L'Orangerie, 903 North La Cienega Boulevard, Los Angeles, CA 90069; telephone 213-652-9770.)

Los Angeles's ever-trendy Melrose Avenue has a new restaurant on the block. Owned by a young Belgian couple, Chapo is a quietly elegant bistro that boasts delicious Belgian-California fare and excellent service. Call 213-655-2924 to make reservations.

Eat in, take out, dine early or late, on a little or a lot. The Trattoria Dell'Arte is *the* spot for the 57th Street crowd in Manhattan. This handsomely appointed place boasts some of the finest and most pleasant service in the city and is handy to Carnegie Hall, as well as to some popular movie theaters. Its imaginatively decorated walls (with artists' anatomical casts) and soft lights provide a delightful setting to enjoy the grazing menu. There's also

delicious Italian meat loaf, roast chicken, sandwiches, pasta and more. Don't miss the paper-thin, just-baked pizzas. (Trattoria Dell'Arte, 900 7th Avenue at West 57th Street, New York, NY 10019; 212-245-9800.)

The restaurant that everyone is talking about in L.A. is Atlas Bar & Grill, the latest scion of restaurateur and impresario Mario Tamayo. Located in the beautifully restored art deco midtown Wiltern Theatre building, the room is styled in a manner that almost defies description. Modern and nostalgic, exciting and comfortable, grand and intimate, it's like a salon, lounge and brasserie rolled into one. The food is also distinctive and eclectic. Standout dishes include a goat cheese and guava paste quesadilla appetizer, cumin-roasted chicken with sautéed onions, and raspberry-rhubarb crumble. And if you don't want to eat, stop by the bar for a cocktail and some terrific people-watching, L.A. style. (Atlas Bar & Grill, 3760 Wilshire Boulevard, Los Angeles, CA 90010; telephone number 213-380-8400.)

🍃 Getaways

Next time you pay a visit to Manhattan, spend the night in style in the new Paramount hotel in the heart of the theater district. Co-owner Ian Schrager (of Studio 54 and New York's Palladium fame) wisely gave the interior design to Philippe Starck. The result is a contemporary yet intimate setting, which includes a state-of-the-art fitness center, a playroom for children and a movie theater. Special weekend rates begin at $90. (Paramount, 235 West 46th Street, New York, NY 10036; 800-225-7474 or 212-764-5500.)

If Martinique is on your itinerary, look into the charming Le Palais Créole hotel in the heart of Fort-de-France. This restored, historic four-story house overlooking Victor Schoelcher Square and the Palace of Justice is within walking distance of shops, museums and restaurants. Room rates range from $70 per night for a single room during off season to $120 per night for a double room during peak season. An on-premises tearoom features creole cuisine. (Le Palais Créole, 26 Rue Perrinon, 97200 Fort-de-France, Martinque, French West Indies; call 596-63-83-33 or FAX 596-71-65-29.)

When you stay at the Melrose, a charming newly renovated Victorian guest house in New Orleans, you are picked up at the airport by limousine (which can also be hired to ferry you around the city). The pampering continues with afternoon cocktails in the parlor or on the veranda overlooking the heated pool. This small inn is an easy walk from the French Quarter. Room rates range from $195 to $395 and include airport pickup, cocktails and a buffet breakfast of New Orleans specialties. (Melrose, 937 Esplanade Avenue, New Orleans, LA 70116; telephone 504-944-2255.)

🍃

Just 90 minutes southwest of the hustle and bustle of New York City lies the pastoral Pennsylvania countryside, where you can restore your spirits, do some serious antique shopping and dine or stay at the charming 250-year-old Black Bass Hotel. The inn's Sunday Champagne brunch is particularly enjoyable. Savor homemade breads, salads and desserts while overlooking the idyllic Delaware River. (Black Bass Hotel, Route 32, Lumberville, PA 18933; telephone 215-297-5770.)

L'Auberge Aux Trois Saisons, a restored seventeenth-century inn in Burgundy, is the perfect spot from which to explore this famous wine region. Tour nearby vineyards and châteaux, enjoy boat tours on the Saône, go aloft in hot-air balloons or take the two-hour drive to Geneva for lunch. Dinners at the inn, prepared by chef-owner Mort Sobel, are deliciously eclectic, drawing on his experiences in South Africa, Turkey, Beverly Hills, Boston, Puerto Rico and Paris. The auberge is open from April 1 to November 1. (L'Auberge Aux Trois Saisons, Le Prémoy, B.P. 6, Dracy-le-Fort, 71640 Givry, France; 85.44.41.58.)

The American European Express (cousin to the famed Orient Express) recently expanded its luxury rail destinations to include a New York-Philadelphia-Chicago route. It had established its reputation with a route between Washington, D.C., and Chicago. Famous for its comfort and first-rate service, the train also provides such indulgences as caviar, Gulf shrimp salad and baby lamb chops. One-way fares start at $525, based on double occupancy. For more information, call 800-677-4233.

Located in the heart of Princeton, New Jersey, The Nassau Inn is, and has been since 1756, a nostalgic gathering place for locals of the university town. Although recently restored, the inn has not lost any of its colonial ambience. The 217 guest rooms are furnished with handsome period pieces, and the main dining room, Palmer's, serves game and produce from local farms. The American-style meals are superb, the setting serene; and the innkeeper, Nelson Zager, is a warm and charming host. (The Nassau Inn, Palmer Square, Princeton, NJ 08542; telephone 609-921-7500.)

You'll be snug and pampered as can be at The Little Inn on the Bay in Newport Beach, California, plus you'll have a gorgeous view of ships, yachts, sailboats and the bustle of seaside life. Included in your stay will be a Continental breakfast, wine and cheese in late afternoon and milk and cookies when you return from your evening out. Within walking distance are such local favorite dining spots as the Bouzy Rouge Cafe, offering tapas, fondues, pizzas, pastas and more. All this adds up to a perfect spot for a relaxing getaway weekend. (The Little Inn on the Bay, 617 Lido Park Dr., Newport Beach, CA 92663; 800-538-4466, or, in California, 800-438-4466. Call the Bouzy Rouge Cafe at 714-673-3440.)

People who travel a lot (and even those who don't) know what a treat it is to find a special hotel that's not in all the guidebooks. Savvy visitors to Los An-geles know that the place to stay is the Sunset Marquis Hotel and Villas just off the Sunset Strip. Quiet and privacy are of prime importance in this enclave, long a favorite of actors, writers and musicians. The facilities, boasting two swimming pools and a delightful garden, are spread over nearly four acres of parklike grounds in a residential neighborhood. There's a lovely dining room and bar, and the sauna, Jacuzzi and exercise room are other appreciated amenities. It's just about the closest thing L.A. has to a country retreat. (Sunset Marquis, 1200 North Alta Loma Road, West Hollywood, CA 90069; 800-858-9758.)

Downtown Los Angeles continues to boom as the financial center for the entire Pacific Rim, and business travelers (plus savvy vacationers) now have a little deluxe hotel right in the heart of the action. It's called Checkers, the latest venture of Bill Wilkinson, the masterful gentleman behind San Francisco's own elegant Campton Place Hotel. Guest rooms have the level of comfort and luxury one would expect from that pedigree, but the other story here is in the dining room—one of the most-talked-about stops in town. Power breakfasters feast on such dishes as eggs scrambled with asparagus and Asiago cheese or duck hash with poached eggs and orange hollandaise. (Checkers, 535 S. Grand Avenue, Los Angeles, CA 90071; 213-624-0000.)

🍎 For the Kitchen & Table

Set the table with a shovel, a pitchfork and a chain saw, and just wait for the smiles to begin. Gardeners, especially, will love this amusing stainless steel flatware. What better way to enjoy the fruits (and vegetables) of their labor? A five-piece place setting costs $60. For more information, contact Jelly Sandwich at 504-522-8752.

Swid Powell's sleek new stainless steel ice cream scoop and pie server, designed by architect Ettore Sottsass for Reed & Barton, are the best excuse we know of for indulging in a slice of pie with ice cream. The set is $85 in fine department stores across the country; call 800-822-1824 for the nearest store.

Create super-stylish settings with accessories from Chateau X. Wrap table napkins (or try their oversize hand-screened "nature napkins") in a ring of "jewels" or a sleigh bell. And to make the mood really sparkle, add their new gold-tinted straw place mats. Suggested retail prices are $25 for a "nature napkin," $15 for a "jewel" napkin ring, $8 for a sleigh bell ring, $60 for four place mats. All available at Macy's New York; selected items from the collection are sold at Neiman-Marcus and Barneys stores.

New hand mixers from both Sunbeam and KitchenAid make baking easier. Sunbeam's electronic Mixmaster ($41.95) has eight speeds and three attachments (in addition to the basic beaters). KitchenAid's sturdy new five-speed Ultra Power Plus ($64.95) is designed for optimal mixing and minimal cleaning. Both are available at selected retailers nationwide.

Cloth kitchen towels are best for the environment (there's no waste), but sometimes paper towels are a must. Conscientious consumers may want to try recycled paper towels. A package of 15 rolls costs $18.95 plus shipping from Co-Op America. And instead of plastic food storage bags, try those made of biodegradable cellulose, a plant fiber. The bags are microwavable, freezable, reusable and keep food just as fresh as plastic. A supply of 50 sandwich bags and 50 two-quart storage bags costs $11.50 plus shipping from Co-Op America. To order, contact Co-Op America Order Service, 49 The Meadows Park, Colchester, VT 05446; 802-655-2975.

Lend a nautical flavor to your next party by using scaled-down versions of boats as serving pieces. The handcrafted 28-inch-long minipirogue and lake skiff are priced at $20 and $50 respectively, plus shipping. Perfect for presenting the catch of the day. For more information, contact Ron Chapman—Shipwright, 324 East Solidelle Street, Chalmette, LA 70043; telephone 504-277-6526.

Royal Copenhagen, famous for its fine hand-painted porcelain, has recently revived the tradition of Danish faience. Their two new patterns, "Golden Summer" and "Blue Pheasant," are richly colored and make a beautiful table. Prices range from $56 for a cup and saucer to $420 for a vase. Write Royal Copenhagen, 27 Holland Avenue, White Plains, NY 10603; or telephone 914-428-8222.

Keep fish and shellfish from falling through the grill with the Griffo-Grill—a 16 × 12-inch black porcelain enamel rustproof rack that fits any conventional gas or charcoal barbecue (and some indoor cooktops). It also works for vegetables, poultry, meats and pizzas. Order no. 2376 for $29.99 plus shipping from The Chef's Catalog, Department PR, 3215 Commercial Avenue, Northbrook, IL 60062; toll free 800-338-3232.

These rainbow-toned vases are a spectacular addition to a mantel, sideboard or buffet table—with or without flowers. Glassblower Robin Mix calls his gracefully designed vessel "Veronese" after the Renaissance artist. Available in a variety of exquisite color combinations, they are $300 each, including shipping. Order from Robin Mix, Route 110, Tunbridge, VT 05077; telephone 802-889-3430.

You don't need to pull out that big, party-size wok when you're in the mood for a small serving of stir-fried veggies. Both All-Clad Metalcrafters and Calphalon have recently introduced easy-to-use stir-fry pans—small skillets with deep, sloping sides. They're perfect for side dishes or solo suppers. The All-Clad stir-fry pan is available in anodized aluminum for $98 or brushed aluminum for $75. Calphalon's classic anodized aluminum ten-inch pan is $52; an eight-inch one is $35. Write to the manufacturers: All-Clad Metalcrafters, RD #2, Canonsburg, PA 15317; Calphalon Commercial Aluminum Cookware Company, P.O. Box 583, Toledo, OH 43693.

The sleek, newly designed coffeemaker from Mr. Coffee brews up to 35 percent faster than conventional machines. It's great for those mornings when you just can't wait for that first cup. Called the "Expert," this model has an adjustable temperature control, so you can keep your coffee as hot as you like. The safety feature will perk you up, too. It shuts off automatically when the pot is empty or in about five hours, whichever comes first. Available in black or white at most department stores for approximately $80. For details, call 800-321-0370.

Tuffnut nutcracker cracks open tough nuts with minimal damage to the meat, thanks to a powerful compression spring handle. Made by Grantz U.K. of England, one of the companies in Prince Charles's Youth Business Trust, it costs $15 from Boston Warehouse, 59 Davis Avenue, Norwood, MA 02062; 617-769-8550.

Ask any chef worth his toque what kind of cookware he (or she) prefers, and you can bet the vote will be copper pots and pans every single time. Now the chore of maintaining these has been cut drastically by Brabant Copper. Their classic cookware is engineered with stainless steel bonded to the copper interior. Unlike silver, nickel or tin, it neither blackens nor wears off. Both the satin copper finish and the stainless interior come clean quickly and easily. These pots and pans last virtually forever and make wonderful gifts for serious cooks. Prices range from $83 for a gratin pan to $263 for a large casserole with lid. Contact North Sea Imports, P.O. Box 151502, Chevy Chase, MD 20825; telephone number 301-933-0144.

❦ *Diet News*

Ben & Jerry's new light frozen desserts are one-third lower in fat and have 40 percent less cholesterol than their original super-premium ice creams. Available in six refreshing flavors at supermarkets nationwide for approximately $2.25 a pint.

Eat Healthy America, a new booklet with good-for-you recipes, is free from the makers of Mazola corn oil. There are simple tips, basic guidelines and recipes in this booklet that will help you keep off unwanted pounds. Write to Mazola FACTS, Department EHA-MC, Box 307, Coventry, CT 06238.

An apple a day? Here's why. You probably already know that apples are high in fiber and low in calories, but there's more. They're also rich in vitamin C, potassium, pectin (which can help lower LDL—the "bad" cholesterol) and boron, a trace mineral that may actually help the body retain calcium.

Organically grown foods not only taste good and are good for you, but using them also supports a cleaner environment (pesticides and herbicides create toxic runoff that can pollute water sources). For a listing of organic growers in your area, call for *The Organic Network,* 517-456-4288. The international directory is $15; directories for most states are $2 each.

Good Sources of Nutrients, a set of 17 fact sheets from the USDA, details the top food sources for minerals, dietary fiber and 16 vitamins; explains the function of nutrients; and provides tips on preparing foods that contain them. To order, send a check for $5 payable to the Superintendent of Documents, Consumer Information Center, Dept. 171W, Pueblo, CO 81009.

The Tufts University Guide to Total Nutrition (Harper & Row, 1990), by Stanley Gershoff, Ph.D., is a solid source of information on healthful eating, diet and exercise, plus the latest news on issues such as caffeine consumption. The book also includes interesting food facts and related trivia.

Did you know that a few tablespoons of sour cream have more saturated fat than a small filet mignon? This fact and other surprising ones are revealed in a video, "Lower Your Cholesterol, NOW!" The 59-minute tape offers advice on reading labels, shopping and cooking. Available for $39.95 plus $3 shipping from Supermarket Savvy, P.O. Box 7069-MMC, Reston, VA 22091; telephone 703-742-3364.

Looking for some pots and pans that will enable you to fry, sauté and stir-fry without a drop of fat? T-Fal might be what you want. Their Ultrabase cookware combines the newest interior and exterior treatments for nonstick cookware. For more information contact T-Fal Corporation, 208 Passaic Avenue, Fairfield, NJ 07004; telephone number 201-575-1060.

The oil-rich avocado yields a perfect fat for salads and sautéing. It is cholesterol free, mildly flavored, low in calories, nongreasy and ideal for high-temperature cooking. It takes 25 avocados to produce a 12.7-ounce bottle of oil from Calavo, which sells in supermarkets for about four dollars.

🍎 Credits and Acknowledgments

The following people and restaurants contributed the recipes included in this book:

A Sousceyrac, Paris, France
Amsterdam's Bar & Rotisserie, New York, New York
Andrew's Restaurant, Honolulu, Hawaii
Aragona's Italian Restaurant, Soquel, California
Ascona Place, Gravenhurst, Ontario, Canada
Baby Routh, Dallas, Texas
Bella Union Restaurant & Saloon, Jacksonville, Oregon
Shelley Berger
Bouligny, New Orleans, Louisiana
Brennan's, Houston, Texas
Bud & Alley's, Santa Rosa Beach, Florida
Cafe Annie, Houston, Texas
Cafe des Artistes, New York, New York
Cauley Square Tea Room, Goulds, Florida
Charlie Trotter's, Chicago, Illinois
Chez Pauline, Paris, France
Chez Raphael, Novi, Michigan
Chez Shea, Seattle, Washington
Chouinard's on Vendue, Charleston, South Carolina
Leonard Cohen
Courtyard Cafe and Bar, New York, New York
Lane Crowther
Daisy Flour Mill, Rochester, New York
Dakota's, Dallas, Texas
Roberto Donna
Sue Ellison
Ellen Faris
Basha Gelman
Harris Golden
The Golden Door, Escondido, California
The Golden Kitchen, Phoenix, Arizona

Gary and Victoria Gott
Grand Bay Hotel, Miami, Florida
Lee Dicks Guice
Zack Hanle
Leslie Taverner Holliday
Hotel Bel-Air, Los Angeles, California
House of Seafood, Kauai, Hawaii
Hugo's, West Hollywood, California
Island Grill, New York, New York
Jean-Louis at Watergate, Washington, D.C.
KKJ and Company, St. Helena, California
Karen Kaplan
Lynne Rossetto Kasper
Jeanne Thiel Kelley
Kenwood Vineyards, Kenwood, California
Kristine Kidd
The King's Cottage, Lancaster, Pennsylvania
Kelley Kraft
L'Ambroisie, Paris, France
L'Assiette, Paris, France
La Veranda, El San Juan Hotel & Casino, San Juan, Puerto Rico
Landau's, Bellevue, Washington
L'Enoteca Pinchiorri, Florence, Italy
Le Bernardin, New York, New York
Le Salon, The Stanhope Hotel, New York, New York
Les Filles du Roy, Montreal, Quebec, Canada
Louie's Backyard, Key West, Florida
Melissa Love
Gilda Lupes
Abby Mandel
Masa's, San Francisco, California
Michael McLaughlin
Chuck McNeil

Merriman's, Kamuela, Hawaii
Miller Howe, Cumbria, England
Jinx and Jefferson Morgan
Selma Morrow
Ellen Ogden
Oliverio's, Royal Oak, Michigan
Patina, Los Angeles, California
R.I.K.'s, West Bloomfield, Michigan
Restaurant Philippine Welser, Innsbruck, Austria
Restaurante Ampurdan, Ampurias, Spain
Martha Reynolds
Betty Rosbottom
John R. Salisbury
Richard Sax
Connie Barbara Schaeffer
Seabourn Spirit, Seabourn Cruise Line
Edena Sheldon
Marie Simmons
Sostanza, Los Angeles, California
David Starr
Stein Eriksen Lodge, Park City, Utah
Swan Court Cafe, Embassy Suites Hotel, Napa California
Syzygy, Aspen, Colorado
Tommy Tang
Sarah Tenaglia
Valentino, Los Angeles, California
Patti and Dick Ward
Wildsee-Schlossl, Seefeld, Austria
The WineSellar & Brasserie, San Diego, California
Ernie Wolfe
Yank's, Beverly Hills, California

"News '90" text supplied by Zack Hanle, Sarah Belk, Steven Raichlen, Richard Sax, Ken Hom, David Ricketts

Foreword and chapter introductions written by Laurie Glenn Buckle

Editorial Staff:
William J. Garry
Barbara Fairchild
Laurie Glenn Buckle

Graphics Staff:
Bernard Rotondo
Sandy Douglas

Copy Editor:
Marilyn Novell

Production:
Joan Valentine

Rights and Permissions:
Gaylen Ducker Grody
Gerri E. Silver

Indexer:
Rose Grant

The Knapp Press
is a wholly owned subsidiary of
KNAPP COMMUNICATIONS CORPORATION

Composition by Andresen Typographics, Tucson, Arizona

This book is set in Sabon, a face designed by Jan Teischold in 1967 and based on early fonts engraved by Garamond and Granjon.